THE ETHICS OF WAR IN ASIAN CIVILIZATIONS

This book explores how issues of ethics in war and warfare have been treated by major ethical traditions of Asia. It looks at six different Asian religious, philosophical and political traditions: Islam, Judaism, Hinduism, Buddhism, China and Japan; and it is organized in three parts according to geography: West Asia, South Asia and East Asia.

While chapters are written by specialists in Asian cultures, some of the conceptual apparatus is drawn from the scholarly discourse on just war developed in the study of the ethical tradition of Christianity. These concepts provide the necessary focus and make comparison across cultural boundaries possible. As a study of the comparative ethics of war, this book opens a discussion about whether there are universal standards in the ideologies of warfare between the major religious traditions of the world. The concept of just war is at the core of the argument. This new approach opens a new field of research on war and ideology.

Torkel Brekke completed his DPhil at the University of Oxford in 1999 and is currently Associate Professor at the Institute of Culture Studies and Oriental Languages at the University of Oslo. His primary research interest is the relationship between religion and politics. Previous publications include *Religious Motivation and the Origins of Buddhism* also published by Routledge and *Makers of Modern Indian Religions* (Oxford University Press, 2002).

THE ETHICS OF WAR
IN ASIAN CIVILIZATIONS

A comparative perspective

Edited by
Torkel Brekke

Routledge
Taylor & Francis Group

LONDON AND NEW YORK

First published 2006
by Routledge
2 Park Square, Milton Park, Abingdon, Oxon, OX14 4RN

Simultaneously published in the USA and Canada
by Routledge
270 Madison Ave, New York NY 10016

Routledge is an imprint of the Taylor & Francis Group

Transferred to Digital Printing 2009

Typeset in Times New Roman by
Keystroke, Jacaranda Lodge, Wolverhampton

British Library Cataloguing in Publication Data
A catalogue record for this book is available from the British Library

Library of Congress Cataloging in Publication Data
The ethics of war in Asian civilisations : a comparative perspective /
edited by Torkel Brekke.
p. cm.
1. Just war doctrine. 2. War–Moral and ethical aspects–Asia.
3. War–Religious aspects. I. Brekke, Torkel.
B105.W3E85 2005
205′.6242′095–dc22
2005001219

ISBN10: 0–415–34292–9 (hbk)
ISBN10: 0–415–54437–8 (pbk)

ISBN13: 978–0–415–34292–6 (hbk)
ISBN13: 978–0–415–54437–5 (pbk)

CONTENTS

List of contributors   vii
Editor's preface   ix
Acknowledgements   xvii

Introduction: comparative ethics and the crucible of war   1
G. SCOTT DAVIS

PART I
West Asia   37

1   The ethics of war in Judaism   39
    NORMAN SOLOMON

2   Islamic tradition and the justice of war   81
    JOHN KELSAY

PART II
South Asia   111

3   Between prudence and heroism: ethics of war in the Hindu
    tradition   113
    TORKEL BREKKE

4   In defense of Dharma: just war ideology in Buddhist Sri Lanka   145
    TESSA BARTHOLOMEUSZ

CONTENTS

PART III
East Asia   **157**

5   Might makes right: just war and just warfare in early medieval
    Japan   159
    KARL FRIDAY

6   The just war in early China   185
    MARK E. LEWIS

    Afterword: ethics across borders   201
    HENRIK SYSE

    Index   206

CONTRIBUTORS

Tessa Bartholomeusz (1958–2001) was Professor of Religion at the Florida State University, Tallahassee. She established a reputation as a leading interpreter of Buddhism through such works as *Women under the Bo Tree* (Cambridge University Press, 1994), *Buddhist Fundamentalisms and Minority Identities in Sri Lanka* (SUNY, 1998), and numerous articles in scholarly journals. Her book, *In Defense of Dharma*, was published by Routledge in 2002. Professor Bartholomeusz also received a number of awards for teaching at Florida State University, served as treasurer for the American Institute of Sri Lanka Studies, and as the book review editor for the *Journal of Asian Studies*.

Torkel Brekke completed his DPhil at the University of Oxford in 1999 and is currently Associate Professor at the Institute of Culture Studies and Oriental Languages at the University of Oslo. His primary research interest is the relationship between religion and politics. Previous publications include *Religious Motivation and the Origins of Buddhism* (RoutledgeCurzon, 2002) and *Makers of Modern Indian Religions* (Oxford University Press, 2002).

G. Scott Davis is Lewis T. Booker Professor of Religion and Ethics at the University of Richmond, Virginia. He obtained an AB summa cum laude from Bowdoin College and a PhD from Princeton. He is author of *Warcraft and the Fragility of Virtue: An Essay in Aristotelian Ethics* (University of Idaho Press, 1992), and editor of *Religion and Justice in the War over Bosnia* (Routledge, 1996). He serves as book discussion editor of the *Journal of Religious Ethics*.

Karl Friday (PhD Stanford, 1989) is Professor of History at the University of Georgia. He has published extensively on Japanese military institutions and traditions. Friday is author of *Hired Swords: The Rise of Private Warrior Power in Early Japan* (Stanford University Press, 1992) and *Legacies of the Sword: The Kashima Shinru and Samurai Martial Culture*, with Professor Seki Humitake (University of Hawaii Press, 1997). Professor Friday's current book project is called *Samurai, Warfare and the State in Early Medieval Japan* (Routledge, 2004, the "Warfare and History" series).

John Kelsay (PhD University of Virginia, 1985) is Richard L. Rubenstein Professor of Religion at Florida State University, Tallahassee. Professor Kelsay's work focuses on religious ethics, particularly in relation to the Islamic tradition. His publications include *Islam and War* (Westminster/John Knox, 1993), *Human Rights and the Conflict of Cultures* (co-authored; University of South Carolina, 1988), and *Just War and Jihad* (co-edited; Greenwood Press, 1991). He is currently working on a book entitled "Religion and the Imperatives of Justice: The Islamic Law of War and Peace", as well as on other projects dealing with intersections between religion and violence in the contemporary world.

Mark E. Lewis (PhD University of Chicago) is Kwoh-ting Li Professor of Chinese Culture at Stanford University. He is author of *Sanctioned Violence in Early China* (SUNY, 1990), *Writing and Authority in Early China* (SUNY, 1999), and *The Construction of Space in Early China* (SUNY, forthcoming). He is currently completing a volume *The Flood Myths of Early China*, as well as the first two volumes of a five-volume history of imperial China to be published by Harvard University Press.

Norman Solomon was born in Cardiff, South Wales, and educated at St. John's College, Cambridge. He was rabbi to Orthodox congregations in Britain until he became founder-Director of the Centre for the Study of Judaism and Jewish/Christian Relations at Selly Oak Colleges, Birmingham. He was Fellow in Modern Jewish Thought at the Oxford Centre for Hebrew and Jewish Studies 1995–2001 and is a member of Wolfson College, Oxford and the Oxford University Teaching and Research Unit in Hebrew and Jewish Studies. He has published several books on Judaism.

Henrik Syse is a postdoctoral fellow at the Ethics Program of the University of Oslo, and a senior research fellow at the International Peace Research Institute, Oslo (PRIO). He has written several articles on the ethics of war and peace, and is also the co-editor (with Gregory Reichberg and Endre Begby) of *The Ethics of War – An Historical Anthology* (Blackwell, 2005). His other publications include *Natural Law, Religion, and Rights* (St. Augustine's Press, 2004).

EDITOR'S PREFACE

This book explores how issues of ethics in war and warfare have been treated by major ethical traditions of Asia. It takes a comparative view of ideologies of war in history. While the chapters are written by people who specialize in Asian cultures, much of the conceptual apparatus is drawn from scholarship on the just war tradition in Christianity. These concepts provide the necessary focus and makes comparison across cultural boundaries possible.

This is not the first book that applies the conceptual framework of Christian just war thinking to non-Christian cultures. Several scholars have maintained that there is a tradition for just war – *jihad* in its diverse meanings and manifestations – in Islamic jurisprudence that is parallel to that found in the Christian just war tradition.[1] This position has been challenged by other scholars.[2] Judaism has also been included in the academic debate about the ethics of war. In my view, scholarship on the ethics of war needs to include other non-Western civilizations in order to reach the broadest possible fundament for cross-cultural comparison. With its emphasis on the just war tradition, the academic study of the ethics of war has harboured an element of Eurocentricism comparable to that found in the field of military history, where this bias is now addressed by leading scholars like Jeremy Black.[3]

This book looks at six different Asian religious, philosophical and political traditions: Islam and Judaism, Hinduism and Buddhism, and China and Japan. When I started working on this project nobody had looked at the ethics of war in the religious traditions of South and East Asia in a systematic, comparative manner. However, the interest in this field seems to be growing. During the last couple of years there have been several conferences and seminars devoted to the topic.

It is to be hoped that the present volume will contribute to the growing interest in the ethics of war. The readers we have in mind are first of all scholars and advanced students working in the fields of comparative ethics, religious studies, war studies and Asian studies. It has been a goal that chapters should be as accessible as possible to non-specialists or scholars from other academic fields. Therefore, the contributors have refrained from using diacritical marks in the few necessary transliterations of words from different languages.

This book is organized in three parts according to geography: West Asia, South Asia and East Asia. Obviously, there is not a perfect match between the geographical organization of the book and the religious and ethical traditions that we look at. For instance, the Islamic tradition covers much of Africa and Southeast Asia in addition to West Asia. Judaism is very much a European tradition, while I include it alongside Islam in the section on West Asia. Hindus may be found in East Africa and North America as well as in the Pacific and the Caribbean. Thus, in many instances we should perhaps have added inverted commas when we talk about Asian civilizations. Still, the fact that these major traditions originated in certain geographical areas allows for such an organization of the book for practical purposes.

The fundamental questions this book seeks to answer are: Do the major Asian civilizations have ethical traditions pertaining to war? To what extent do these traditions correspond to the Christian thinking on just war (*jus ad bellum*) and just warfare (*jus in bello*)? To what extent can these traditions be used to illuminate the Western tradition of just war? With more philosophical expertise we might also ask whether the possible parallels between different cultures have any relevance for the cross-cultural legitimization of the ethics of war. However, the contributors to this volume are first and foremost historians and philologists.

Each chapter of this book is written by a specialist in a particular tradition. The contributors have been asked to seek systematically in the available literature of their culture of specialization and make the tradition answer quite specific questions: Do we find ideas of just cause in the moral tradition in question? This is the point on which Asian civilizations seem to deviate most from the Christian just war tradition. In many cases ideas of just cause may be implicit in the discourse on war and statecraft. For instance, the actions of the sovereign may be perceived as inherently just and such implicit assumptions are natural issues of discussion for the chapters. Several important questions are linked to the general question of just cause. For example: Can we identity themes like right authority or right intention? Does the tradition in question distinguish between *jus ad bellum* and *jus in bello*, just war and just warfare? This question is important if we wish to compare the Asian traditions with Christian just war thinking.

The discussion of *jus in bello* turned out to be relevant to all chapters in this book. Indeed, it seems that all cultures have some ideas of what behaviour is immoral, unheroic or criminal on the battlefield. Again, reference to concepts from the just war will be useful. For instance, what does the tradition in question have to say about the treatment of non-combatants? Some of our chapters conclude by addressing the basic question of whether a particular ethical tradition has produced a discourse comparable to the just war. This does not amount to a simple yes or no in most cases but rather takes the form of a discussion of whether the comparison seems meaningful or relevant. However, on matters concerning *jus ad bellum* the data seem to reveal some fundamental differences between civilizations. In the ethical traditions of Christianity, Judaism and Islam there is great interest in questions of *jus ad bellum*, while there seems to be an almost complete lack of interest in the same in other traditions. Thus, it seems that a major question for research in the ethics of war should be: Why were Christians, Jews and Muslims so interested in matters of *jus ad bellum* and why did Indian, Chinese or Japanese writers take so little interest in the same questions?

A secondary issue is the possible implications of our results on modern problems. In other words, what is the possible relevance, beyond the purely academic, of our exploration of the ethics of war in ancient Asian traditions? Does our exploration of the ethics of war in Asian civilizations have any bearing on the questions of armed conflict today? J. T. Johnson concludes his book on morality and contemporary warfare with an argument for "a more thorough exploration of the moral traditions of the world's civilizations, in order to identify and understand the conception of war and its limits to be found in each one".[4] According to Johnson, moral reflection on war can support the development of a strengthened international consensus by exploring avenues for conversation among moral traditions worldwide and by developing those commonly held features that tend toward restraint in the resort to war and the limitation of the conduct of war.[5] Scholars of comparative ethics are not alone in holding such views about the relevance of the study of war. In his far-ranging critique of the modern Clausewitzean philosophy of war, which dominated Western military thinkers in the twentieth century, the military historian J. Keegan concludes that future peacekeepers have much to learn from alternative military cultures, both that of the Orient and that of the primitive world.[6] There is a need to rediscover the wisdom of restraint in warfare, he says, and to reject the view that war and politics belong within the same continuum. We might add that Hans Morgenthau, one of the founding fathers of classical realism in the study of international relations, saw the study of ancient civilizations as important to political theory because "human nature, in which the laws of politics have their roots, has not changed since the classical philosophies of China, India, and Greece endeavored to discover these laws".[7]

Perhaps the discussion of the relevance of the comparative ethics of war can be connected explicitly to the present situation. We are witnessing tremendous changes in the international system. Some argue that 1989 was more important than 1789 or 1815 because it marked the end of the balance-of-power-system in Europe.[8] Some argue that the modern state is in decline.[9] Even the moderate Javier Solana indicated in 1998 that the Westphalian system was outdated and incapable of meeting present problems.[10] But the conflicts of the 1990s also showed that the world is a long way from developing a new system that limits and regulates international conflicts. What is the role of ethics in this situation? J. Bryan Hehir has pointed to two issues that will determine the future role of the just war ethic.[11] First, the status of sovereignty is shifting. State sovereignty has been eroded by interlinked political trends, economic integration and by the strategic vulnerability of the nuclear age. But the most important challenge to the principle of sovereignty may be the global debate on ethics and human rights and its political consequences. The tension between state sovereignty and the imperative of humanitarian intervention is certainly one of the most problematic dilemmas of international relations today. Second, according to Hehir, the nature of war is changing. Low-intensity civil wars, fought with low-technology weapons, causing great suffering for civilians, dominate the international picture. This is a fact that has been commented on by a number of writers.

Part of the explanation for this transformation is the fact that the political role of religious and ethnic identities has grown during the last couple of decades.[12] The universal religious revival and its political impact are global trends and there are good reasons to look for the causes of these changes in the context of globalization.[13] The most glaring manifestations of the new political roles of religious and ethnic identities are the wars and conflicts fuelled by identity politics in Europe, in Africa and in Asia. There is a new complexity to the new conflicts. The new actors were bands of armed criminals, guerrillas, paramilitary units, police forces and break-away units of regular armies.[14] In the light of these changes in the nature of armed conflict, the relevance of our exploration of the ethics of war goes beyond the purely academic. The developments in world politics can only bode well for the field of comparative religious ethics, as Simeon O. Ilesanmi says.[15]

I believe that a thorough investigation of the ethics of war in different cultures might yield answers to the questions of whether the core principles of the ethics of war are universal. For instance, if we find that all traditions condemn the killing of innocent bystanders as immoral or criminal, is it not fair to use such a fact to counter claims of relativism in global discourse about ethics across cultures? At this point, I have moved into the territory of the philosophers, a territory which is unfamiliar to me. Indeed, one of the problems with the field of comparative ethics is that one should ideally be both a philosopher and a historian. In an attempt to solve this problem, I have asked two philosophers to contribute to this book.

In the Introduction, G. Scott Davis presents some of the basic questions of the comparative ethics of war. His chapter is also a broad overview of the development of just war thinking in Europe from the Romans until modern times. This historical background is important in our investigation of Asian civilizations because our vocabulary is drawn from the Christian tradition and one of our tasks is to determine whether we can find concepts in other traditions that correspond or overlap with those of the just war tradition. In the Afterword, Henrik Syse addresses some of the general moral questions raised by our historical studies: How can we find resources within the various traditions for recognizing human dignity beyond one's own "in-group" and how can we all come to take seriously the gravity of taking life? Both Professor Davis and Dr Syse are philosophers and it is the hope of the editor that their chapters at the beginning and the end of this book will provide the right philosophical context for our six historical chapters.

Chapter 1 by Norman Solomon is about Judaism. He points out that to understand how Judaism handles the ethics of war, we need to review sources from the earliest scriptures to the literature of contemporary Israel. This is what Solomon does and this is where his chapter takes the study of the ethics of war in Judaism a step forward from the books and articles that restrict their investigation to Old Testament theology.

Chapter 2 on Islam by John Kelsay moves our focus further away from Christian Europe. Kelsay looks at the practice of Shari'a reasoning as a transgenerational conversation. The career of Shari'a reasoning with respect to war provides a good example of both continuity and change built into the system. Kelsay presents Islamic discussions about *jus ad bellum* and *jus in bello* in the sources that he examines.

Chapter 3 on Hinduism by the editor Torkel Brekke moves the focus further away from Europe. Brekke argues that there are two opposed strands in the ideology of war in Hindu India, which he calls heroism and prudence. He argues that the interaction of these two strands of ethical thought produce a characteristic and somewhat ambivalent tradition of the ethics of war in India.

Chapter 4 on Buddhism in Sri Lanka is written by Tessa Bartholomeusz. The sad fact of her death meant that she was never able to complete her chapter. Instead, we have decided to reprint her article *In Defense of Dharma*, which was published in the *Journal of Buddhist Ethics* (1999, vol. 6). In that article, which was based on interviews of Buddhists in Sri Lanka, Tessa Bartholomeusz observed that the same stories and legends could be used by Buddhists both to support and oppose the war against the Tamil separatists. This fact seemed to indicate that the Buddhists of Sri Lanka follow an ethical particularism rather than an ethical system of absolutes. Perhaps the widely differing views on the war, all based on a Buddhist world view, show that the search for a consistent Buddhist ethics is futile?

Chapter 5 on Japan by Karl Friday looks at the development of the famous warrior order that developed in the Heian period (794–1185). Friday challenges the assumption among scholars of Japan that early samurai warfare was regulated by a set of gentlemanly rules and norms. Such rules have been identified because scholars expected to find them, Friday asserts. In fact, warriors of the Heian and Kamakura periods were far less gentlemanly than often assumed. Thus, Europe and Japan evolved in opposite directions in the centuries we often call the high Middle Ages in Europe. European warfare became more controlled and restricted, whereas in Japan the opposite was the case.

Chapter 6 on China is by Mark E. Lewis, who offers a thorough investigation of the concept *yi bing*. *Yi bing* came to serve as a rubric for ideas that are comparable to the Christian just war, Lewis writes. According to the *yi bing* doctrine war was justifiable as punishment to suppress revolt or criminality. The ideas about the just or righteous war developed in China during the centuries leading up to the first unified empire in 221 BC and they remained important into the twentieth century.

Each chapter has a bibliography. The bibliographies are meant as a guide to students and scholars who want information about secondary literature on the ethics of war in the different cultures and regions treated in this book. The bibliographies are not exhaustive on matters of primary material nor on secondary sources in non-European languages. For complete references to primary material readers should consult the individual chapters and their endnotes.

Notes

1 Khadduri, Majid (1955) *War and Peace in the Law of Islam*. Baltimore, MD: Johns Hopkins University Press. Kelsay, John (1990) "Religion, Morality, and the Governance of War: The Case of Classical Islam." *Journal of Religious Ethics* 18(2): 123–39; Kelsay, John and Johnson, James Turner (eds.) (1991) *Just War and Jihad. Historical and Theoretical Perspectives on War and Peace in Western and Islamic Traditions*. New York: Greenwood.
2 Tibi, Bassam (1996) "War and Peace in Islam" in *The Ethics of War and Peace*, edited by Terry Nardin. Princeton, NJ: Princeton University Press: 128–45.
3 See Black, Jeremy (2004) *Rethinking Military History*. London and New York: Routledge, esp. ch. 3.
4 Johnson, James Turner (1999) *Morality and Contemporary Warfare*. New Haven, CT: Yale University Press: 227.
5 Ibid.
6 Keegan, John (1994) *A History of Warfare*. London, Victoria Books: 392.
7 Morgenthau, Hans (1973) *Politics Among Nations* fifth edition. New York: Alfred Knopf: 4.
8 Cooper, Robert (2003) *The Breaking of Nations. Order and Chaos in the Twenty-first Century*. London: Atlantic Books: 3.
9 Creveld, Martin van (1999) *The Rise and Decline of the State*. Cambridge: Cambridge University Press.
10 Solana, Javier (1998) "Securing Peace in Europe." Speech by Dr. Javier Solana, Secretary General of NATO, at the Symposium on the Political Relevance of the 1648 Peace of Westphalia. Münster, 12 November.
11 Hehir J. Bryan (1992) "Just War Theory in a Post-Cold War World." *Journal of Religious Ethics* 20(2): 237–65.
12 See, for instance, Berger, Peter (1999) *The Desecularization of the World. Resurgent Religion and World Politics*. Washington, DC: William B. Eerdmans Publishing.
13 For an early theory about the links between globalization and religious resurgence, see Robertson, Roland and Chirico, JoAnn (1985) "Humanity, Globalization, and Worldwide Religious Resurgence: A Theoretical Exploration." *Sociological Analysis* 46(3): 219–42. See also Beyer, Peter (1994) *Religion and Globalization*. London: Sage Publications.
14 Some important formulations of this theme: Huntington, Samuel (1993) "The Clash of Civilizations?" *Foreign Affairs* 72(3): 23–49. Juergensmeyer, Mark (1993) *The New Cold War: Religious Nationalism Confronts the Secular State*. Berkeley: University of California Press. Kaldor, Mary (1999) *New and Old Wars. Organized Violence in a Global Era*. Cambridge: Polity Press. Kepel, Gilles (1994) *The Revenge of God: The Resurgence of Islam, Christianity and Judaism in the Modern World*, trans. by Alan Braley. University Park: Pennsylvania University Press.
15 Ilesanmi, Simeon O. (2000) "Just War Theory in Comparative Perspective. A Review Essay." *Journal of Religious Ethics* 28(1): 140.

Bibliography

Berger, Peter (1999) *The Desecularization of the World. Resurgent Religion and World Politics*. Washington, DC: William B. Eerdmans Publishing.
Beyer, Peter (1994) *Religion and Globalization*. London: Sage Publications.
Black, Jeremy (2004) *Rethinking Military History*. London and New York: Routledge, esp. ch. 3.

EDITOR'S PREFACE

Cooper, Robert (2003) *The Breaking of Nations. Order and Chaos in the Twenty-first Century*. London: Atlantic Books: 3.

Creveld, Martin van (1999) *The Rise and Decline of the State*. Cambridge: Cambridge University Press.

Hehir, J. Bryan (1992) "Just War Theory in a Post-Cold War World." *Journal of Religious Ethics* 20(2): 237–65.

Huntington, Samuel (1993) "The Clash of Civilizations?" *Foreign Affairs* 72(3): 23–49.

Ilesanmi, Simeon O. (2000) "Just War Theory in Comparative Perspective. A Review Essay." *Journal of Religious Ethics* 28(1): 140.

Johnson, James Turner (1999) *Morality and Contemporary Warfare*. New Haven, CT: Yale University Press: 227.

Juergensmeyer, Mark (1993) *The New Cold War: Religious Nationalism Confronts the Secular State*. Berkeley: University of California Press.

Kaldor, Mary (1999) *New and Old Wars. Organized Violence in a Global Era*. Cambridge: Polity Press.

Keegan, John (1994) *A History of Warfare*. London: Vintage Books.

Kelsay, John (1990) "Religion, Morality, and the Governance of War: The Case of Classical Islam." *Journal of Religious Ethics* 18(2): 123–39.

Kelsay, John and Johnson, James Turner (eds.) (1991) *Just War and Jihad. Historical and Theoretical Perspectives on War and Peace in Western and Islamic Traditions*. New York: Greenwood.

Kepel, Gilles (1994) *The Revenge of God: The Resurgence of Islam, Christianity and Judaism in the Modern World*, trans. by Alan Braley. University Park: Pennsylvania University Press.

Khadduri, Majid (1955) *War and Peace in the Law of Islam*. Baltimore, MD: Johns Hopkins University Press.

Morgenthau, Hans (1973) *Politics Among Nations*, fifth edition. New York: Alfred Knopf: 4.

Robertson, Roland and Chirico, JoAnn (1985) "Humanity, Globalization, and Worldwide Religious Resurgence: A Theoretical Exploration." *Sociological Analysis* 46(3): 219–42.

Solana, Javier (1998) "Securing Peace in Europe." Speech by Dr. Javier Solana, Secretary General of NATO, at the Symposium on the Political Relevance of the 1648 Peace of Westphalia. Münster, 12 November.

Tibi, Bassam (1996) "War and Peace in Islam" in *The Ethics of War and Peace*, edited by Terry Nardin. Princeton, NJ: Princeton University Press: 128–45.

ACKNOWLEDGEMENTS

The publishers would like to thank the following for permission to reprint their material: the *Journal of Buddhist Ethics* for kind permission to reprint Tessa Bartholomeusz, 'In Defense of Dharma', *Journal of Buddhist Ethics*, 1999, vol. 6.

Every effort has been made to contact copyright holders for their permission to reprint material in this book. The publishers would be grateful to hear from any copyright holder who is not here acknowledged and will undertake to rectify any errors or omissions in future editions of this book.

There are a number of people who deserve thanks for their help and advice with this volume. First of all, I would like to thank the contributors to the book for their patience with the editor. I started working on this project in 1999 and the work has been interrupted many times. Consequently, this book has come into being slowly and the main reason is conflicting professional obligations both at the University of Oslo and outside. I would like to thank my former supervisor in Oxford, Professor Richard Gombrich for his support in many aspects of my research. I would also like to thank Professor Olle Qvarnström and Professor Paul Dundas for advice on Jainism and war. I would like to thank Georg Von Simson, formerly professor of Sanskrit at the University of Oslo, for his generous help with my work on the Hindu tradition. I would like to thank Dr. Iver B. Neumann of the Norwegian Institute of Foreign Affairs for reading an early version of the chapter on Hinduism. Thanks also to Greg Reichberg and Henrik Syse at the Peace Research Institute of Oslo (PRIO) for discussions on the comparative ethics of war. I would like to thank Professor John Baines of the Faculty of Oriental Studies, the University of Oxford for generous help. I am grateful to the Norwegian Ministry of Defence and the Christian Michelsen's Institute for generous grants. Thanks also to the *Journal of Military Ethics* for letting me use some pages from a previous article in the chapter on Hinduism.

And, as always, thanks to Margrete, Kristian and Iris for their patience and support.

INTRODUCTION

Comparative ethics and the crucible of war

G. Scott Davis

Michael Howard takes the title of his recent essay, *The Invention of Peace*, from the nineteenth-century jurist and historian of comparative law Henry Maine, who wrote that "war appears to be as old as mankind, but peace is a modern invention."[1] We moderns tend to assume that the great wars of the nineteenth and twentieth centuries were aberrant eruptions marring the peaceful status quo, but the opposite better describes the long view. Outside the Garden of Eden, human communities have always been involved in political conflict and that conflict has regularly escalated to the use of lethal force, both within the community and between communities. The ways in which peoples have both justified and constrained the use of such force are windows into how they see themselves and the other peoples with whom they share, often reluctantly, the world around them. To watch the changes that develop in even a single society's understanding of war is to watch that society being born and reborn.[2] To juxtapose different societies and their distinct ways of understanding war, as Clifford Geertz once said of anthropology, is "not to answer our deepest questions, but to make available to us answers that others, guarding other sheep in other valleys, have given, and thus to include them in the consultable record of what man has said."[3] In this introduction I want to do three things. First, I plan to sketch the ways in which the ancient Greeks and their legatees discussed the restraint of war. Second, I will provide a sketch of contemporary just war thinking. Finally, I want to make some suggestions about comparative ethics and the restraint of war.

From Achilles to Jesus

The evidence of classical literature makes it seem like the ancient Greeks and Romans were obsessed with political violence. Yet "despite the massive concern with war in ancient historical writing," writes M. I. Finley, "it is significant that the analysis of causation failed to progress much. The 'fruit', Momigliano wrote, that Thucydides and his followers reaped 'is not very impressive' . . . Roman historians were not much better, nor were Plato and Aristotle in their theoretical reflections."[4]

In large measure, Finley suggests, this results from "the 'naturalness' of warfare both as a means of acquisition and as one way of achieving other objectives."[5] War in the abstract stood in no more need of explanation than eating and drinking. The shield Hephaestus forges for Achilles in *Iliad* XVIII depicts two cities. The first might seem to be a city at peace, but that is only because there is a procedure for adjudicating "the blood-price for a kinsman just murdered."[6] Such procedures are always unstable and that first city may soon resemble the second, circled by "a divided army gleaming in battle-gear, and two plans split their ranks, to plunder the city or share the riches with its people."[7] Power and glory are all that matter for real heroes. The poem opens with Achilles disgraced and there is no sense that his initial wrath is misplaced. It is his refusal to accept Agamemnon's gifts in book IX that leads Patroclus to beg for Achilles' armor and thus seal both their fates. Sarpedon, son of Zeus yet soon to die by Patroclus's hand, sums up the situation for his companion Glaucus:

> Ah my friend, if you and I could escape this fray and live forever, never a trace of age, immortal, I would never fight on the front lines again or command you to the field where men win fame. But now, as it is, the fates of death await us, thousands poised to strike, and not a man alive can flee them or escape – so in we go for attack! Give our enemy glory or win it for ourselves.[8]

Such is the fate of all warriors. The virtues of Homer's nobility are pride, strength, and cunning. The proper exercise of those virtues results in riches and glory. Who is the chief commander is a matter of fate. So is the length of a life. To be cut down in battle is not something the warrior can always avoid, but as long as he fights the good fight he has lived the good life.

Homer provides portraits of the despicable on both sides. Thersites is "insubordinate," the "ugliest man who ever came to Troy . . . taunting the king with strings of cutting insults" and when Odysseus has had enough he whacks him with the speaker's scepter and Thersites "squatted low, cringing, stunned with pain, blinking like some idiot rubbing his tears off dumbly with a fist. Their morale was low but the men laughed now."[9] Even more revolting is the Trojan Dolon, whose fear for his life leads him to betray his own people. Diomedes and Odysseus milk him for as much information as they need, then, "just as Dolon reached up for his chin to cling with a frantic hand and beg for life, Diomedes struck him square across the neck – a flashing hack of the sword – both tendons snapped and the shrieking head went tumbling in the dust."[10] Better to be Sarpedon dead than Dolon alive.

The moral world of Homer is one where commoners and their worries don't count for much. If they misbehave, as do the women of Odysseus' house, they can be disposed of without a second thought.[11] But before Odysseus returns to reclaim his house and wife, and to dispatch the suitors and their sluts, he catalogs a set of "alternative life styles," none of which is worthy of a warrior. It frequently surprises students how little a role Odysseus' famous wanderings play in Homer's epic: four out of 24 books; 75 pages in Fagles's translation, which runs to almost 500. In many ways the Lotus-eaters are the scariest of all:

> who had no notion of killing my companions, not at all, they simply gave them the lotus to taste instead . . . Any crewmen who ate the lotus, the honey-sweet fruit, lost all desire to send a message back, much less return, their only wish to linger there with the Lotus-eaters, grazing on lotus, all memory of the journey home dissolved forever.[12]

"Grazing" is the operative word here. Humans eat, drink, and tell tales; livestock grazes. It is the hope of returning to genuinely human life that keeps him going.

From Homer to Thucydides we jump at least 300 years into an entirely different moral world: no more superheroes and demi-gods. What prompts the Peloponnesian War are fears about the balance of power.[13] But, as Yvon Garlan notes, the wars of the Greeks and Romans, early and late, were hedged round with rules guaranteed by the gods. "The ancients," he writes, "could not imagine a true war that was not limited in time by declarations, agreements, and symbolic acts."[14] For Greeks and Romans war displays a "sacral rhythm" which moves from the sacred precincts to the councils of the people to a solemn declaration, all under the aegis of the gods. Wars were interrupted "to observe a sacred truce during the great panhellenic festivals."[15] Wars were ended by solemn oaths guaranteed by the gods. The political order "was converted into a three-sided contract by the intervention of sacred powers."[16]

The laws of war were also guaranteed by the gods. Anything dedicated to them was absolutely immune for attack. Not only the priests of the temples, but everything "which belonged to the gods (sanctuaries, temples, altars, wealth, flocks and lands) or fell under their protection (tombs, certain types of monuments, sometimes even entire towns)" was out of bounds, at least in theory; "men sometimes forgot the terrible punishment meted out to Ajax by Athena for having brutally torn the prophetess Cassandra from her Trojan temple."[17] Ambassadors, because they were traditionally priests, were immune. Duty required that battle be followed immediately by the burial of the dead. In early times, according to Garlan, trophies were dedicated to the gods, though by the time of the Empire they had become symbols of personal glory.[18]

Such was the situation when the Romans became the lords of the Mediterranean. Even at the time of Jesus the Romans, with their punctilious commitment to the demands of law, couched war in ritual context. A generation or two ago it was common to think that early Christianity "condemned warfare and military service on grounds that were essentially 'pacifist.'"[19] Hunter surveys a number of volumes that have changed the perspective on military service. John Helgeland's studies of the Roman army suggest that Christians had been serving in the army since at least the middle of the second century.[20] Origen's apology, while insisting that Christians may not serve, explains this as a function not of a general Christian pacifism, but of their religious vocation. "If Celsus wishes us to be generals," he writes, "let him realize that we do this . . . Our prayers are made in secret in the mind itself, and are sent up as from priests on behalf of the people in our country."[21]

Ambrose and Augustine, writing after the conversion of the emperors, theologically ratify a situation that had been uncertain since the persecutions under Diocletian in the late third and early fourth centuries. In letter 189 to Boniface, military governor of Numidia, Augustine exhorts him not to "think that no one who serves as a soldier, using arms for warfare, can be acceptable to God."[22] Augustine goes on to enumerate the devout soldiers of the New Testament and to explain that Christian soldiers "don't seek peace in order to stir up war; no – war is waged in order to obtain peace." Furthermore, "it ought to be necessity, and not your will, that destroys an enemy who is fighting you. And just as you use force against the rebel or opponent, so you ought now to use mercy towards the defeated and the captive."[23] Augustine had elaborated his view of war as a tragic necessity, inevitable given human sinfulness, in his *Contra Faustum* of 398. A few years before his death, in the famous book XIX of his *City of God*, he repeats it. The real evils of war are the vices that motivate human beings to anti-social behavior. All that the soldier can do is serve in good conscience, abjuring hate and blood lust, to subdue disturbers of the peace and preserve the fragile order that is all we can manage in our earthly pilgrimage.[24] Charlemagne had the works of Augustine read to him at meals.[25]

The Christian church on peace and war, 975–1274

The legacy of late antiquity and the Patristic age, with regard to war as with so much else, was deeply ambiguous. Priests and monks were themselves understood in military terms. As Richard Southern puts it:

> The monks fought battles quite as real, and more important, than the battles of the natural world; they fought to cleanse the land from supernatural enemies. To say that they prayed for the well-being of the king and kingdom is to put the matter altogether too feebly. They fought as a disciplined élite, and the safety of the kingdom depended on their efforts.[26]

The year 975 is generally taken to mark the opening of the "peace of God" movement in tenth-century France. In part this seems to have been a practical movement to bring sanctions against robbers and thieves who plundered both the church and the common people. At the same time, it was an early step in the emerging reform movement, attempting to establish at least the basic parameters within which citizens of the earthly city could pursue their vocation as "sons of peace."[27]

The peace of God movement led directly into the "truce of God," which attempted to legislate those days of the week and year during which force of any kind could be employed. Here also, vows were made in public assembly, in the presence of relics of the saints, thereby invoking divine authority and sanction against all who might threaten the truce. There seems to have been widespread popular support for the notion that God and the saints would stand up for the weak against the predations of the strong. The social consequence of the peace, however, was to protect church land and to place the lesser nobles directly under the authority of the greater. It is not impossible that the result was greater peace, in the sense of order, but this came at the expense of the freedom of the common people.[28]

On 27 November 1095, at Clermont, Pope Urban II exhorted those who had broken the peace to become soldiers of Christ, pledged to retake the Holy Land from the Turks.[29] The various local peaces were extended throughout France, whence the leadership was expected to come, and bands of pilgrim soldiers for God began to move east in the spring of 1096. It is unlikely that there was anything like a theory of crusading at the end of the eleventh century. After the crusaders managed to capture Jerusalem, in July of 1099, many tried to explain, and thereby justify, the success of the First Crusade. The available paradigms for war in the service of God were those of the Hebrew Bible. The crusaders were like the children of Israel, led out of Egypt to establish a holy kingdom and to rid the land of the enemies of God. But unlike the ancient Israelites, the followers of Christ had a duty to protect the land where he died for their salvation, in particular to place the Holy Sepulcher in Jerusalem firmly in the hands of Christ's followers.

The distinction between just war and holy war, of which the crusade is supposedly the prime example, is more trouble than it was ever worth.[30] Wars of self-defense, or to recover property, were clearly just. Wars of expansion and enrichment were suspect, though their ends might make them more credible and an upright authority might guarantee their character. To be authorized and guided by God, as the early interpreters of the crusades held those enterprises to be, could not be anything but just. But whether there could be such a war in a post-biblical epoch was another matter. "To Anselm, or to Peter Damian," writes Richard Southern, "the crusade made no appeal." He goes on to cite Anselm's exhortation to "abandon that Jerusalem that is now not a vision of peace but tribulation."[31] But the contemporary *Song of Roland* portrayed upright churchmen winning personal glory in the fight against the heathens. Clergy carrying arms was dubiously legal, though some did.[32] In any event, the clergy on crusade thought their enterprise a just one and prayed God for its success and the success of the various lords they served. This was generally not thought in any way in tension with the demands of Christian vocation.

Since the land was, so to speak, bought and paid for with the blood of the Redeemer, the crusade differed from the wars of the biblical Judges in being a *reassertion* of divine right. Mere possession did not constitute a legitimate holding, despite the long hiatus between Muslim control and the mounting of the crusade. The crusaders's goal was liberation, not only of the Holy Sepulcher, but of those Christians, pilgrims and natives, who had been abused by unbelievers. From the French perspective, the First Crusade stood in the tradition of justice derived from the Roman tradition and the writings of the Latin fathers, notably Augustine.[33]

Criticism of the crusades emerged particularly in the wake of the failed Second Crusade, preached by St. Bernard in 1146. But such criticism as there was seems rarely to have been directed against the idea of war itself. Individual failures might be seen as trials sent from God or as punishments for sin.[34] This was the judgment of Bernard himself and became the standard response to setback in the subsequent centuries. Later criticism was directed against particular crusaders or clerics who abused their power for personal gain, but here again, few seemed to impugn the idea.[35]

In March of 1272, Pope Gregory X called a council at Lyons for May of 1274. He solicited briefs on three issues: the prospects for a renewed crusade, relations with the Greek church, and the need for church reform. Humbert of Romans, past master general of the Dominicans, responded with his *Opera Tripartitum*.[36] For Humbert, most of the reasons given for rejecting a crusade stem from sinful self-indulgence or unbelief. Arguments that the crusade is not compatible with Christian peacefulness he meets with what had become standard responses. The Muslims are actively persecuting Christians, some of whom convert to avoid mishap. The land really belongs to Christ and his followers, from whom it was unjustly taken six hundred years earlier. Thus genuine knights of Christ should welcome the opportunity to enter into battle, not only for the sake of Christ, but to accumulate the divine blessing that will open the way to paradise. Not only that, but a Christian defeat of the Muslims might hurry them on the way to conversion, demonstrating that there is no aid to be found in Muhammad. Thus war would be an act of charity directed toward non-believers. Should the crusader be enriched by the way, that was no harm.[37]

Thomas Aquinas and the just war tradition

All the advocates of crusade, whether it was crusade to the east or against European heretics, perceived the endeavor as just. What we call the just war tradition is an attempt to clarify the conditions which must be met for a war to be fought in good conscience. What makes the achievement of Aquinas so impressive is that his account of war and the use of force generally is informed by a systematic moral psychology and account of the virtues based on the work of Aristotle.

Thomas's older contemporaries tended to rely more on the traditional Augustinian arguments. For Thomas, the human being is born into a social context and dependent on that local community for being trained up into the practical and intellectual virtues. If the individual is lucky enough to be born into a Christian community, the cardinal virtues of prudence, temperance, courage, and justice will be informed by the theological virtues of faith, hope, and charity. The human act moves from the excitation of the appetites by physical stimulus, to the contemplation of an action. If the act in question meets the conditions of virtue, then the inner act of will initiates the outward action in pursuit of the good in question. That external forces or limits may frustrate the act is sometimes fortunate and sometimes tragic, but our judgment of the individual depends on the kinds of acts he or she characteristically wills and pursues.[38]

This general account becomes specific in the second part of the second part of Thomas's *Summa Theologiae*, which discusses the details of Christian life in terms of the theological and cardinal virtues. The account of war comes in the discussion of charity, specifically of those vices that are contrary to charity.[39] Hatred, apathy, and envy may each, in its way, subvert charity. When concern for self leads to the neglect of the neighbor's good you have discord, and discord gives rise to contentiousness. As sides form there is the prospect of schism, a specific form of prideful contentiousness that puts the spiritual well-being of the community in jeopardy. This leads to the possibility of war.

When Thomas turns to war he presupposes the larger moral theory already laid out, so when he says that war can, in theory, be just he means that it is the sort of action that can be praiseworthy when, to paraphrase Aristotle, it is undertaken by the right people, for the right reasons, and in the right way. This doesn't mean that war is desirable in itself, which would be absurd, or that any war always manages to meet the conditions of justice. In fact, given the perverseness of the fallen human will, it is reasonable to assume that even a war that was in principle just would be fraught with instances of self-serving and vice. The crusader chronicles are awash in murderous bloodletting, not least the accounts of the sack of Constantinople in 1204. Aquinas is not denying or making light of these facts. He is, rather, asking whether and under what conditions sinful humanity can resort to armed force.

The answer is that resort to force is just when it meets three conditions. First, war can only be undertaken as a public act, under the aegis of whatever public authority is duly constituted to provide for the common good. Private use of organized force is always illicit. Mob violence, vigilante "justice," feuds, and the like are inherently vicious and could, in any event, not properly be called war. As always, of course, there are likely to be grey areas, a fact that would have been most clear to medieval people. So, while there might be no properly constituted authority with the power to raise an army, invasion by Viking or Mongol might lead to the spontaneous formation of a militia, a perfectly legitimate move to protect the common good at short notice.

There must, furthermore, be a just cause to enter into war. Thomas explicates this as "those who are attacked are attacked because they deserve it on account of some wrong they have done." This admits of two interpretations, only one of which is consonant with Aquinas's account of political authority. On the one hand, it might appear that anyone who commits a malicious act subjects himself to correction. This would seem to lay a foundation for crusading, given the view that the Muslims of the Holy Land wrested the territory from its previous, Christian, rulers by force. Such a view would seem to be justified when Thomas quotes Augustine's description of "a just war as one that avenges wrongs, that is, when a nation or state has to be punished either for refusing to make amends for outrages done by its subjects, or to restore what it has seized injuriously." Not only that, but Thomas has earlier written, seemingly with approval, that Christians wage war with unbelievers to prevent them from hindering the practice of the faith.[40]

On the other hand, the authority of the ruler derives from human law. The purpose of law is to constrain the wayward and disorderly, essentially a supplement to the education that the more virtuous received from their parents.[41] This constraint extends only to external acts that threaten the peace and public order. Unlike the natural law, the laws of particular human communities, indeed the communities themselves, are fleeting and changeable. Their authority extends primarily to the acts of their citizens and only secondarily to events removed in time and place. Thus, without saying so directly, Thomas rejects both the original exhortation to crusade put forward by Urban II and the reassertion of those justifications by his brother Humbert.

The third condition for a just war, that "the right intention of those waging war is required, that is, they must intend to promote the good and to avoid evil,"[42] raises the barrier still higher. Not only must the wrong be one directed at a particular human community, over which the proponent of war has jurisdiction, but the enterprise must be directed toward rectifying a particular evil, without employing any wicked means. Thomas's justification of crusading, then, only extends to those Christians who are themselves being oppressed for the practice or preaching of their faith.

In context, this was no negligible constraint. There had, through the eleventh century, been a steady stream of pilgrims from Europe to Jerusalem, which flow was only in part curtailed by the crusades. The indigenous Christian communities of the eastern Mediterranean had suffered little at Muslim hands, even after the onset of the crusades. In fact, in the decades just before the arrival of the crusaders, the non-orthodox Christians of Anatolia had backed the emerging Seljuk Turks as a welcome relief from the oppression of the Byzantines.[43] In 1229 the aspiring emperor Frederick II negotiated a truce with the sultan, guaranteeing Christian freedom of worship throughout Syria, for which he was roundly excoriated by the Christian patriarch of Jerusalem. After the Mongol conquest of Baghdad in 1258 the Christians were in better shape than the Sunni Muslims, owing to the fact that the new ruler's wife was a Nestorian Christian. Another Dominican respondent to Gregory X's call for briefs, William of Tripoli, reported that the indigenous Christians disapproved of the crusades as an impediment to good business.[44] In short, while war against unbelievers was in theory supportable, the facts argued against it. For Thomas, judgment and action always take place in specific contexts and if all the conditions for right action are not met, the act is defective.[45]

Thomas's three conditions for *jus ad bellum* (justice in going to war) lie at the heart of subsequent just war thinking. The remaining *ad bellum* criteria – proportionality of war to injury, last resort, and reasonable hope of success – are simply demands of prudence. Anyone who would undertake war in the absence of such conditions would by that very fact convict himself of malicious belligerence. But it remains to consider the restraints that must be observed in prosecuting a war, what came to be called the *jus in bello* criteria for maintaining a just war. Here again it is important to recall that all the conditions must be met for a war to be just and defect at any point renders the enterprise blameworthy. So in considering whether subterfuge and ambush are legitimate tactics in war, Thomas notes that there is a distinction between lying or promise-breaking and concealment. The first sort of deception requires the deliberate use of wicked means and is never acceptable. Concealment, on the other hand, is a legitimate dictate of prudence.

Wicked means may never be used in any circumstances. This includes targeting the innocent to achieve a military objective. Thomas makes a clear distinction between private and public persons in noting that "if a private person uses the sword by the authority of the sovereign or judge, or if a public person uses it through zeal for justice . . . then he himself does not 'draw the sword', but is commissioned by another to use it, and does not deserve punishment."[46] The logic of the argument is clear. A sovereign is commissioned by the people to pursue and protect the common good. Those in authority may, in turn, commission previously private individuals to use deadly force on behalf of the public. By being incorporated into a public instrument private persons become part of a whole. So when the soldier attacks another soldier, he acts legitimately and the killing is not malicious. This is true even if the *jus ad bellum* criteria are not met; it does not lie within the authority of the individual soldier to determine whether or not there is just cause, right intent, and the like. Unless an order or tactic is manifestly unjust the soldier may, in good conscience, follow orders. The defect in the action falls on the head of the commander.[47] Soldiers, then, can only kill other soldiers. The army is the instrument with which the aggressor inflicts his injury and the instrument by which the aggression is repulsed. In later work this will come to be known as the *in bello* criterion of "discrimination," which condemns any attack on non-combatants.

Of course, it would be absurd to pretend that wars take place without civilian casualties, even in the more restricted context of medieval warfare. In his discussion of self-defense Thomas elaborates what comes to be called the principle of "double effect." This much misinterpreted principle is not intended by Aquinas as the introduction of some arcane, much less arbitrary, theoretical justification for doing evil. He is, rather, making explicit something that is generally taken for granted when we assign responsibility. "A single act," he writes, "may have two effects, of which one alone is intended, whilst the other is incidental to that intention."[48] Consider, for example, any competition for an academic position. One graduate student may know that a friend is competing for the same job, but as long as she behaves honestly and in good faith, she deserves no blame if she succeeds. By extension, when the private person resists his attacker with reasonable force there is no malice, even if the attacker dies.

Soldiers using otherwise legitimate means, particularly in modern warfare (though even medieval archers often missed the mark), should realize that non-combatants in proximity to the fighting run a risk of injury. Therefore they must use their weapons in ways that discriminate between legitimate objects: combatants, their weapons, and the materials that make aggression possible. When soldiers fire at legitimate targets, with reasonable weapons, and hit civilian bystanders, it is tragic but not culpable.[49] It is no counter-argument that what is reasonable is often a matter of judgment. We exercise the virtues of prudence, justice, and courage to determine where to draw the line. Thomas's Aristotelianism is not designed to eliminate judgment but to clarify it. Nor is it relevant that people lie or dissemble about their real intentions. The fact remains, if known only to God.

Aquinas was on his way to attend Gregory's council at Lyons when he died, in March of 1274. He had apparently intended to address the issue of Latin–Greek relations, since he was travelling with a copy of his *Against the Errors of the Greeks*, composed a decade earlier. There is no way to be sure what he might have said on Gregory's proposed crusade. But his account of the ethics of war rapidly became the benchmark discussion. No previous author so fully integrated the problem of war into a comprehensive moral psychology and political theory. Virtuous people make reasonable laws to facilitate the business of the commonwealth. All are essential, but first among equals is virtue, which is essential to making good laws and pursuing the right sort of business. The account provided by Aquinas remained the standard for the next 300 years.[50]

From the death of Aquinas to the Second Scholastic

The most notable event in the subsequent century was the appearance of the first independent legal treatise on war, that of John of Legnano, who taught both civil and canon law at the University of Bologna from the 1350s until his death in 1383.[51] While students of law had addressed issues of war from Gratian on, the discussions are generally jumbled and philosophically unstructured. Thomas Aquinas was particularly dismissive of the authority of lawyers. But the concerns of lawyers are of necessity the concerns of the society and a look at John of Legnano is an entry into a new vocabulary emerging in the later Middle Ages. The first thing to remark is the very wide scope John gives to the concept of war. There is, to begin, a distinction between spiritual and corporeal war. Spiritual war at the celestial level seems to be the struggle of the individual against the limit placed and judgment passed on human life by God. At the human level, spiritual war reflects the Pauline struggle between the law of God and the law operative in the body.[52] Corporeal war comprises not only what Thomas means by war – which John calls "universal corporeal war" – but the conflicts of individuals that result in reprisals and duels.

Though John cites Aristotle, Augustine, and Aquinas in those chapters where he talks about virtue, courage, and justice in general, questions of legal authority and obedience dominate the work. Following the discussion of mercenaries, for example, is the question "whether those who die in war are saved?"[53] The answer is that those who die in war for the Church are saved, while those who die in another sort of lawful war are saved only on condition that they are without mortal sin. "But if they fall in an unlawful war," he insists, "though that be their only mortal sin, they perish." Thus to have a legal obligation to a lord may be morally binding, on pain of loss of livelihood, while to venture forth, if the war is unlawful, may jeopardize eternal life. The disparate legal judgments, from differing times and places, often leave it unclear how to resolve whether or not an action is lawful and who is bound by it, morally or legally. So when John asks "whether a vassal is bound to help his lord against his father, or a father against his son?" several texts seem to say that the feudal oath takes precedent while another gloss "somewhat inclines to the contrary view." John concludes, not very helpfully, that "I should think that the quality of the assistance to be rendered should be considered."[54]

For Thomas, human law should be in the service of the common good, pursued in accord with the virtues. Any obligation must be analyzed in the context of justice and the common good. What the son owes to the father in virtue of his gift of life, nurture, and stewardship can never, for Aquinas, following Aristotle, be repaid. It is only if the father were to become vicious and inimical to the common good that the son could ever be required to take sides against him and then only if the son had a public role like that of a policeman. This should not be taken to imply that all issues can be resolved independent of the law. Any extended human community will require some body of law to negotiate day-to-day existence and some judicial body to consider findings of fact in the light of that law. The point is only that the law does not float free of the community's pursuit of the common good. When justice seems to be at odds with the letter of the law, the virtuous judge exercises equity to maintain our collective commitment to justice and the common good.[55]

Contrast this with John's account of dueling. On his usage the duel is a "particular war," specifically "a corporeal fight between two persons, deliberate on both sides, designed for compurgation, glory, or exaggeration of hatred."[56] All such endeavors would clearly violate Thomas's rejection of brawling and private killing. Even the duel of compurgation, by which John means the *lex duellorum*, a duel to vindicate one's position before a court of law, is explicitly ruled out. For while it may take place as a public proceeding under the rules of a court of law, it is a form of divination and improperly involves demanding a judgment from God.[57] Thus the fact that the Lombard law permitted such duels in 20 cases is inconsequential and John's discussion of champions, the organization of the duel, and who should strike first (cf. chaps. 176–194), for instance, are of merely antiquarian interest.[58]

The rise of the lawyers did not signal the end of theological treatment of war. In the course of the fourteenth and fifteenth centuries Thomas is not the only theological authority invoked in discussing war. In the *Question at Vespers* of 1512, Jacques Almain writes rather baldly that "Scotus's assertion in question 3 of distinction 15 [of his commentary on Peter Lombard's *Sentences*] is quite false, that it is not legitimate for anyone whatever to kill by public authority other than in the cases excepted by God from the commandment 'Thou shalt not kill.'"[59] The implication is that, at least for the purposes of disputation, there is a tradition of invoking John Duns Scotus against the just war arguments of Aquinas. In his discussion of the Decalogue, Scotus argues that the sixth commandment, along with the rest of the second tablet, is not properly speaking part of the natural law. From this it would seem to follow that once the commandment is issued it must be understood as direct divine legislation, which remains binding unless and until there is a dispensation issued by God. The implication is that this extends to all killing, including wars of self-defense and the execution of criminals.[60]

Against this Almain invokes Aquinas explicitly for the legitimacy of excising the diseased part and thus, by analogy, for the praiseworthiness of killing the dangerous criminal. Furthermore, the community acts in accord with practical reason when it delegates this authority to the prince, who acts to protect the common good. Almain insists that, while the delegation of authority is positive, Thomas is right to say that it is natural for human beings to form communities and that it accords with practical reason to create things like police forces and armies. Since these various forces are ordered to a specific, communal end, they await no direct command, even that of God, for their reasonable use.

The pre-eminence of St. Thomas in moral theology was an explicit tenet of the movement known as the "Second Scholastic" and associated with a group of Parisian trained Spanish Dominicans a bit younger than Almain. The best known are Francisco de Vitoria and Domingo de Soto. Vitoria and Soto were both active critics of Spanish practice and policy in the recently discovered New World. It is, in fact, for his *Inquiry on the Indians* that Vitoria remains the most widely known and widely read figure of the Second Scholastic. Following Thomas, Vitoria begins by noting that there is some doubt as to the propriety of Spanish conduct in the newly discovered lands and that in such cases neither the royal counsellors nor lawyers are competent to judge a case which rightly falls to the moral theologian.[61] Vitoria reviews the possible titles that Spain might have to dominion in the New World and finds them wanting, concluding that, in the main, Spanish treatment of the New World natives has been illicit and immoral. Neither the king nor the pope is a universal sovereign. Given the existence of recognizable indigenous communities, the representatives of the king had no authority to intervene in their lives or appropriate their properties. Adventurers such as the brothers Pizarro, whose depredations were manifestly vicious, should be strongly sanctioned by the king and his ministers and Vitoria even suggested, though only in oblique terms, that reparations might be in order.[62]

Vitoria follows Thomas in insisting that, while the Spaniards have in principle a right to preach the Gospel, and that the natives incur mortal sin in failing to believe, this sin is wholly intelligible given the context and does not license any war by the Spaniards. If they must resort to arms in self-defense, that force should extend only to their protection and if they succeed in suppressing an attack they are still not allowed to carry war to the natives. Nor is it just to despoil them or to place them in servitude, even were the intent to make them more receptive to the Gospel. There is no justice in conversion by the sword.[63]

In the 1540s the humanist and royal chronicler Juan Ginés de Sepúlveda invoked the Aristotelian doctrine of "natural slavery" to claim that the Spanish conquests were just. Sepúlveda argued that the native Americans lived a life so crude and lacking in the basic amenities of civilization that it was an act of Aristotelian justice and Christian charity to subdue them to a higher civilizing force. The Dominican Bartolomé de Las Casas, who had long been active in the native cause, objected strenuously and succeeded in having Sepúlveda's book suppressed in Spain. Soto, who convened the conference on publishing the volume, summarized the competing arguments and shortly thereafter, in his work on justice, not only reiterated the position of Vitoria, but pointed out that even the least sophisticated among the Indians was no more a natural slave than the peasants and simple-minded of Spain itself, whom nobody thought could rightfully be enslaved.[64] In their discussions of Spanish injustice in the New World, Vitoria and Soto displayed the practical applicability of just war thinking as formulated by Thomas Aquinas. While recognizing the importance of legal issues, those findings were clearly subordinate to those of moral theology.

The triumph of the lawyers

The legal and moral traditions proceeded in parallel for the next 250 years, but more and more the just war tradition of Aquinas and the Second Scholastic came to be identified with Catholic Orthodoxy and to be replaced, when questions of justice came up at all, by the legal paradigm as developed by the Dutch humanist Hugo Grotius. Grotius dutifully acknowledges the work of Aquinas and Vitoria, but it is a mistake to locate his work in their tradition. First, he reflects the anti-Aristotelian turn of the humanist tradition. Grotius's anti-Aristotelian program comes out clearly in *The Law of War and Peace*, which first appeared in 1625.[65] There he writes that Aristotle's supremacy in the intellectual world has been so tyrannical "that Truth, to whom Aristotle devoted faithful service, was by no instrumentality more repressed than by Aristotle's name!"[66] The source of his anti-Aristotelianism is not altogether clear, but the result is the traditional lawyerly goal of reducing the exercise of prudence and equity in favor of a strict deduction of application from law. By eliminating the Aristotelian appeal to the virtues it is much easier to put forward "the humanist tradition, which applauded warfare in the interests of one's *respublica*, and saw a dramatic moral difference between Christian, European civilization and barbarism."[67]

Grotius's earlier volume, *De Jure Praedae*, shows him doing something quite new when compared to Vitoria. He combines the Stoic account of human nature with a lawyerly desire to see ethics in terms of a hierarchy of laws, rules, and principles governing the exchange of goods in an orderly social machine. From the Stoics Grotius takes the notion that God's will is the law and that it is expressed in the design of creation. Central to all animals, including humans, is the urge to self-preservation. Humans are also endowed with reason and an inclination to sociability. "We are born," he writes, "for a life of fellowship."[68] So we are impelled by nature toward the creation of a social order. At the same time, nature demands that we take whatever means are necessary to maintain our security. The result is that we contract with our fellows to establish a system of laws and the instruments for their enforcement. Grotius elaborates a legal structure of nine rules and 13 laws from which, he maintains, various theses and their corollaries may be shown to follow.[69]

Specifically, Grotius hopes to justify the recent Dutch seizure of a Portuguese vessel. Because evil deeds must be corrected, the good pursued, and the care of the common good maintained by all citizens, "a private war is undertaken justly in so far as judicial recourse is lacking."[70] Because the Spanish have, for a sustained period of time, injured the interests of the Dutch generally and because the Spanish cannot be brought to cease from their abuses, it is legitimate that prizes should be taken when possible.[71] Thus, this particular prize is legitimate and the Dutch should "defend the right of commerce against every possible injury."[72]

Turning, in his *Law of War and Peace*, to the indigenous peoples of the non-Christian world, Grotius rejects the arguments of Vitoria and Soto:

> Regarding such barbarians, wild beasts rather than men, one may rightly say what Aristotle wrongly said of the Persians . . . that war against them was sanctioned by nature; and what Isocrates said, in his *Panathenaic Oration*, that the most just war is against savage beasts, the next against men who are like beasts.
>
> (1925: II, 40)

This is doubly appropriate when such barbarians violate the natural law, for "they [Vitoria *et al.*] claim that the power of punishing is the proper effect of civil jurisdiction while we hold that it also is derived from the law of nature.[73] Grotius may use the language of Aquinas and his Spanish followers, but it is a language that has become vastly more permissive than the older school. And it paves the way for supposedly liberal thinkers such as John Stuart Mill to write as if it were obvious that Africans, Indians east or west, and similarly barbaric peoples must fall under western tutelage before they can enjoy the benefits of liberty. Thus Mill, writing two and a half centuries after Grotius, can take it as "hardly necessary to say that this doctrine is meant to apply only to human beings in the maturity of their faculties . . . Despotism is a legitimate mode of government in dealing with barbarians."[74]

The consolidation of the Westphalian system, the expansions of colonial empire, the age of revolution, and the struggle to maintain the balance of power in the seventeenth, eighteenth, and nineteenth centuries left the classic just war tradition in the dust. Questions of law and contract, on the one hand, and liberty and nationalism, on the other, dominate arguments of rhetoric of the late eighteenth and the nineteenth centuries. Serious political thinkers, such as the young Henry Kissinger, take as their ideal the practical political machinators of the post-Napoleonic era. Kissinger's *A World Restored*, based on his 1954 Harvard dissertation, maintains that "the test of a statesman, then, is his ability to recognize the real relationship of forces and to make this knowledge serve his ends."[75] The realism of Kissinger, in the history of political thought, is the flip side of John Dewey's idealism.

War and justice in twentieth-century thought

In the first half of the twentieth century the natural law approach to the ethics of war was dismissed by most American political thinkers. "During the nineteenth century," writes John Dewey, "the notion of natural law in morals fell largely into discredit and disuse outside the orthodox moralists of the Catholic church . . .

Even when retained, as in some texts, it was in perfunctory deference to tradition rather than as a living intellectual force."[76]

The alternative to natural law occupied Dewey for much of his career, particularly after the start of the First World War. His *German Philosophy and Politics* of 1915 is not generally thought one of his most compelling volumes. Nonetheless, Jo Ann Boydston writes that, "although in later years this book has been generally conceded to be among Dewey's least valuable, reviewers praised it at the time of its publication."[77]

One who did not, however, was W. E. Hocking. Dewey, as Hocking rightly reads him, sees a direct connection between Kant's categorical imperative and German militarism. "Can anyone with the slightest historical justice," asks Hocking rhetorically, "credit the German government of to-day with following *this* Kantian principle?" Hocking closes with the accusation that German behavior is, in fact, "pragmatic, which is what *Realpolitik* essentially means."[78] Dewey, rather obviously irked, responds that "Professor Hocking has not grasped my position."[79] *German Philosophy and Politics*, while inspired by the European conflict, is a case-study in moral theory, designed to articulate Dewey's sense "that there are no such things as pure ideas of *pure* reason."[80] Ideas are themselves expressions of living individuals and communities coming to grips with a concrete situation. When the social world is orderly it is not necessary, nor are people ordinarily inclined, to reflect in depth on the norms and ideals embodied in social life. In times of flux, however, ordinarily stable beliefs and inferences fall into question. War, thus, opens a window on the relation between ideas and action.

Alan Ryan, a sympathetic reader of *German Philosophy and Politics*, describes it as "one of the most striking (though not strikingly persuasive) books Dewey ever wrote,"[81] and attributes the failure of the argument, at least in part, to the fact that Dewey "relied rather too heavily" on the German military theorist Friedrich von Bernhardi.[82] But this, I think, misses Dewey's point. At the turn of the century Bernhardi was in charge of war history for the German General Staff. By 1909 he was commanding general of the Seventh Army. His *On War Today* (of which *Germany and the Next War* is volume two) has been described by Michael Howard as "brilliant and heterodox," containing "a great deal of shrewd tactical analysis."[83] The text went through nine editions in the two years before the war and shortly after the opening of hostilities the young Walter Lippmann, later to assist in formulating Wilson's "fourteen points," wrote that "we were all surprised at the war, stunned at the idea that such things could happen. And then we took to reading Bernhardi . . . and we discovered that this war had been a long time in the minds of the men who know Europe."[84] Whatever the actual motives of individual agents in the field, Bernhardi is a Weberian "ideal type," playing the role of Benjamin Franklin in Dewey's account of the Kantian ethic and the spirit of militarism.

Dewey argues that interpreting morality on the model of law, whether it be that of the philosopher-king, the Christian god, or the rational intellect, risks turning the strategies of a particular time and place into superhumanly established and maintained norms. When this illusion becomes the norm it stifles our ability to innovate and experiment with alternative approaches. As in Weber's account of the spirit of capitalism, an all-encompassing idea – here Kant's cosmopolitan vision of perpetual peace – is transformed into its opposite. War, now, "is to national life what the winds are to the sea, 'preserving mankind from the corruption engendered by immobility.' "[85]

Against "*a priorism*" Dewey advocates "a radically experimental philosophy,"[86] but he denies the European identification of "Americanism" with "a crude empiricism and a materialistic utilitarianism."[87] It is closer, surprisingly, to the position of Burke. What inspires Dewey to identify with Burke is the conservative icon's rejection of "metaphysical abstraction" and his insistence on grounding the moral life in the contingencies of shared experience. What distinguishes American liberalism from British conservatism is the fact that "America is too new . . . we have not the requisite background of law, institutions and achieved social organization."[88] Not only that, "but in our internal constitution we are actually interracial and international."[89] Only with violent internal upheaval could we attain the sort of cultural and historical homogeneity that renders Burke's conservatism plausible.

The moral life of democracy is one that fosters "the fruitful processes of co-operation in the great experiment of living together . . . a future in which freedom and fullness of human companionship is the aim, and intelligent cooperative experimentation is the method."[90] Only in the service of these democratic ideals is it legitimate to break the peace; only in furtherance of these ideals, Dewey ultimately wants to say, can a democratic community enter into the present war. His willingness to support the war effort was always predicated on this democratic *jus ad bellum* and he was deeply disappointed with the outcome of the war. Dewey's stance against the League of Nations and his involvement with the "outlawry of war" movement reflect this disappointment.[91] Philosophically, however, it was a descent into nonsense. Dewey writes that:

> The Committee for the Outlawry of War had strenuously opposed making a distinction between aggressive and defensive wars, point out that all nations claimed that their own wars were defensive and holding to the idea that it was the institution of war and not particular wars which were to be outlawed.[92]

At the time he vilified international law as implicated in the "war system."[93] Having rejected the just war tradition, Dewey, America's leading public intellectual in the first half of the twentieth century, leaves us with a stark contrast between pacifism and an aggressive Euro-American will to power.

Almost a decade later, Dewey reverted to the position he held prior to his outlawry of war period. "War with a totalitarian power," he insists, "is war against an aggressive way of life that can maintain itself in existence only by constant extension of its sphere of aggression."[94] This totalitarian challenge is a direct attack on the virtues of democracy. While not to be welcomed, much less sought out, this sort of war is part of our democratic commitment "to unceasing effort to break down the walls of class, of unequal opportunity, of color, race, sect, and nationality, which estranges human beings from one another."[95] When confronted with war the pragmatist swings between democratic, then pacifist, then back to democratic idealism.

Ethics and war in a nuclear age: the return of the just war tradition

If ever a day changed everything, it was 6 August 1945. "Little Boy" and "Fat Man" were astounding in their economy and their aftermath; but for the Japanese, the terror had already become routine. The dropping of the atomic bomb was the culmination of six months of firebombing:

> The most careful count, done by the Japanese themselves, produced fewer losses than the Americans estimated, but either number is horrific: 240,000 to 300,000 dead (mostly civilians), approximately 2.5 million homes destroyed, and more than 8 million refugees. Of 71 Japanese cities, only 5 escaped substantial damage – and two of these were Hiroshima and Nagasaki.[96]

The firebombing of Japan brought to the Pacific theater tactics that had already been roundly condemned in the European. In the Catholic world, the American Jesuit John Ford had condemned the firebombing of Germany along lines that continued the analysis of Aquinas and the Second Scholastic. "No proportionate cause," Ford concluded, "could justify the evil done; and to make it legitimate would soon lead the world to the immoral barbarity of total war."[97] A few years later, the British philosopher Elizabeth Anscombe protested giving an Oxford honorary to Harry Truman on the grounds that he was a mass murderer.[98] In 1961, Anscombe joined with a distinguished group of British Catholics to train the resources of just war thinking on the emerging policy of deterrence by mutually assured destruction.[99]

In the United States, Catholic moral thought was viewed with suspicion by the mostly Protestant mainstream and Dewey's invocation of democratic values hardly seemed adequate to deal with the situation. So, at least, it seemed to Paul Ramsey. In 1961, he shocked the Protestant establishment by turning away from the pragmatic realism of Reinhold Niebuhr and embracing, with some modifications, the tradition of Vitoria. Ramsey recast the just war theory in an Augustinian mold, insisting on the centrality of *agape*, the other regarding love that demands of public officials a commitment to the welfare of their neighbors, even if it requires the exercise of deadly force. On this version, Aquinas's Aristotelian moral psychology is relegated to the background and the just war tradition after Augustine becomes a matter of clarifying the principles that inform Christian love of neighbor.[100]

As opposition to the war in Vietnam gathered momentum, Ramsey and the just war tradition generally came to be seen as tools of the right wing establishment. In

1977, Michael Walzer published his own reworking of the just war tradition, pitched to the social democratic left. Walzer was reacting to his own sense that the anti-war movement of the mid-1960s did not have an adequate vocabulary to explain what was wrong with the war in Vietnam and what was right about nuclear deterrence. Like Ramsey, Walzer had little use for the Aristotelian background of Aquinas and the Second Scholastic, identifying himself with a legal paradigm grounded in the contractarian tradition of Grotius, Hobbes, and Rousseau. For Walzer, the "war convention" stipulates the intuitive ideals for fighting a just war, and we then elaborate the modifications of that convention forced on us by the necessities of war, culminating in "supreme emergency," which licenses illegal acts in order to protect our basic values, but only so long as is necessary to put down the threat and restore the rule of law.

However interpreted, the just war criteria have become the starting points, on the left and right, for discussing the ethics of war. Advocates and critics of the American actions in the first Gulf War agreed that the *jus ad bellum* requires:

1   right authority
2   just cause
3   right intention
4   last resort
5   reasonable hope of success
6   proportionality of injury to the consequences of war.[101]

Both sides also insisted that the just prosecution of a war satisfy the *jus in bello* demands of:

1   discrimination, subject to the reasonable allowance of double effect
2   proportion, in the sense of limiting damage to the importance of a particular action for securing the ends of war.

These are the minimal conditions for justice. Players on the international stage are always at liberty to hold themselves to a higher standard through signing on to international treaties and joining international organizations, but such alliances are conditional. For just war thinkers, the demands of justice are not.

Ethics, war, and the perils of comparison

The twenty-first-century promises to be more multi-cultural than any since the advent of modernity, with the voices and vocabularies of many traditions demanding to be heard. How these alternative voices shape the thought and practice of the next few decades defies prediction, but making a start on grasping those vocabularies should not be postponed. Based solely on the history of the western just war tradition, the student of comparative ethics ought to recognize that there are at least three models, broadly speaking, for understanding ethics: the legal paradigm; the virtue, or character, paradigm; and the economic paradigm.

The legal paradigm finds it natural to speak of law, a lawgiver, and a community bound to observe the law. In the western tradition, the oldest continuous version of this model is that found in Hebrew Scripture. The creator issues commands, first to Adam and Eve, later to Noah and Abraham, and finally to Moses. God has the authority to issue these laws because, as creator, he is ultimately the owner of his creation. Despite the clear demands of his law, humans continually fail to observe them, which typically leads to some sanction. Thus Adam and Eve are expelled from the Garden, all but Noah and his family are expunged from creation, Abraham is tested and found worthy, and the people of Israel, despite their apostasy at Sinai, receive the 613 commandments of Torah.

The best critic of ethics as law is Aristotle himself. The *Nicomachean Ethics* sees law as a product of individual societies, seeking to formulate a code of public behavior, such as the constitution of Athens, that facilitates the pursuit of what the community cares about. Such constitutions presuppose at least a rudimentary consensus about the kind of people valued, the kind of behavior to be praised and blamed, and the sort of polis that should be fostered. For such communities there is no need to ask about universal reason; what matters is the shared reasons they give each other either for applauding or condemning what goes on among them. The character and virtues of both the individuals and the group as a whole are what give the law meaning.

The "economic paradigm" treats ethics along the lines of contracts and exchanges. We have seen in Grotius that individuals find themselves under the law, but only as a result of an implicit agreement motivated by nature. What the law must acknowledge are the rights, as well as the duties, secured in the initial contract. John Rawls, the most important recent contract theorist, argues that to achieve fairness the contract must be negotiated, conceptually speaking, from an original position where the parties do not know where they will end up in the social order. Once the basic structure of justice is in place, goods are negotiated in the public square on the basis of fairness.[102] When it comes to war, Rawls simply identifies himself with the contractarian approach of Walzer.[103]

While Rawls proposes his theory of justice as an alternative to utilitarianism, utilitarians such as Peter Singer agree that:

> an ethical principle cannot be justified in relation to any partial or sectional group . . . Ethics requires us to go beyond 'I' and 'you' to the universal law, the universalisable judgment, the standpoint of the impartial spectator or ideal observer, or whatever we choose to call it.[104]

What leads Singer to utilitarianism is the sense that Rawls does not provide credible guidance in justifying the ways we balance competing interests to satisfy our intuitions about what is best. Utilitarianism, despite its critics, at least gives some direction to what counts as the best consequences. Ultimately, right action is a matter of balancing aggregate goods over individual evils. When we want to draw a line, it becomes, as for Rawls, a matter of negotiating where the attempt to maximize goods must be limited. So, while Singer follows Seneca in seeing infanticide as the compassionate solution to "the problem posed by sick and deformed babies," he hastens to add that "killing an infant whose parents do not want it dead is, of course, an utterly different matter."[105]

It would be a mistake to think that comparative ethics is simply a matter of attaching these labels to this or that author in this or that tradition. Most traditions will display features of all three. Classical Judaism, for example, might be thought of as standing foursquare in the legal paradigm, but it is hardly to be divorced from the prophetic tradition, calling Israel to be the sort of people God wants them to be. At the same time, opening the Mishnah at random will likely confirm the importance of rights and fairness in the exercise of the law. For example, at Sanhedrin 3.1: "Cases concerning property are decided by three judges. Each suitor chooses one and together they choose another. So R. Meir. But the Sages say: The two judges choose yet another."[106] If there is already this mix of paradigms in the foundational text of classical Judaism, we should hardly be surprised if its contemporary branches divide up with even greater complexity. No theory or method can get around the fact that human acts are always performed in a particular time and place and that interpreting those acts requires some entry into language and context.

At the most general level, interpretation is a matter of what Donald Davidson calls "triangulation." Imagine two individuals who do not as yet share a language encountering each other on the seashore. They may respond to each other in many different ways, putting both in possession of three bits of information: his own response, the response of the other, and the environment that provokes the response. Assuming they have the time and inclination, the two can, by a familiar process of backing and forthing, move closer to getting the responses to match up. By itself, this sort of triangulation may not be sufficient to identify precisely what the other thinks, wants, feels or believes, but it "is necessary if there is to be any answer at all to the question what its concepts are concepts of."[107] Once their responses are regularly predictable they can undertake cooperative actions together. After that, it's a gray line where we say the one has learned the other's language.

Still, as Wittgenstein put it, "one human being can be a complete enigma to another." But this doesn't refer to some sort of Cartesian privacy. Rather:

> We learn this when we come into a strange country with entirely strange traditions; and, what is more, even given a mastery of the country's language. We do not *understand* the people. (And not because of not knowing what they are saying to themselves.) We cannot find our feet with them.[108]

The source of the problem is not one of radical translation. It lies in the "entirely strange traditions." R. C. Zaehner, for example, was a prodigious linguist, but he never seems to have felt at home with the rituals of purity and concern for pollution evident in the traditions he studied. In his introduction to Zoroastrianism he:

omits all account of the elaborate system of taboo worked out in the *Videvdat* . . . and maintained down to the present day by the orthodox. This I have done because it is of no interest to the general reader and because it is the least attractive and the least worthwhile aspect of an otherwise attractive religion.[109]

He says similar things about Hinduism in various places. In his sketch of Hinduism he refers the reader to the Abbe Dubois's *Hindu Manners, Customs, and Ceremonies*, first published in English in 1816, "as still the most exhaustive treatment of a subject scarcely touched on in this book."[110] In this Zaehner is simply the heir, perhaps odd for a Catholic convert, to a modern "tendency to suppose that any ritual is empty form."[111] The result is that Zaehner never learns how the language of pollution, ritual, and sacrifice hang together in the life of his subjects. As far as day-to-day existence goes, he never finds his feet with them.[112]

Herbert Fingarette's *Confucius: The Secular as Sacred* transformed the study of Confucianism, and comparative religious ethics, by reading the *Analects* not as the "archaic irrelevance" of a "prosaic and parochial moralizer,"[113] but as the work of a social visionary trying to articulate a way to see Lu and its neighboring principalities as a cultural whole, worthy of preservation in a period of warring states and social turmoil. Of the three ways, generally speaking, that individuals can be brought to cooperate, two – coercion and contract – are inherently unstable. By seeing the practices that secure order as "an inheritance through accepted tradition,"[114] Confucius succeeded in persuading subsequent generations that "the dignity peculiar to man and the power associated with this dignity could be characterized in terms of holy rite."[115]

Fingarette articulates the interrelated vocabulary of ceremony – *li, jen, shu*, etc. – as an alternative to the ethics of law and guilt, or that of utility and contract, prevalent in Anglo-American moral theory. While he is committed to the practices, and some of the positions, of the Anglo-American philosophical tradition,[116] Fingarette is profoundly dissatisfied with moral theory done in the:

> language of choice and responsibility as these are intimately intertwined with the idea of the ontologically ultimate power of the individual to select from genuine alternatives to create his own spiritual destiny, and with the related ideas of spiritual guilt, and repentance or retribution for such guilt.[117]

Whether they used a language like ours or not, the people of ancient China faced problems not wholly unlike their contemporaries to the west. "Some men," Fingarette remarks, "were more responsible than others in Confucius's day as in ours. It is also obvious that men made choices in ancient China."[118] The point is to see how other people thought about their lives and to see what light that sheds on our ways of thinking about our lives. His Confucius sees "the flowering of humanity in the ceremonial acts of men."[119] This is, if you like, a Chinese ethic of character, for whose adherents it is both a duty and an honor to become the sort of person who wants to continue the way of the ancestors. This sort of person needs no fear of human or superhuman sanction or reward to do what needs to be done.[120]

Fingarette's engaged, sympathetic rereading is only the first step in finding our feet in comparative ethics. In the last century the flowering of social anthropology made it progressively easier to grasp how what might seem entirely alien to the foreign visitor could be second nature to the locals. Ethnographic classics by E. E. Evans-Pritchard, Godfrey Lienhardt, and others allowed the sympathetic reader to feel, if not exactly at home, an honored guest in some very alien environments.[121] But Mary Douglas may have done more than anyone to shake the modern psychologism that makes it easy to think other cultures are undeveloped versions of our own.[122]

By using her fieldwork among the Lele of the Kasai to generate an alternative reading of the abominations of Leviticus she highlighted the importance of social norms and categories in shaping perception.[123] She made it impossible to read cavalier dismissals of ritual practice like those of Zaehner as anything other than the product of blinkered parochialism. Later works trained the anthropological lens on our own classificatory practices, suggesting that what appear to us to be natural and unreflective responses to our environs are themselves products of the languages and habits we're trained into from birth.[124]

At the same time Douglas was developing a nuanced, fieldwork savvy version of Durkheim, Clifford Geertz was doing much the same for Max Weber. In his early essays, Geertz saw himself as working on "a kind of prototheory . . . of a more adequate analytic framework."[125] By 1967, he had begun to worry less about social theory and more about constructing perspicuous narratives that brought out the workings of the different societies he observed. In his Terry Lectures, Geertz "attempted to lay out a general framework for the comparative analysis of religion and to apply it to a study of the development of a supposedly single creed."[126] While not averse to the Durkheimian approach of Douglas,[127] Geertz sees Weber as providing a more subtle entry into the complications introduced by change over time. To take the most famous of Weber's case studies, the Reformed asceticism of Calvin's Geneva was embraced as an ideal by followers in Holland, Scotland, and England. That asceticism was popularized in English by Bunyan's *Pilgrim's Progress*, which Weber describes as "by far the most widely read book of the whole Puritan literature."[128]

In less than a hundred years, Benjamin Franklin, the son of one of Bunyan's Puritan contemporaries, would be perpetrating hoaxes, counselling revolutionaries, and giving canonical expression to an American ethic of capitalist thrift. Nothing, it would seem, could be further from the ethos of *Pilgrim's Progress* than Franklin's utilitarian deism. Yet, Weber argues, the ideas of Calvin and Bunyan held within themselves the seeds of "present-day capitalism . . . into which the individual is born, and which presents itself to him, at least as an individual, as an unalterable order of things in which he must live."[129] Regardless of its adequacy as history, what impresses Geertz is Weber's ability to link ideas to social change, which then produces new ideas. Because human beings are constantly attempting to figure out what's going on around them, ideas are constantly being interpreted, invented, and rearranged in response to the "problem of meaning."[130]

The 1970s found Geertz hoping "to draw large conclusions from small, but very densely textured facts; to support broad assertions about the role of culture in the construction of collective life by engaging them exactly with complex specifics."[131] By the time Geertz delivered the Storrs Lectures in 1981, his quick term for these complex specifics had become "local knowledge." "Law," he writes, "is local knowledge; local not just as to place, time, class, and variety of issue, but as to accent – vernacular characterizations of what happens connected to vernacular imaginings of what can."[132] Learning the language of legal judgment is as much a matter of triangulation as it is for the language of perception. Any theory of law, if meant to account for how people in different times and places go about enforcing their demands on each other and solve, or resolve, matters in dispute, would have to be so general as to be of very little descriptive use. Those trained up in one or more of the schools of Islamic law, Shari'a, may have serious doubts about the procedures of someone trained up in Indic law, with "its animating idea, *dharma*."[133] Both could easily be flumoxed by people discussing *adat*, a word of Arabic origins, meaning something like "custom," in an unnamed Balinese village in 1958.[134]

Geertz tells the story of Regreg and his lost wife to put on display the ways that wrinkles in one system cannot easily be ironed out by another. Regreg's kin-group was too weak to force his wife's abductor/boyfriend to return her. When he bucked the system of *adat*, apparently in a fit of peek, Regreg was shunned, left to wander "homeless, about the streets and courtyards of the village like a ghost, or more exactly like a dog."[135] When "the highest ranking traditional king on Bali, who was also, under the arrangements in effect at the time, the regional head of the new Republican government, came to beg Regreg's case,"[136] the local council refused to allow Regreg back. The new law was lovely, but not applicable. This local judgment, Geertz wants to insist, reflects its own "legal sensibility: one with form, personality, bite, and, even without the aid of law schools, jurisconsults, restatements, journals, or landmark decisions, a firm, developed, almost willful awareness of itself."[137] The moral of Geertz's effort "to render anomalous things in not too anomalous words"[138] is that we have no choice but to locate our own traditions and institutions among the various historically, politically, accidentally shaped alternatives. To attempt to wish this fact away "in a haze of forceless generalities and false comforts" is neither particularly scientific or much help in imagining "principled lives we can practicably lead."[139]

For those of us who stay fairly close to home, Geertz can agree with Fingarette that "precisely because we of the West are so deeply immersed in a world conceived in just such terms" as those found in the tradition that runs from the Greeks, through the Christians, to contemporary moral theory, "it is profitable for us to see the world in quite another way."[140] Geertz's critique of legal, and other, theorists intersects

Fingarette's critique of Anglo-American moral theorists. When, in the essays that make up his most recent collection, Geertz describes himself as an "anti anti-relativist" it is not because he thinks anything goes, but because "looking into dragons, not domesticating or abominating them, nor drowning them in vats of theory, is what anthropology has been all about."[141] Translated into ethics and politics, this amounts to an argument:

> that political theory is not, or anyway ought not to be, intensely generalized reflection on intensely generalized matters, an imagining of architectures in which no one could live, but should be, rather, an intellectual engagement, mobile, exact, and realistic, with present problems.[142]

This is, in a nutshell, what reflection on the purposes and limits of war has always been, East and West.

Notes

1 Howard, Michael (2000) *The Invention of Peace: Reflections on War and International Order*, Oxford: Oxford University Press: 1. Throughout my citations are to authors by date of work and page. In instances where convention dictates, I cite the traditional form, e.g. Aristotle by Bekker number and Aquinas by part, question, article.
2 Three authors dominate the current scene in Anglo-American military history. Michael Howard has already been mentioned. His 1976 volume, a brief sketch of the changing face of European war, remains a classic: Howard, Michael (1976) *War in European History*, Oxford: Oxford University Press. John Keegan surveys the entire history of how human beings have made war: Keegan, John (1993) *A History of Warfare*, New York: Alfred A. Knopf. Victor Hanson has not only contributed much to the study of ancient Greek warfare, but his recent volumes on war, society, and democratic values are brilliant if controversial, covering political implications of the history of western war from antiquity to the present: Hanson, Victor Davis (1989) *The Western Way of War: Infantry Battle in Classical Greece*, New York: Knopf and (1999) *The Soul of Battle: From Ancient Times to the Present Day, How Three Great Liberators Vanquished Tyranny*, New York: Free Press.
3 Geertz, Clifford (1973) *The Interpretation of Culture*, New York: Basic Books: 30.
4 Finley, M. I. (1985) *Ancient History: Evidence and Models*, New York: Viking Penguin: 70.
5 Ibid.: 71.
6 *Iliad* I. 582. Homer, *Iliad*, trans. Robert Fagles, introduction and notes Bernard Knox, New York: Viking, 1990.
7 *Iliad* II. 593–595.
8 *Iliad* XII, 374–380.
9 *Iliad* II, 246–316.
10 *Iliad* X, 523–527.
11 *Odyssey* XXII, 459–499. Homer, *Odyssey*, trans. Robert Fagles, introduction and notes Bernard Knox, New York: Viking, 1996.
12 *Odyssey* IX, 102–110.
13 *History of the Pelopponeisian War*, I, 23. Thucydides, *The Landmark Thucydides: A Comprehensive Guide to the Peloponnesian War*, ed. Robert Strassler, intro. Victor Davis Hanson, New York: Free Press, 1996.

14 Garlan, Yvon (1975) *War in the Ancient World: A Social History*, trans. Janet Lloyd, New York: W. W. Norton: 41.

15 Ibid.: 50.

16 Ibid.: 55.

17 Ibid.: 58.

18 Ibid.: 63.

19 Hunter, David G. (1992) "A Decade of Research on Early Christian and Military Service," *Religious Studies Review* 18(3): 87.

20 Helgeland, John, with Robert J. Daly, and J. Patout Burns (1985) *Christians and the Military: The Early Experience*, Philadelphia, PA: Fortress Press: 21–34.

21 Origen, *Contra Celsum*, ed. and trans. Henry Chadwick, Cambridge: Cambridge University Press, 1953: VIII, 73.

22 Augustine of Hippo, *Political Writings*, ed. and trans. by E. M. Atkins and R. J. Dodaro, Cambridge: Cambridge University Press, 2001: 216.

23 Ibid.: 217.

24 Markus, Robert (1983) "St. Augustine's Views on the 'Just War'" in W. J. Shiels (ed.) *The Church and War*, Oxford: Basil Blackwell: 4–12.

25 Becher, Matthias (2003) *Charlemagne*, trans. David S. Bachrach, New Haven, CT: Yale University Press: 5.

26 Southern, Richard W. (1953) *The Making of the Middle Ages*, New Haven, CT: Yale University Press: 224.

27 Head, Thomas and Richard Landes (eds.) (1992) *Peace of God: Social Violence and Religious Response in France around the Year 1000*, Ithaca, NY: Cornell University Press: 3ff.

28 Ibid.: 41–57, 308–326.

29 Riley-Smith, Jonathan (1986) *The First Crusade and the Idea of Crusading*, Philadelphia: University of Pennsylvania Press: 13. The literature on the crusades is enormous. Jonathan Riley-Smith (1987) *The Crusades: A Short History*, New Haven, CT: Yale University Press is a survey by the most influential recent student of the crusades. It has a helpful discussion of the literature, including primary sources in translation. His 1999 volume brings together essays on various aspects of the crusades by many of the most important other students of the topic: Riley-Smith, Jonathan (ed.) (1999) *The Oxford History of the Crusades*, Oxford: Oxford University Press.

30 The *locus classicus* for this distinction is Bainton, Roland H. (1960) *Christian Attitudes toward War and Peace: A Historical Survey and Critical Re-evaluation*, New York: Abingdon Press. It repeats an argument originally made in 1942 (Johnson, James Turner (1975) *Ideology, Reason, and the Limitation of War*, Princeton, NJ: Princeton University Press: 134–146). James Johnson returns to the problems with Bainton's approach in his 1997 (*The Holy War Idea in Western and Islamic Traditions*, University Park: Pennsylvania State University Press), which also provides a helpful survey of Muslim and Christian sources. H. E. J. Cowdrey makes telling, if philosophically suspect, use of the distinction in Bull, Marcus and Norman Housley (eds.) (2003) *The Experience of Crusading, I: Western Approaches*, Cambridge: Cambridge University Press: chapter 11.

31 Southern 1953: 50.

32 Brundage, James A. (1969) *Medieval Canon Law and the Crusader*, Madison: University of Wisconsin Press: 28–29, 32; Bull and Housley 2003: 147–156.

33 Riley-Smith 1986: 111.

34 Ibid.: 133.

35 Throop, Palmer A. (1975) *Criticism of the Crusade: A Study of Public Opinion and Crusade Propaganda*, Philadelphia, PA: Porcupine Press, which originally appeared

in 1940, sees criticism of the crusades as widespread. Riley-Smith and, following him, his student Elizabeth Siberry, reject Throop's argument. See Siberry, Elizabeth (1985) *Criticism of Crusading, 1095–1274*, Oxford: Oxford University Press. They see such criticism as there was as very much a minority position, usually directed toward particular offenses. But all parties agree that it was a particularly heated issue for Dominicans, at home and abroad.

36 Throop 1975: 148. Penny Cole has discussed Humbert's earlier compendium *On Preaching the Cross against the Infidel Saracens and the Pagans* in considerable detail (Bull and Housley: chapter 10). She refers to E. T. Brett (1985) *Humbert of Romans: His Life and Views of Thirteenth Century Society*, Toronto: Pontifical Institute of Medieval Studies. I have not yet been able to consult this volume.

37 Needless to say, Muslims and other inhabitants of the eastern Mediterranean and Palestine didn't see things quite this way. Francesco Gabrieli presents translations from Muslim historians of the time. See Gabrieli, Francesco (1969) *Arab Historians of the Crusades*, trans. E. J. Costello, Berkeley: University of California Press. Amin Maalouf tells the story as it appears to a Muslim reading those histories in Maalouf, Amin (1985) *The Crusades through Arab Eyes*, trans. Jon Rothschild, New York: Schocken Books. Further technical bibliography may be found in the bibliography of Riley-Smith 1999: 407–408.

38 The literature on St. Thomas is vast, even when restricted to English language publications. The standard translation of the *Summa Theologiae* (*ST* from now) is the older one by the English Dominicans, which first appeared between 1913 and 1926 and has been many times reprinted. A new generation of English Dominicans produced a bilingual edition in 60 volumes between 1964 and 1973. This last, often referred to as the Blackfriars edition, is less literal but, given the facing text, is often more helpful for close readings. Many volumes have very useful appendices. Bibliographical details on the primary texts may be found in Weisheipl, James A. (1974) *Friar Thomas D'Aquino: His Life, Thought, and Works*, Garden City, NY: Doubleday and in Torrell, Jean-Pierre (1996) *Saint Thomas Aquinas, Vol. I: The Person and His Work*, trans. Robert Royal, Washington, DC: Catholic University of America Press. As for secondary reading, very little is non-controversial, so I will simply record that my reading leans heavily on Chenu, Marie-Dominique (1964) *Toward Understanding St. Thomas*, trans. A. M. Landry and D. Hughes, Chicago, IL: Henry Regnery. This is supplemented by the self-consciously Aristotelian reading of Ralph McInerny. See McInerny, Ralph (1980) "The Principles of Natural Law," reprinted in Charles E. Curran and Richard A. McCormick (eds.) *Natural Law and Theology*, Mahwah, NJ: Paulist Press, 1991: 139–156. See also McInerny, Ralph (1982) *Ethica Thomistica: The Moral Philosophy of Thomas Aquinas*, Washington, DC: Catholic University of America Press. The most recent edition of McInerny 1982 leaves out the discussion based on his 1980 essay. An important recent volume is Bowlin, John (1999) *Contingency and Fortune in Aquinas's Ethics*, Cambridge: Cambridge University Press. Pope brings together essays by diverse hands to provide a comprehensive and detailed account of Thomas's ethics in Pope, Stephen J. (ed.) (2002) *The Ethics of Aquinas*, Washington, DC: Georgetown University Press.

39 Thomas treats homicide generally under the aegis of justice. Sinners may be killed by the public authority if there is a public danger and execution is necessary to preserve the common good. Thomas invokes the medical analogy, arguing that the situation is like that of a rotten or corrupt limb that threatens the whole of the body. Under those conditions it is "praiseworthy and healthy that it be cut off" (*ST* 2a2ae, 64, 2). Still, he insists, even in self-defense it is illicit for a private person to intend to kill his attacker. The innocent are never to be attacked directly, though judges and executioners incur no guilt in the case where an innocent is convicted through due process (*ST*, 2a2ae, 64, 6).

40 *ST*, 2a2ae, 10, 8.

41 *ST*, 1a2ae, 95, 1.

42 *ST* 2a2ae, 40, 1.

43 Holt, P. M., A. K. S. Lambton, and Bernard Lewis (eds.) (1970) *The Cambridge History of Islam*, 2 vols, Cambridge: Cambridge University Press: I, 233ff.

44 Throop 1974: 120–124; but see Siberry 1985: 208.

45 *ST*, 1a2ae, 19–20.

46 *ST*, 2a2ae, 40, 1 ad 1.

47 Cf. *ST*, 1a2ae, 19, 5–6.

48 *ST*, 2a2ae, 64, 7.

49 Pillage is a special problem. The pillaging and plunder of non-combatants is clearly wicked but was extremely widespread. As Robert Stacey puts it, "neither soldiers nor the lawyers and judges who adjudicated the resulting disputes over plunder paid the slightest attention to such immunities" (1994) "The Age of Chivalry," in Howard *et al.* (eds.) *The Laws of War: Constraints on Warfare in the Western World*, New Haven, CT: Yale University Press: 35) Also see Keen, Maurice (1984) *Chivalry*, New Haven, CT: Yale University Press: 227–237.

50 For many in the Catholic tradition Aquinas's moral theology, or some version of it, remains the dominant moral paradigm. There is some irony in the fact that, from his own perspective, Thomas's *Summa Theologiae* was a failure. Thomas had hoped to provide a comprehensive overview of theology. In the decades after his death, much of the Aristotelian realism that sets the background for Aquinas's moral theology was rejected. But the second part of the *Summa Theologiae* circulated as a manual for casuistry, bereft of its larger intellectual framework. The works of Leonard Boyle are fundamental to understanding the fate of Thomas's moral theology, particularly "The Setting of the *Summa Theologiae* of Saint Thomas," now reprinted, with some slight additions, in Pope 2002: 1–16. Further of Boyle's articles are collected in Boyle, Leonard E. (1981) *Pastoral Care, Clerical Education and Canon Law, 1200–1400*, London: Variorum Reprints. His "Saint Thomas Aquinas and the Third Millennium" was delivered as a plenary address to an audience of Dominican educators in April 1999, just six months before his death. It is a fine summary statement of the innovative character of the *Summa Theologiae* as a contribution to the "cura animarum" (http:// www.op.org/DomCentral/trad/boyle3mill.htm).

51 John of Legnano seems little studied beyond the work that went into the Carnegie endowment translation and the article by McCall. See John of Legnano (1917) *De Bello, De Represalis et De Duello*, ed. T. E. Holland, trans. J. L. Brierly, Oxford: Oxford University Press for the Carnegie Endowment for International Peace. See McCall, John (1967) "The Writings of John of Legnano with a List of Manuscripts," *Traditio* 23: 415–437. Jonathan Barnes mentions him in his essay (1982) "The Just War" in Norman Kretzmann *et al.* (eds.) *The Cambridge History of Later Medieval Philosophy*, Cambridge: Cambridge University Press: 771–784. John provided much of the material for Honoré Bonet's *Tree of Battles*, for which see Johnson (1975): 57–72. See Contamine, Philippe (1984) *War in the Middle Ages*, trans. Michael Jones, Oxford: Basil Blackwell, chap. 10. Note that, while "Bonet" appears in the notes and bibliography, the body of the text has "Bovet" for reasons I cannot discern.

52 Romans 7: 22–23.

53 Chap. 65.

54 Chap. 35.

55 *ST*, 2a2ae, 120, 1–2.

56 Chap. 169.

57 *ST*, 2a2ae, 95, 8 ad 3.

58 That John declines to follow Thomas here may stem from the fact that he seems to have been an avid astrologer. See chaps. 5–6.

59 Kraye, Jill (ed.) (1997) *Cambridge Translations of Renaissance Philosophical Texts, Vol. 2: Political Philosophy*, Cambridge: Cambridge University Press: 17.
60 This will become a standard move in the anti-Aristotelian approach to ethics known as "voluntarism." But this is a slippery term and, were it not part of the literature, we would probably be better off without it. Bonnie Kent sketches the spectrum of positions in her (1995) *Virtues of the Will: The Transformation of Ethics in the Late Thirteenth Century*, Washington, DC: Catholic University of America Press. She also provides a helpful introduction to Scotus's moral thought in Williams, Thomas (ed.) (2003) *Cambridge Companion to Duns Scotus*, Cambridge: Cambridge University Press. The primary locus for Scotus's moral thought is Wolter, Alan (1997) *Duns Scotus on the Will and Morality: Selected and Translated with an Introduction*, ed. William Frank, Washington, DC: Catholic University of America Press.
61 Vitoria, Francisco (1991) *Political Writings*, ed. and trans. Anthony Pagden and Jeremy Lawrence, Cambridge: Cambridge University Press: 234. The translation of Pagden and Lawrence has now become the standard. For a discussion of Vitoria's text and earlier translations see their introduction, pp. xiii–xxxviii. I do not think they are the most theologically or philosophically sensitive of Vitoria's readers. For my reasons see (1997) "Conscience and Conquest: Francisco de Vitoria on Justice in the New World," *Modern Theology* 13(4): 475–500.
62 Victoria 1991: 333.
63 Ibid.: 286.
64 Davis, G. Scott (1999) "Humanist Ethics and Political Justice: Soto, Sepulveda, and the 'Affair of the Indies,'" *Annual of the Society of Christian Ethics* 19: 193–212.
65 Grotius's works have had a complex publishing history. Richard Tuck argues that the text known as *De Jure Praedae Commentarius*, begun about 1608, was thought of by Grotius as *De Indis* and intended as a response to Vitoria. (Tuck, Richard (1993) *Philosophy and Government, 1572–1651*, Cambridge: Cambridge University Press: 170ff.; Tuck, Richard (1999) *The Rights of War and Peace: Political Thought and the International Order from Grotius to Kant*, Oxford: Oxford University Press: 80ff.) But more important is Tuck's argument that *De Indis* lays the foundation for the more famous *De Jure Belli et Pacis*, particularly in its first edition of 1625. The subsequent editions, Tuck suggests, modify the argument to make it "appear more acceptable to the Aristotelian, Calvinist culture of his opponents within the United Provinces." I cite the Carnegie translation of *De Jure Praedae* by page number and the translation of *De Jure Belli et Pacis* by book and section.
66 Grotius, Hugo (1925) *De Jure Belli et Pacis Libri Tres*, vol. 2, trans. Francis W. Kelsey, Oxford: Oxford University Press: Pro., 42.
67 Tuck 1999: 78.
68 Grotius, Hugo (1950) *De Jurae Praedae*, vol. 1, trans. Gwladys Williams, Oxford: Oxford University Press: 13.
69 Grotius 1950, appendix A: 369–370.
70 Ibid.: 95.
71 Ibid.: 167.
72 Ibid.: 365.
73 Grotius 1925: II, 40.
74 Mill, John Stuart (1989) *On Liberty and Other Writings*, ed. Stefan Collini, Cambridge: Cambridge University Press: 13.
75 Kissinger, Henry (1957) *A World Restored: Metternich, Castlereagh, and the Problems of Peace, 1812–1822*, Boston, MA: Houghton Mifflin: 325.
76 Dewey, John (1923) "Ethics and International Relations" reprinted in (1929) *Characters and Events: Popular Essays in Social and Political Philosophy*, ed. J. Ratner, New York: Henry Holt: 804–814: 806–807.

77 Dewey, John (1979) *The Middle Works, 1899–1924*, vol. 15, ed. J. A. Boydston, Carbondale, IL: Southern Illinois University Press: 486.

78 Hocking, William Ernest (1915) "Political Philosophy in Germany," reprinted in Dewey (1979): 473–477: 475.

79 Dewey, John (1915a) "Reply to William Ernest Hocking's 'Political Philosophy in Germany,'" reprinted in Dewey (1979): 418–420: 418.

80 Dewey, John (1915) *German Philosophy and Politics*, reprinted in Dewey (1979): 134–204: 141.

81 Ryan, Alan (1995) *John Dewey and the High Tide of American Liberalism*, New York: W. W. Norton: 169.

82 Ibid.: 186.

83 Paret, Peter (1986) *Makers of Modern Strategy: From Machiavelli to the Nuclear Age*, Princeton, NJ: Princeton University Press: 908–909.

84 Lippmann, Walter (1970) *Early Writings*, with introduction and annotations by Arthur Schlesinger, Jr., New York: Liveright: 13.

85 Dewey 1915: 197.

86 Ibid.: 201.

87 Ibid.: 200.

88 Ibid.: 202.

89 Ibid.: 203.

90 Ibid.: 203–204.

91 Westbrook, Robert B. (1991) *John Dewey and American Democracy*, Ithaca, NY: Cornell University Press: 274.

92 Dewey, John (1933) "Outlawry of War" reprinted in (1986) *The Later Works, 1925–1953*, vol. 8, ed. J. A. Boydston, B. Walsh, and H. F. Simon, Carbondale, IL: Southern Illinois University Press: 17.

93 Dewey 1923: 655.

94 Dewey, John (1942) "The One-World of Hitler's National Socialism" reprinted in Dewey 1979: 446.

95 Ibid.: 446.

96 Murray, Williamson and Allan R. Millett (2000) *A War to be Won: Fighting the Second World War*, Cambridge, MA: Harvard University Press: 507.

97 Miller, Richard (ed.) (1992) *War in the Twentieth Century: Sources in Theological Ethics*, Louisville, KY: Westminster/John Knox Press: 170.

98 Ibid.: 237–246.

99 Stein, Walter (ed.) (1961) *Nuclear Ethics and Christian Conscience*, London: The Merlin Press.

100 See Davis, G. Scott (1992) *Warcraft and the Fragility of Virtue*, Moscow, ID: University of Idaho Press.

101 As I mentioned above, for the Aristotelian tradition only the first three are strictly required. Nonetheless, it is important to keep in mind that other approaches to just war thinking don't share my Aristotelian commitments. James Childress's "Just War Criteria" is a well-respected non-Aristotelian approach (Miller 1992: 351–372). For an Aristotelian reading of Childress see Davis 1992: 103–110. What different thinkers list as the *jus ad bellum* criteria is, ultimately, not nearly as important as the distinction between thinkers who think war can be just, and thus on occasion the right and the good thing to do, and those who, as Childress sometimes seems to, think of war as a justifiable evil, which is sometimes necessary to prevent even worse evils. See the exchange that comprises Childress, James (1997) "Nonviolent Resistance, Trust and Risk-Taking Twenty-five Years Later," *Journal of Religious Ethics* 25(2): 213–222; Johnson, James Turner (1998) "Comment," *Journal of Religious Ethics* 26(1): 219–222; and Davis, G. Scott (1999a) "Research Note," *Journal of Religious*

Ethics 27(2): 369–374, as well as Ilesanmi, Simeon (2000) "Just War Tradition in Comparative Perspective: A Review Essay," *Journal of Religious Ethics* 28(1): 139–155.

102 Cf. Rawls, John (2001) *Justice as Fairness: A Restatement*, Cambridge, MA: Harvard University Press: 168–176.

103 Rawls, John (1999a) *Collected Papers*, ed. Samuel Freeman, Cambridge, MA: Harvard University Press: 95, n. 8.

104 Singer, Peter (1993) *Practical Ethics*, second edition, Cambridge: Cambridge University Press: 11–12.

105 Ibid.: 173–174.

106 Danby, Herbert (1933) *The Mishnah, Translated from the Hebrew with Introduction and Brief Explanatory Notes*, Oxford: Oxford University Press: 385.

107 Davidson, Donald (2001) *Subjective, Intersubjective, Objective*, Oxford: Oxford University Press: 119.

108 Wittgenstein, Ludwig (1958) *Philosophical Investigations*, second edition, ed. R. Rhees and G. E. M. Anscombe, trans. Anscombe, Oxford: Basil Blackwell: II, xi.

109 Zaehner, R. C. (1961) *The Dawn and Twilight of Zoroastrianism*, New York: G. P. Putnam's Sons: 16.

110 Zaehner, R. C. (1962) *Hinduism*, Oxford: Oxford University Press: 198.

111 Douglas, Mary (1966) *Purity and Danger: An Analysis of Concepts of Pollution and Taboo*, London: Routledge: 62.

112 An alternative to Davidson's treatment of interpretation that is capturing much attention is the "inferentialism" of Robert Brandom. Richard Rorty and Jeffrey Stout deploy Brandom with interesting results in their contributions to Frankenberry, Nancy (ed.) (2002) *Radical Interpretation in Religion*, Cambridge: Cambridge University Press. Stout's contribution has been integrated into Stout, Jeffrey (2003) *Democracy and Tradition*, Princeton, NJ: Princeton University Press. This can be read as an extended exercise in the inferential analysis of moral traditions.

113 Fingarette, Herbert (1972) *Confucius: The Secular as Sacred*, New York: Harper & Row: vii.

114 Ibid.: 62.

115 Ibid.: 63.

116 Ibid.: 11, n. 6.

117 Ibid.: 18.

118 Ibid.: 18–19.

119 Ibid.: 78.

120 I am not suggesting that all interpreters of Chinese thought have embraced Fingarette's reading of Confucius. On the other hand, as preeminent a Sinologist as Angus Graham writes that Fingarette "revitalized all our thinking about the sage" (Graham, A. C. (1989) *Disputers of the Tao: Philosophical Argument in Ancient China*, La Salle, IL: Open Court: 23). Such important interpreters of Chinese thought as Henry Rosemont and Roger Ames reflect on Fingarette's work in Bockover, Mary (1991) *Rules, Rituals, and Responsibility: Essays Dedicated to Herbert Fingarette*, La Salle, IL: Open Court. Geaney, Jane (2000) "Chinese Cosmology and Recent Studies in Confucian Ethics," *Journal of Religious Ethics* 28(3): 451–470 is a review of more recent work in Confucian ethics.

121 Douglas, Mary (1999) *Implicit Meanings: Selected Essays in Anthropology*, second edition, London: Routledge: 188.

122 Ibid.: 108–110.

123 Douglas 1966: 42–58.

124 Douglas, Mary (1996) *Natural Symbols: Explorations in Cosmology*, new edition, London: Routledge: 20–36; Douglas 1999: 231–313; Stout, Jeffrey (2001) *Ethics*

after Babel, with a New Postscript by the Author, Princeton, NJ: Princeton University Press: 145–160, 353–355.

125 Geertz, Clifford (1973) *The Interpretation of Culture*, New York: Basic Books: 141.
126 Geertz, Clifford (1971) *Islam Observed: Religious Development in Morocco and Indonesia*, Chicago: University of Chicago Press: v.
127 See Geertz 1973: 142ff.
128 Weber, Max (1992) *The Protestant Ethic and the Spirit of Capitalism*, trans. Talcott Parsons, with intro. by Anthony Giddens, London: Routledge: 63. If anything, Weber underplays the impact of *Pilgrim's Progress*. Until the end of the nineteenth century, Bunyan's allegory was the second most widely read book in English. Roger Sharrock, one of Bunyan's recent editors, writes that "it has penetrated into the non-Christian world; it has been read by cultivated Moslems during the rise of religious individualism within Islam, and at the same time in cheap missionary editions by American Indians and South Sea Islanders. Its uncompromising evangelical Protestantism has not prevented it from exercising an appeal in Catholic countries" (Bunyan, John (1965) *The Pilgrim's Progress*, edited with introduction and notes by Roger Sharrock, Harmondsworth: Penguin Books: 7).
129 Weber 1992: 19.
130 Geertz 1973: 104.
131 Ibid.: 28.
132 Geertz, Clifford (1983) *Local Knowledge: Further Essays in Interpretive Anthropology*, New York: Basic Books: 215.
133 Ibid.: 195.
134 Ibid.: 175–176.
135 Ibid.: 177.
136 Ibid.: 178.
137 Ibid.: 179.
138 Ibid.: 225.
139 Ibid.: 234.
140 Fingarette 1972: 18.
141 Geertz, Clifford (2000) *Available Light: Anthropological Reflections on Philosophical Topics*, Princeton, NJ: Princeton University Press: 63–64.
142 Ibid.: 259.

Bibliography

Aristotle (2000) *Nicomachean Ethics*, trans., with introduction, notes, and glossary, by Terence Irwin, second edition, Indianapolis, IN: Hackett Publishing.

Augustine of Hippo (2001) *Political Writings*, ed. and trans. by E. M. Atkins and R. J. Dodaro, Cambridge: Cambridge University Press.

Bainton, Roland H. (1960) *Christian Attitudes toward War and Peace: A Historical Survey and Critical Re-evaluation*, New York: Abingdon Press.

Barnes, Jonathan (1982) "The Just War," in Norman Kretzmann, Anthony Kenny, and Jan Pinborg (eds.) *The Cambridge History of Later Medieval Philosophy*, Cambridge: Cambridge University Press, pp. 771–784

Becher, Matthias (2003) *Charlemagne*, trans. David S. Bachrach, New Haven, CT: Yale University Press

Bockover, Mary (1991) *Rules, Rituals, and Responsibility: Essays Dedicated to Herbert Fingarette*, La Salle, IL: Open Court.

Bowlin, John (1999) *Contingency and Fortune in Aquinas's Ethics*, Cambridge: Cambridge University Press.

G. SCOTT DAVIS

Boyle, Leonard E. (1981) *Pastoral Care, Clerical Education and Canon Law, 1200–1400*, London: Variorum Reprints.

Boyle, Leonard E. (1999) "Saint Thomas Aquinas and the Third Millennium" now at http://www.op.org/DomCentral/trad/boyle3mill.htm

Bull, Marcus and Norman Housley (eds.) (2003) *The Experience of Crusading, I: Western Approaches*, Cambridge: Cambridge University Press.

Bunyan, John (1965) *The Pilgrim's Progress*, edited with introduction and notes by Roger Sharrock, Harmondsworth: Penguin Books.

Chenu, Marie-Dominique (1964) *Toward Understanding St. Thomas*, trans. A. M. Landry and D. Hughes, Chicago, IL: Henry Regnery.

Chenu, Marie-Dominique (2002) *Aquinas and His Role in Theology*, trans. P. Philibert, Collegeville, MN: Liturgical Press.

Childress, James (1997) "'Nonviolent Resistance, Trust and Risk-Taking' Twenty-five Years Later," *Journal of Religious Ethics* 25(2): 213–22.

Contamine, Philippe (1984) *War in the Middle Ages*, trans. Michael Jones, Oxford: Basil Blackwell.

Danby, Herbert (1933) *The Mishnah, Translated from the Hebrew with Introduction and Brief Explanatory Notes*, Oxford: Oxford University Press.

Davidson, Donald (2001) *Subjective, Intersubjective, Objective*, Oxford: Oxford University Press.

Davis, G. Scott (1991) "'Et quod vis fac': Paul Ramsey and Augustinian Ethics," *Journal of Religious Ethics* 19(2) Fall: 31–69.

Davis, G. Scott (1992) *Warcraft and the Fragility of Virtue*, Moscow, ID: University of Idaho Press.

Davis, G. Scott (1997) "Conscience and Conquest: Francisco de Vitoria on Justice in the New World," *Modern Theology* 13(4): 475–500.

Davis, G. Scott (1999) "Humanist Ethics and Political Justice: Soto, Sepulveda, and the 'Affair of the Indies,'" *Annual of the Society of Christian Ethics* 19: 193–212.

Davis, G. Scott (1999a) "Research Note," *Journal of Religious Ethics* 27(2): 369–74.

Dewey, John (1915) *German Philosophy and Politics*, reprinted in Dewey (1979): 134–204.

Dewey, John (1915a) "Reply to William Ernest Hocking's 'Political Philosophy in Germany,'" reprinted in Dewey (1979): 418–20.

Dewey, John (1923) "Ethics and International Relations," reprinted in Dewey (1929): 804–14.

Dewey, John (1929) *Characters and Events: Popular Essays in Social and Political Philosophy*, ed. J. Ratner, New York: Henry Holt.

Dewey, John (1933) "Outlawry of War," reprinted in Dewey (1986): 13–18.

Dewey, John (1942) "The One-World of Hitler's National Socialism," reprinted in Dewey (1979): 421–46.

Dewey, John (1979) *The Middle Works, 1899–1924*, vol. 15, ed. J. A. Boydston, Carbondale, IL: Southern Illinois University Press.

Dewey, John (1986) *The Later Works, 1925–1953*, vol. 8, ed. J. A. Boydston, B. Walsh, and H. F. Simon, Carbondale, IL: Southern Illinois University Press.

Douglas, Mary (1966) *Purity and Danger: An Analysis of Concepts of Pollution and Taboo*, London: Routledge.

Douglas, Mary (1996) *Natural Symbols: Explorations in Cosmology*, new edition, London: Routledge.

Douglas, Mary (1999) *Implicit Meanings: Selected Essays in Anthropology*, second edition, London: Routledge.

Fingarette, Herbert (1972) *Confucius: The Secular as Sacred*, New York: Harper & Row.

Finley, M. I. (1985) *Ancient History: Evidence and Models*, New York: Viking Penguin.

Frankenberry, Nancy (ed.) (2002) *Radical Interpretation in Religion*, Cambridge: Cambridge University Press.

Gabrieli, Francesco (1969) *Arab Historians of the Crusades*, trans. E. J. Costello, Berkeley, CA: University of California Press.

Garlan, Yvon (1975) *War in the Ancient World: A Social History*, trans. Janet Lloyd, New York: W. W. Norton.

Geaney, Jane (2000) "Chinese Cosmology and Recent Studies in Confucian Ethics," *Journal of Religious Ethics* 28(3): 451–70.

Geertz, Clifford (1971) *Islam Observed: Religious Development in Morocco and Indonesia*, Chicago, IL: University of Chicago Press.

Geertz, Clifford (1973) *The Interpretation of Culture*, New York: Basic Books.

Geertz, Clifford (1983) *Local Knowledge: Further Essays in Interpretive Anthropology*, New York: Basic Books.

Geertz, Clifford (2000) *Available Light: Anthropological Reflections on Philosophical Topics*, Princeton, NJ: Princeton University Press.

Graham, A. C. (1989) *Disputers of the Tao: Philosophical Argument in Ancient China*, La Salle, IL: Open Court.

Grotius, Hugo (1925) *De Jure Belli et Pacis Libri Tres*, vol. 2, trans. Francis W. Kelsey, Oxford: Oxford University Press.

Grotius, Hugo (1950) *De Jurae Praedae*, vol. 1, trans. Gwladys Williams, Oxford: Oxford University Press.

Hanson, Victor Davis (1989) *The Western Way of War: Infantry Battle in Classical Greece*, New York: Knopf.

Hanson, Victor Davis (1999) *The Soul of Battle: From Ancient Times to the Present Day, How Three Great Liberators Vanquished Tyranny*, New York: Free Press.

Hanson, Victor Davis (2001) *Carnage and Culture: Landmark Battles in the Rise of Western Power*, New York: Doubleday.

Head, Thomas and Richard Landes (eds.) (1992) *Peace of God: Social Violence and Religious Response in France around the Year 1000*, Ithaca, NY: Cornell University Press.

Helgeland, John, with Robert J. Daly, and J. Patout Burns (1985) *Christians and the Military: The Early Experience*, Philadelphia, PA: Fortress Press.

Hocking, William Ernest (1915). "Political Philosophy in Germany," reprinted in Dewey (1979): 473–77.

Holmes, Arthur F. (ed.) (1975) *War and Christian Ethics*, Grand Rapids, MI: Baker Book House.

Holt, P. M., A. K. S. Lambton, and Bernard Lewis (eds.) (1970) *The Cambridge History of Islam*, 2 vols, Cambridge: Cambridge University Press.

Homer (1990) *The Iliad*, trans. Robert Fagles, introduction and notes Bernard Knox, New York: Viking.

Homer (1996) *The Odyssey*, trans. Robert Fagles, introduction and notes Bernard Knox, New York: Viking.

Howard, Michael (1976) *War in European History*, Oxford: Oxford University Press.

Howard, Michael (2000) *The Invention of Peace: Reflections on War and International Order*, Oxford: Oxford University Press.

Howard, Michael, George J. Andreopoulos, and Mark R. Shulman (eds.) (1994) *The Laws of War: Constraints on Warfare in the Western World*, New Haven, CT: Yale University Press.

Hunter, David G. (1992) "A Decade of Research on Early Christian and Military Service," *Religious Studies Review* 18(3).

Ilesanmi, Simeon (2000) "Just War Tradition in Comparative Perspective: A Review Essay," *Journal of Religious Ethics* 28(1): 139–55.

John of Legnano (1917) *De Bello, De Represalis et De Duello*, ed. T. E. Holland, trans. J. L. Brierly, Oxford: Oxford University Press/Carnegie Endowment for International Peace.

Johnson, James Turner (1975) *Ideology, Reason, and the Limitation of War: Religious and Secular Concepts, 1200–1740*, Princeton, NJ: Princeton University Press.

Johnson, James Turner (1997) *The Holy War Idea in Western and Islamic Traditions*, University Park, PA: Pennsylvania State University Press.

Johnson, James Turner (1998) "Comment" *Journal of Religious Ethics* 26(1): 219–22.

Keegan, John (1976) *The Face of Battle*, New York: Viking.

Keegan, John (1993) *A History of Warfare*, New York: Alfred A. Knopf.

Keen, Maurice (1984) *Chivalry*, New Haven, CT: Yale University Press.

Kent, Bonnie (1995) *Virtues of the Will: The Transformation of Ethics in the Late Thirteenth Century*, Washington, DC: Catholic University of America Press.

Kissinger, Henry (1957) *A World Restored: Metternich, Castlereagh, and the Problems of Peace, 1812–1822*, Boston, MA: Houghton Mifflin.

Kraye, Jill (ed.) (1997) *Cambridge Translations of Renaissance Philosophical Texts, Vol. 2: Political Philosophy*, Cambridge: Cambridge University Press.

Lippmann, Walter (1970) *Early Writings*, with introduction and annotations by Arthur Schlesinger, Jr., New York: Liveright.

Little, David and Sumner B. Twiss (1978) *Comparative Religious Ethics: A New Method*, New York: Harper & Row.

Maalouf, Amin (1985) *The Crusades through Arab Eyes*, trans. Jon Rothschild, New York: Schocken Books.

McCall, John (1967) "The Writings of John of Legnano with a List of Manuscripts," *Traditio* 23: 415–37.

McInerny, Ralph (1980) "The Principles of Natural Law," reprinted in Charles E. Curran and richard A. McCormick (eds.) *Natural Law and Theology*, Mahwah, NJ: Paulist Press, 1991, pp. 139–56.

McInerny, Ralph (1982) *Ethica Thomistica: The Moral Philosophy of Thomas Aquinas*, Washington, DC: Catholic University of America Press.

Markus, Robert (1983) "St. Augustine's views on the 'Just War,'" in W. J. Shiels (ed.) *The Church and War*, Oxford: Basil Blackwell.

Mill, John Stuart (1989) *On Liberty and Other Writings*, ed. Stefan Collini, Cambridge: Cambridge University Press.

Miller, Richard (ed.) (1992) *War in the Twentieth Century: Sources in Theological Ethics*, Louisville, KY: Westminster/John Knox Press.

Murray, Williamson and Allan R. Millett (2000) *A War to be Won: Fighting the Second World War*, Cambridge, MA: Harvard University Press.

Origen *Contra Celsum*, ed. and trans. Henry Chadwick, Cambridge: Cambridge University Press, 1953.

Paret, Peter (1986) *Makers of Modern Strategy: From Machiavelli to the Nuclear Age*, Princeton, NJ: Princeton University Press.

Pope, Stephen J. (ed.) (2002) *The Ethics of Aquinas*, Washington, DC: Georgetown University Press.

Rawls, John (1971) *A Theory of Justice*, Cambridge, MA: Harvard University Press.

Rawls, John (1999) *The Law of Peoples*, Cambridge, MA: Harvard University Press.

Rawls, John (1999a) *Collected Papers*, ed. Samuel Freeman, Cambridge, MA: Harvard University Press.

Rawls, John (2001) *Justice as Fairness: A Restatement*, Cambridge, MA: Harvard University Press.

Riley-Smith, Jonathan (1986) *The First Crusade and the Idea of Crusading*, Philadelphia, PA: University of Pennsylvania Press.

Riley-Smith, Jonathan (1987) *The Crusades: A Short History*, New Haven, CT: Yale University Press.

Riley-Smith, Jonathan (ed.) (1999) *The Oxford History of the Crusades*, Oxford: Oxford University Press.

Ryan, Alan (1995) *John Dewey and the High Tide of American Liberalism*, New York: W. W. Norton.

Scott, James Brown (1917) "Preface of the General Editor" to Iohannis de Lignano, *De Bello, de Represaliis, et de Duello*, ed. T. E. Holland, Oxford: Oxford University Press/ Carnegie Endowment for International Peace.

Siberry, Elizabeth (1985) *Criticism of Crusading, 1095–1274*, Oxford: Oxford University Press.

Singer, Peter (1993) *Practical Ethics*, second edition, Cambridge: Cambridge University Press.

Southern, Richard W. (1953) *The Making of the Middle Ages*, New Haven, CT: Yale University Press.

Southern, Richard W. (1970) *Western Church and Society in the Middle Ages*, London: Penguin Books.

Stein, Walter (ed.) (1961) *Nuclear Ethics and Christian Conscience*, London: The Merlin Press.

Stout, Jeffrey (2001) *Ethics after Babel, with a New Postscript by the Author*, Princeton, NJ: Princeton University Press.

Stout, Jeffrey (2003) *Democracy and Tradition*, Princeton, NJ: Princeton University Press.

Throop, Palmer A. (1975) *Criticism of the Crusade: A Study of Public Opinion and Crusade Propaganda*, Philadelphia, PA: Porcupine Press.

Thucydides (1996) *The Landmark Thucydides: A Comprehensive Guide to the Peloponnesian War*, ed. Robert Strassler, intro. Victor Davis Hanson, New York: Free Press.

Torrell, Jean-Pierre (1996) *Saint Thomas Aquinas, Vol. I: The Person and His Work*, trans. Robert Royal, Washington, DC: Catholic University of America Press.

Tuck, Richard (1993) *Philosophy and Government, 1572–1651*, Cambridge: Cambridge University Press.

Tuck, Richard (1999) *The Rights of War and Peace: Political Thought and the International Order from Grotius to Kant*, Oxford: Oxford University Press.

Vitoria, Francisco (1991) Political Writings, ed. and trans. Anthony Pagden and Jeremy Lawrence, Cambridge: Cambridge University Press.

Weber, Max (1992) *The Protestant Ethic and the Spirit of Capitalism*, trans. Talcott Parsons, with intro. by Anthony Giddens, London: Routledge.

Weisheipl, James A. (1974) *Friar Thomas D'Aquino: His Life, Thought, and Works*, Garden City, NY: Doubleday.

Westbrook, Robert B. (1991) *John Dewey and American Democracy*, Ithaca, NY: Cornell University Press.

Williams, Thomas (ed.) (2003) *Cambridge Companion to Duns Scotus*, Cambridge: Cambridge University Press.

Wittgenstein, Ludwig (1958) *Philosophical Investigations*, second edition, ed. R. Rhees and G. E. M. Anscombe, trans. Anscombe, Oxford: Basil Blackwell.

Wolter, Alan (1997) *Duns Scotus on the Will and Morality: Selected and Translated with an Introduction*, ed. William Frank, Washington, DC: Catholic University of America Press.

Zaehner, R. C. (1961) *The Dawn and Twilight of Zoroastrianism*, New York: G. P. Putnam's Sons.

Zaehner, R. C. (1962) *Hinduism*, Oxford: Oxford University Press.

Part I

WEST ASIA

1

THE ETHICS OF WAR IN JUDAISM

Norman Solomon

Definitions: sources and how to read them

By "ethics" I mean "norms of behaviour", whether they are formulated as laws, or as ethical or moral principles.

"Judaism" is the religion of the Jews, more properly called "Rabbinic Judaism". It is *not* to be identified with "Old Testament Theology". Judaism, like Christianity, has deep roots in the Hebrew Scriptures ("Old Testament"), but it interprets those scriptures along lines classically formulated by the rabbis of the Babylonian Talmud, completed shortly before the rise of Islam.

The Talmud is a reference point rather than a definitive statement; Judaism has continued to mature right up to the present time. To get some idea of how Judaism handles the ethics of war, we have to review sources from the earliest scriptures to the literature of contemporary Israel, a period of three thousand years; there is continuity, but also substantial change.

The Bible (Old Testament, or Hebrew Scriptures) is a collection of books compiled over more than a millennium. It describes the ruthless wars waged by the Israelites against the Canaanites, and it encompasses the vision that "nation shall not lift sword unto nation" (Isaiah 2:4; Micah 4:3). People turn to scripture for guidance, but it has to be interpreted; its range is wide, and our language and our culture are quite different from those in which the Bible was written. How do we read an ancient text in a modern context? Within the Jewish tradition, the Talmud and other works of the rabbis guide the reading.

The Bible reports, for instance, that Jacob's sons slaughtered the inhabitants of Shechem on account of the rape of their sister, Dinah, by their leader's son. Are we to interpret this as a model of righteous zeal, or as a grave aberration? From the text itself we would not know. Later Jewish tradition, however, regarded the massacre as a crime, or at best as an act requiring exceptional justification.[1]

The rabbis gave privileged status within the Bible to the "Torah of Moses", that is, the books Genesis, Exodus, Leviticus, Numbers and Deuteronomy. Laws may be derived from these books, but not from elsewhere in scripture. Deuteronomic legislation, rightly interpreted, is normative; the behaviour of, e.g. King David, is not, and may indeed be open to criticism in the light of Torah legislation.

Consequently, the legislation concerning warfare in Deuteronomy 20 assumes considerable significance in rabbinic thinking, as it was later to do amongst Christians. How has it been interpreted?

The passage, a "military oration",[2] is concerned with what jurists would later refer to as *jus in bello* rather than *jus ad bellum*; it regulates conduct in war, but does not specify conditions under which it is appropriate to engage in war. It distinguishes between (a) the war directly mandated by God against the Canaanites and (b) other wars. This is something like the distinction made in early modern Europe between religious wars (wars of the Church) and wars of the Prince.[3]

Deuteronomy's *jus in bello* is of two kinds. War against the Canaanites is based on the *herem*, or holy ban; it is a war of extermination that knows no bounds (verses 15–18). Justification – a sort of *jus ad bellum* – is offered, on the grounds that these nations might teach Israel "abominations" and lead them to sin (verse 18).[4] No restraints are indicated.

However, "normal" war is subject to several restraints:

- The war is to be fought only by those who are courageous, possessing faith in God, and who do not have a commitment such as a new house, vineyard or wife (verses 1–10).
- An offer of peace is to be made to any city which is besieged, conditional on the acceptance of terms of tribute (10, 11).
- Should the city refuse the offer of peace the males are put to the sword, the females and small children are taken captive, and the city plundered.
- Food trees may not be cut down in prosecution of the siege (19, 20).
- 21:10–14 offers some amelioration of the status of the female captive.

According to a rabbinic observation, based on Joshua 11:19, "No city made peace with the Israelites, save the Hivites who lived in Gibeon", an offer of peace was made to the Canaanites, too.[5]

We must be careful not to read later concepts into the text. For instance, someone might read the commandment to spare the lives of women and children as a primitive form of non-combatant immunity, all adult males being regarded by default as combatants. But the Deuteronomic context is not about the human rights of citizens of an opposing state, but about whether Israelites might retain heathen women and children as booty (in war against the Canaanites women come under the *herem* ban and must be killed).

Likewise, the commandment not to cut down fruit trees has been utilized as a "proof-text" for environmental responsibility in time of war; in its context, however, it is a counsel of prudence, that the conquering army should not destroy its own potential food sources.

Also, the distinction we take for granted between defensive and offensive wars may be inappropriate in the context of the ancient Near East and much of pre-modern (and sadly some modern) society, just as it would be inappropriate if we were speaking of animal societies in which territorial or sexual competition reigns. If you do not take the initiative, someone else will; you eat, or you are eaten.

As to *jus ad bellum*, many biblical passages indicate the need for a *casus belli*, though the Bible does not articulate principles from which we might judge whether a particular cause was justified. If God issued explicit instructions, that would constitute adequate justification. However, God conspicuously does *not* rely on divine fiat alone when he commands the Israelites to conquer the "promised land," but vindicates it with the claims that (a) He has condemned the Canaanites on account of their immorality[6] and (b) if left, they might "contaminate" the Israelites.

Here again, extrapolation is dangerous. Malachi prophesies "The Lord will rule the whole earth" (Malachi 14:9), but nowhere in the Bible or in rabbinic[7] tradition does this translate into a general "holy war" against idolaters beyond the borders of Israel.[8] When Christians and subsequently Muslims abandoned Jewish "particularism" they extrapolated the concept of "holy war" to the international level; a nation might initiate war against another in order to bring it to the "true faith". Reacting to this tendency, the Dominican theologian Franciscus de Victoria (?1486–1546) supports his "natural law" arguments against war for religion by a direct appeal to the Hebrew scriptures:

> [E]ven in the Old Testament, where much was done by force of arms, the people of Israel never seized the land of unbelievers either because they were unbelievers or idolaters or because they were guilty of other sins . . . but because of either a special gift from God or because their enemies had hindered their passage or had attacked them.[9]

We will not explore the extent to which the provisions of Deuteronomy governed Israelite activities in the biblical period; at least one biblical scholar has argued that these provisions were the "radicalism of the writing desk," a retrojection by authors attempting to bolster the covenantal consciousness of Israel.[10] Still, it is worth noting that at least two kings – Saul and Ahab – were reprimanded by prophets for challenging the ruthlessness of the Deuteronomic position,[11] and that the prophet Amos (chapter 1) condemns several nations for atrocities committed in wars against each other.[12]

We focus rather on the "reception history" of the chapter, that is the way in which it was taken up and reinterpreted within rabbinic Judaism, from the time of the Mishna (about 200 CE) onwards. The rabbis would not criticize Deuteronomy, for they regarded it as the direct word of God; rather, they express their unease with the plain meaning of its words by interpreting in a different sense. Likewise, they would not exonerate Saul for his remissness in destroying the Amalekites, since the Bible states that he was deservedly punished; but they retell the story in a way that is sympathetic to Saul and articulates their own puzzlement at the command to destroy Amalek:

> "And he strove[13] in the valley (1 Samuel 15:5)." Rabbi Mani says, "Concerning the inheritance.[14] For when the Holy One, blessed be He, said to Saul, "Go, smite Amalek . . ." (15:3) he said, Surely, if the Torah

says that if someone kills even one person a calf's neck must be broken,[15] how much more so for all these people, and if the adults have sinned, what about the children! A heavenly voice issued forth and said, "Do not be over-righteous".

(Ecclesiastes 7:16)[16]

The "heavenly voice" here is put on the defensive; it is Saul whose moral reasoning is made to appear correct.

Rabbinic readings of scripture

If we regard the revolts of Judea against Rome from 70 CE onwards[17] as wars of national liberation, the last *offensive* war of Jews against a foreign power was most probably Alexander Jannai's Transjordanian campaign *c.*75 BCE, a campaign characterized by Alexander's ruthless extermination of tribes who refused to accept Judaism;[18] even that campaign could, at a stretch, be regarded as defensive.

The War Rule ("War of the Sons of Light against the Sons of Darkness") of the Dead Sea Scrolls[19] illustrates apocalyptic thinking, or rather imagination, in the late first century BCE. Its adaptation of Deuteronomy to the wars against the "Kittim" (Romans), though utilizing some Roman military terminology, has little to do with the conduct of any real war.

By the time the Mishna and its associated classical formulations of rabbinic Judaism were compiled Jews had lost political independence; the sparse discussion of war in this literature lacks firm contact with contemporary reality. There are rationalizations of biblical narrative, selective recollection of the revolts against Rome, and apocalyptic speculation about Messianic wars. Only in the exposition of Deuteronomy 20 do we find elements of legislation on warfare, but even this is historical reconstruction or messianic speculation, not the operational law of an actual society.

We shall now review some of the rabbinic comments and observations that were to acquire significance when Jews in later ages sought guidance on the conduct of and justification for war.

Bearing arms – honour or shame?

Some time between the Fall of Jerusalem in 70 CE and the Bar Kochba Revolt against Rome of 131–135, Eliezer ben Hyrcanus debated with the other sages (rabbis) whether a man might adorn himself with weapons in the public domain on the Sabbath even when not required for defence. Their apparently technical debate on an obscure point in Sabbath law proceeds from a deep difference in attitude to the bearing of arms. To the majority sages the bearing of arms, though necessary for defence, disgraces the wearer; but Eliezer, a staunch Jewish nationalist, regarded the bearing of arms as honourable.[20]

Exemption

King Asa of Judah suffered gout[21] (1 Kings 15:23). Rava, a fourth-century Babylonian sage, speculated that this was a divine punishment because he had conscripted "disciples of the sages" into his army.[22] This is a clear, if infrequently cited, precedent for the exemption of "clerics" from military service.[23]

Distancing from the world of the Bible

Deuteronomy unequivocally calls for a war of extermination against the inhabitants of the "promised land": "You shall annihilate them – Hittites, Amorites, Canaanites, Perizzites, Hivvites, Jebusites – as the Lord your God commanded you, so that they may not teach you to imitate all the abominable things that they have done for their gods and so cause you to sin against the Lord your God" (Deuteronomy 20:17, 18). What was to stop this verse becoming a general warrant for genocide?

Limitations are set within the text itself, which limits the herem to the "seven nations".[24] But this would leave open the question of identification, and it would be only too easy to categorize a potential enemy as belonging to one or other of the despised nations. In fact the determination was made around the year 100 CE by a Palestinian rabbi, Joshua ben Hananiah, that "Sennacherib mixed up all the nations", that is, that no one can any longer be identified with the nations of earlier times; hence, the specific laws pertaining to those nations cannot be invoked.[25]

The rabbis tone down the severity of the plain biblical text of Deuteronomy in two ways:

1　They argue, against the plain sense, that offers of peace were to be made even to the Canaanites.
2　They rule, rather impractically, that in wars other than those of the original conquest, if a town was placed under siege an escape route was always to be provided.[26]

This, at least, is what emerges from the halakhic, or legal, texts. Unfortunately the waters are muddied by the symbolic or typological interpretation that occurs in aggadic (non-legal) texts.

Rabbinic texts refer to Rome, and later to Christendom generally, as "Edom";[27] Islam is (more plausibly) Ishmael. It may well be that the early use of "Edom" for Rome was purely homiletic,[28] not intended as a literal assertion of Roman genealogy, let alone as a normative statement; at no time has it been suggested that Deuteronomy 23:7, 8 should be applied to Romans, or to Christians.

Even more radically, the hasidic rabbi Yehuda Leib Alter of Gora Kalwaria (d. 1905) interpreted every statement about war in the Torah as symbolizing the internal battle against the tendency to evil.[29]

On the other hand, extreme right rhetoric in modern Israel has sometimes identified the country's Palestinian enemies as "children of Esau" or even

"Amalekites", contrary not only to the facts of history but to *halakha* itself.[30] Such talk underlay the ideology of Meir Kahane (1932–1990) and his "Kach" movement; it led Baruch Goldstein and his accomplices to shoot a number of Arabs at worship at Abraham's tomb in Hebron in February 1994, precisely on the festival of Purim which is linked with a reading about Amalek, and it inspired Yigal Amir to assassinate Israeli Prime Minister Yitzchak Rabin "as a traitor" on 4 November 1995.

Goldstein was denounced with shocked horror even by the mainstream Orthodox. Jonathan Sacks, for instance, Chief Rabbi of the (Orthodox) British United Hebrew Congregations, vigorously denounced the attack as a travesty of Jewish values, and declared: "Violence is evil. Violence committed in the name of God is doubly evil. Violence against those engaged in worshipping God is unspeakably evil." The Chief Rabbis of Israel were equally forthcoming.

That Kahane's movement was eventually disqualified by the Israeli Central Election Committee[31] and his followers outside Israel denied the possibility of Israeli citizenship, and that action was taken several times by the Israeli authorities against "celebrations" in honour of Goldstein, is confirmation of the distance put by the rabbis and Jews generally between the world of the Bible and our contemporary world; the rules of war enjoined against the ancient Canaanites are inapplicable to the contemporary situation. Kahanism did not perish with the assassination of its founder; it remains the creed of a small but vociferous minority that waxes and wanes in direct proportion to Palestinian terrorist activity.

Classification of wars, and competent authority

Reflecting on biblical history, the rabbis distinguished between *milhemet hova* (obligatory war) and *milhemet reshut* (optional war):

> Rava said: All agree that Joshua's war of conquest was *hova* (obligatory) and the expansionist wars of David were *reshut* (optional). But they differ with regard to [the status of] a pre-emptive war intended to prevent idolaters from attacking them.[32]

There is some resonance here with the Roman notion of *bellum justum*, though the rabbinic classification is into obligatory and optional rather than just and unjust.[33] A defensive war is obligatory (just); a pre-emptive war *might* be.[34]

On the other hand, the "expansionist wars of David" are seen as more questionable, notwithstanding Psalm 18:48, "He has subdued nations beneath my feet".[35] Elsewhere the Talmud insists that the king would need to seek authorization from the Great Court of 71 justices, as well as divine approval through the oracle[36] of the High Priest, before engaging in such a war.[37] As these institutions have not existed for 2,000 years the definition of "competent authority" virtually rules out the possibility of non-defensive war; there is no Jewish equivalent to the process by which some seventeenth-century English Puritans declared wars to be "commanded by God" simply because they were deemed by the leadership to be in conformity with God's will.[38]

The Talmudic distinction between *kibbush yahid* (individual conquest) and *kibbush rabim* (public conquest) may indicate the need for popular support in addition to the other requirements.[39]

Self-defence and proportionality

Genesis 32 relates how Jacob, a fugitive for many years in the house of Laban, returns home with his family, and as he reaches the border meets his brother Esau with 400 men. "And Jacob feared greatly and was distressed" (Genesis 32:7).

> Said Rabbi Judah bar Ilai: fear and distress are not the same thing. He was afraid lest he be killed, and distressed that he might have to kill someone.[40]

Jacob, on this reading, does not doubt that in self-defence, including the defence of his family, it might be his duty to kill even his own brother, however much it would distress him.

This homily is supported in the legal system of the *halakha*. Defence, including self-defence, is not so much a *right* as a *duty*. The principle of self-defence is derived from Exodus 22:1, understood by the rabbis as referring to a thief who breaks in with intent to kill should he be discovered; *ha-ba l'horg'kha hashkem l'horgo* "If someone comes to kill you, kill him first". Proportionality follows from Exodus 22:2: "If the sun has risen on him, there shall be blood-guilt for him . . ."; as the rabbis express it, "Does the sun rise only on him? [Surely not. But the verse teaches:] if it is as clear as day to you that he does not come in peace (i.e. that he is ready to kill), kill him, but otherwise not".[41]

The duty to defend a threatened victim, even at the expense of the life of the aggressor, is derived somewhat more tortuously from the case of the betrothed rape victim (Deuteronomy 22:25–27). Scripture itself compares rape to murder, and implies that if anyone heard the victim cry out he should have defended her, if need be by slaying the rapist. The same would apply to any other *rodef* (pursuer), for instance someone intent on murdering another person. But what, asks the Talmud, if the victim could be saved by "one of his limbs", i.e. without killing him. Then the saviour would himself be guilty of murder if he killed the attacker.[42] This last caveat establishes the principle of proportionality.

These texts are set in the criminal code, not among the laws pertaining to war. Later authorities extrapolate from personal to collective self-defence, that is war designed to defend society as a whole, or its most cherished values. This is analogous to the way in which Christians such as Ambrose and Augustine argued that "Christian love" mandated not only personal defence of individual Christians but military defence of Christian society.[43]

Accepting the "Yoke of the Nations"

Since the abortive revolts of the late Roman Empire Jews have reconciled themselves to minority status, and rarely if ever rioted or engaged in open revolt, let alone terrorist acts, against their oppressors. Whether out of conviction or through duress they have taken to heart Jeremiah's words, "Seek the peace of the city to which I have exiled you and pray to the Lord for it, for in its peace will you find peace" (Jeremiah 29:7), embodied in the somewhat Hobbesian rabbinic dictum, "Pray for the welfare of the government, for if not for fear of it one man would swallow the other alive".[44]

This resigned attitude is expressed in a Midrash on Song of Songs 2:7: "I adjure you, daughters of Jerusalem, by the gazelles and hinds of the field, do not awaken nor stir my beloved until she desires."

> Rabbi Helbo said: There are four oaths here. He adjured Israel not to rebel against the [oppressing] nations, not to force the End, not to reveal the mysteries [of Torah] to the nations, and not to go up [to the land of Israel] from the diaspora in [military] formation . . . Rabbi Onia says [the oaths] correspond to the four who [attempted to] force the End but stumbled: one in the days of Amram, one in the days of Dinai, one in the days of Bar Koziba, and one in the days of Shutelah ben Ephraim.[45]

Helbo, a third-early fourth-century Babylonian who migrated to Palestine, interprets the Song as an allegory of the love of God and Israel; the awakening of the beloved, that is the restoration of Israel through God's love, is not to be forced.[46] This relatively obscure Midrash (it does not figure in the Talmud) was cited by anti-Zionist rabbis who opposed the setting up of a secular Jewish state which would have to rely on military force for its defence.[47]

Compassion

After a crushing defeat Ben-Hadad, king of Syria, sought refuge with the victor Ahab, king of Israel; his advisers had counselled him that Israelite kings were *malkhei hesed* "merciful kings"(1 Kings 20:31). Ahab was reprimanded by the prophet for affording refuge to Ben-Hadad on this occasion, and the consequences were disastrous. More recently, however, the reputation of the Israelite kings for showing compassion has been a source of pride, and has been cited as an indication that even in wartime compassion should be shown to one's enemies if circumstances are such that it will not undermine the war aim.

Philo of Alexandria, writing early in the first century with an eye to gentile as well as Jewish readership, refers the provisions for non-Canaanite war in Deuteronomy 20 to those who revolt from an alliance, implying that wars of conquest or aggression are never sanctioned; he stresses the restraint to be shown by Israel in first offering peace. The women are in any event to be spared "as in virtue of their natural weakness they have the privilege of exemption from war service":[48]

All this shows clearly that the Jewish nation is ready for agreement and friendship with all like-minded nations whose intentions are peaceful, yet is not of the contemptible kind which surrenders through cowardice to wrongful aggression.[49]

In the Middle Ages there were rabbis, for instance the thirteenth-century author of *Sefer ha-Hinukh*, who argued (rather like Philo, whose work was unknown to him) that the rationale of less-than-total war against the "other nations" was to instil compassion, for "it is fitting for us, the holy seed, to act [with compassion] in all matters, even towards our idolatrous enemies".[50]

Amongst those exempted from participation in *milhemet ha-reshut* is "he who is afraid or of tender heart" (Deuteronomy 20:8). Tosefta attributes to José ha-Gelili (second century) the interpretation "Even if he is mightiest of the mighty and strongest of the strong, but compassionate (*rahaman*), he should return from the lines".[51] Of course, by *rahaman* José may mean no more than "soft-hearted", and may consider it a defect rather than a virtue; there seems little justification to use his words, as some have done, to argue for compassion in the conduct of war.

Environment

When you are at war, and lay siege to a city . . . do not destroy its trees by taking the axe to them, for they provide you with food.

(Deuteronomy 20:19)

In its biblical context this is a counsel of prudence rather than a principle of conservation; Israelites are enjoined to use only "non-productive" trees, that is non fruit-bearing trees, for their siege works. However, rabbinic tradition has applied it generally as a prohibition of waste, and modern Jewish environmentalists have quarried this tradition in support of their pleas for conservation.

It does provide an additional argument against warfare, and raises the question of whether there is some limit to the amount of environmental degradation that might be caused even in pursuit of a just war. Was the defoliation of the forests of Vietnam acceptable even if the war aims were agreed? Irrespective of the human suffering caused, could it ever be acceptable to have recourse to nuclear weapons, seeing that their use would severely damage the environment? The works of Artson and Landes give some indication of the range of Jewish views on these matters; while the duty of conserving nature is universally acknowledged, there is disagreement over how this duty should be balanced against the duty of defence of human life.

Arms trade

The Mishna ruled, "One may not sell bears or lions, nor anything that may harm the public, to [gentiles]".[52] A discussion in the Talmud on whether iron lamps may be sold to gentiles, seeing that the material could be reworked into weapons "that harm the public", is cut short by the interjection "But nowadays that we sell them . . ." to which Rav Ashi replies: "To the Persians, who protect us."[53] Evidently, Jews felt it appropriate to sell arms to Persians in the fourth century; the remark of the Tosafists that "It would seem that nowadays we are permitted for the same reason . . ." shows that the same business was afoot in thirteenth-century Rhineland. These are among precedents cited by Chaim David Halevi (b. 1925), then Sefardi Chief Rabbi of Tel Aviv/Jaffa, in his responsum, published shortly after the Yom Kippur War of 1973, on whether the sale of arms by Israel to friendly countries is permissible under the *halakha*.[54]

Although for almost 2,000 years Jews were rarely involved as principals in war, they often played a subsidiary role in finance and supply. Isaac Abravanel himself is said to have loaned 1½ million gold ducats to Ferdinand and Isabella to pursue the war with Granada (1491–92). More recently, in the seventeenth and eighteenth centuries, Jews were very prominent as military contractors (purveyors of livestock, fodder, food, uniforms, etc.). Among the most famous army contractors for pay and supplies in eighteenth-century England were Sir Solomon de Medina, the associate of Marlborough, and Abraham Prado. In all these cases it is difficult if not impossible to assess the extent to which Jews were acting under duress, or in the perceived interest of their own communities, rather than on the basis of some freely embraced religious principle.

Some medieval Jewish views

Prior to the rise of Islam there were several independent Jewish tribes in Arabia and North Africa, such as the Himyarite kingdom of South Arabia. The sixth-century Jewish poet Samuel Ibn Adiya, whose "poetry ranks with the finest heroic traditional Arabic battle poetry of the pre-Islamic period and shows little trace of Jewish origins and themes", enjoyed a reputation for loyalty that was proverbial.[55] The Quran records Muhammed's negotiations and battles with some of the Arabian Jewish tribes, and from Arab sources we learn about the activity of Jewish Berber tribes such as the Aurés, led by the female warrior Kahina Dahiya,[56] which for a time in *c*.700 successfully resisted the advance of Hasan ibn al Numan through the Maghreb and into Spain. Unfortunately, literary records are scant for all of these, as for the short-lived kingdom of Khazaria,[57] and from none of them can we garner information on distinctively Jewish religious thinking about war.

Otherwise, though there are numerous references to Jewish mercenaries throughout the pre-modern period, and occasional references to organized armed defence,[58] Jews were not collectively involved in warfare other than as bystanders and incidental victims. No mainstream Jew was called upon, in a real-life situation, to determine whether to engage in war or how to prosecute it. Nevertheless, there was reflection on earlier sources and on future "messianic" wars, and a handful of Jewish religious leaders were sufficiently close to political reality to devote serious attention to the ethics of war.

Shmuel ha-Nagid

Shmuel (Samuel) ha-Nagid, also known as Ismail ibn Nagrela (993–1055/6), was vizier to kings Habbus and Badis of Granada, and a Hebrew poet and scholar of distinction. He is probably unique among medieval Jews as military commander of a Muslim army.

Samuel nowhere expressly justifies his involvement on behalf of his dissolute master in the internecine wars of Muslim Spain. Presumably he accepts war as an unfortunate fact of life, and is prepared to discharge his responsibility towards his prince in the interest of protecting his own community. He may even have entertained illusions that he was commencing the messianic wars.[59]

But if his war poems fail to address the moral problems of warfare they certainly address the emotional, spiritual and ritual issues:

> War at the outset is like a beautiful maid
> With whom everyone wishes to flirt
> At the end it is like a despised hag
> Bringing tears and sadness to whomever she meets.[60]

There are prayers before a battle, commitment to the will of God, thanksgiving for victory, a declaration that throughout the battle he has faithfully observed the Sabbath and Festivals – his hint that others were "less scrupulous"[61] rather suggests that Jewish mercenaries formed part of the forces under his command.[62]

Netanel ibn Fayyumi

The Yemenite Jewish philosopher Netanel ibn Fayyumi (d. c.1165), explicitly following the lead of Bahya ibn Paquda (eleventh-century Spain), distinguishes between external and internal obedience to God, the latter being the "duties of the heart":[63]

> The external consists in carrying out the law revealed to the prophets
> – peace be unto them! – in such matters as circumcision, fasting, alms-
> giving, the pilgrimage, the holy war, and what is similar in the practice
> of zizith, tephilin, succah, lulab, mezuzoth, and the other mizvoth, which
> are set forth in the Books of the Law.[64]

Netanel was writing in Arabic, and uses the Arabic term *jihad*, translated by Levine as "holy war". Perhaps Netanel had picked up the broader Islamic concept of *jihad* as struggle, effort, readiness to commit totally to God's work. *Milhama* ("war") figures frequently in the Jewish vocabulary, even in the Talmud, as a metaphor for the excited debate of scholars; several medieval polemical tracts have titles incorporating the metaphor. On the other hand, since the list is of "external" duties as opposed to attitudes ("duties of the heart"), *jihad* here may be not a metaphor, but a hint to Jews that they, too, given the appropriate conditions, have a duty to fight for their faith just as Muslims do; the hint was not picked up by later authorities.

Maimonides

Moses Maimonides (1135/8–1204), or Rambam, as he is generally known, compiled in the 1160s a comprehensive Code of Law incorporating a section titled "The Laws of Kings and their Wars". He did not aim in this work to formulate an original theory of war, but to articulate the rabbinic tradition. Occasionally, he exceeds his brief; expounding the biblical verse (Deuteronomy 20:8) that lays down that one who is afraid, lacking in courage, should return from the muster (7:15), he writes:

> "What man is there that is fearful and faint-hearted?" This is to be taken at its face value, [of one who] lacks the courage to withstand the rigours of war. Once he engages in the rigours of war he should rely on "the Hope of Israel" (God), his saviour in times of distress, and know that he is engaging in war for the Unity of the Name. He should take his life in his hands, neither fear nor tremble, not think of his wife or children, but erase their memory and all considerations other than war from his mind. Whoever starts to consider and think [of other matters] in war transgresses a prohibition, as it is said "Let not your heart be faint, and do not fear, tremble or be in dread of them". Moreover, he bears responsibility for the blood of all Israel, and if he does not win, or fails to exert himself to the utmost, it is as if he spilled the blood of everyone . . . he who fights courageously and fearlessly with the sole intention of sanctifying the Divine Name will certainly suffer no harm, but will build a lasting Jewish home . . . and earn the [rewards of the] World to Come.[65]

This may echo some Islamic interpretations of *jihad*, but has little connection either with Maimonides' rabbinic sources or with the more restrained portrayal of the virtuous leader by the Muslim philosopher Al-Farabi for whom Maimonides elsewhere professes a high regard.[66]

Another significant deviation from the rabbinic sources concerns the exemption from warfare of those who devote their life to God. The context is the biblical command that the tribe of Levi, who are designated as teachers, should not be apportioned land or receive the spoils of war.[67] Maimonides introduces with the phrase "It appears to me" three paragraphs that lack any source in earlier rabbinic literature. They read in part:

> Why did the tribe of Levi have no right to a share in the Land and spoils of war with their brethren? Because they were singled out to serve God, to teach His upright ways and true judgements to the public . . . so they were set apart from the ways of the world, and did not wage war like the

rest of Israel nor inherit [the Land] nor acquire rights through physical exertion. But they are the Lord's army . . . and He, blessed be He, grants their rights.

And not only the tribe of Levi, but any human being whose spirit and intellect move him to stand before God and to serve and know Him, and who walks uprightly as God has made him, and casts aside the designs of men, is a most holy person; God is his portion for ever and will grant his needs in this world as he granted the Priests and Levites.[68]

This has been cited by modern Israeli rabbis in justification of the exemption from military service of yeshiva students and others who devote their life to the study of Torah. Since Maimonides pointedly uses the expression *kol ba'é 'olam* (any *human being*) rather than "any Israelite" he implies that the immunity of clerics and the like on the opposing side is to be respected (provided, of course, that they are non-combatants).

Like his European contemporary Gratian (mid-twelfth century) and later Thomas Aquinas (1225–74), who grant non-combatant immunity only to clerics and bishops,[69] Maimonides grants immunity only to those devoted to the service of God not to non-combatants in general. He presumably has in mind Rava's remark, cited above, that king Asa was punished for enlisting the "disciples of the sages". If so, the reason for exemption is not that such people do not bear arms, but because they are holy, removed from mortal concerns. So it does not follow that immunity would be granted to other non-combatants such as merchants and peasants listed in the treatise *De Treuga et Pace*[70] proclaimed by Pope Urban II at the Council of Clermont (1095) and incorporated in the canon law under Gregory IX (1227–41).

In a section of his later, philosophical work, *A Guide for the Perplexed*, Maimonides again summarizes the commandments under 14 heads, but omits the commandments relating to kings and war. Elsewhere in the work, in the context of idolatry, he briefly justifies the genocide of the Canaanites:

Do you not see in the texts of the Torah, when it commanded the extermination of the *seven nations* and said *thou shalt save alive nothing that breatheth*, that it immediately follows this by saying: *That they teach you not to do after all their abominations, which they have done unto their gods and so ye sin against the Lord your God?* Thus it says: do not think that this is hard-heartedness or desire for vengeance. It is rather an act required by human opinion, which considers that everyone who deviates from the way of truth[71] should be put an end to and that all obstacles impeding the achievement of perfection that is the apprehension of Him, may He be exalted, should be interdicted.[72]

This is a doctrine of "right intent", as it was later characterized by Thomas Aquinas.[73] It is not the only occasion on which Maimonides interprets a biblical command as concession to human weakness;[74] he is extending the Talmudic rationale of the limited permission to cohabit with a captive woman.[75]

Maimonides' overall view seems to be that war is a sad fact of life, a consequence of the moral and intellectual failings of human beings; the Torah regulates it, making due allowance for frail human nature, in accordance with divine compassion, which demands the elimination of evil, the source of which is idolatry. It is perhaps in his assertion of the need for the ruthless destruction of idolatry that Maimonides reflects most strongly the influence of his Muslim environment; however, he does not suggest that Jews have a duty to go out into the world actively to seek and destroy idolatry.

Nahmanides

Nahmanides (1194–1270), or Ramban, as he is generally known, was a rabbi and exegete in Catalonia; he completed his *Commentary on the Torah* in Palestine, where he ended his days having fled Spain in the aftermath of the 1263 Disputation in Barcelona.

His comment on Deuteronomy 23:10 "You shall guard yourself from every evil thing" carries a ring of personal observation:

> Scripture warns [us to be especially careful] at times when sin is common. It is well known that when groups go to war they eat every abominable thing, steal, do violence, and are not ashamed even to commit adultery and other detestable things, so that even the most naturally upright of men is enveloped in violence and anger when setting off to battle against an enemy. Therefore scripture warns, "You shall guard yourself from every evil thing" . . . for "the Lord your God is in the midst of your camp" (verse 15).

This comment is cited by contemporary Israelis in support of the notion of "purity of arms" which we shall meet later.

In opposition to Maimonides, Nahmanides lists "conquest of the land" amongst the 613 commandments.[76] Almost certainly, as many commentators have insisted, his use of the term *kibbush* (conquest) denotes "living in", "settlement", not military conquest.

Gersonides and Arama

Some recent writers have stated that the Provençal mathematician, astronomer, philosopher and biblical commentator Levi ben Gershom (also known as Ralbag, Leo Hebraeus, or Gersonides, 1288–1344) maintained that in the Last Days Israel would inherit their land in a manner not involving warfare. This is wishful thinking. What he actually wrote was that God delayed fulfilment of his promise to Abraham in order to bring it to fruition in the most beneficial way possible; this will happen in the time of the Messiah, and there will be no *subsequent* war, since then all humankind will worship one God together.[77] This was also wishful thinking.

The Spanish theologian and commentator Isaac Arama (*c*.1420–94) incorporates at least two powerful homilies on the value of peace and the virtue of its pursuit in his Commentary on the Torah.[78] Specifically, he contends that the Torah's commandment to proclaim peace requires:

> Entreaties and supplications offered in the most conciliatory possible way, in order to turn their hearts . . . for this follows necessarily from the human wisdom of peace, and the Divine will consent . . . For if we find that He commanded "You shall not destroy its tree [that is, that found in the city of the enemy], to lift against it an axe" [Deuteronomy 20:19], all the more so should we take care not to commit damage and destruction to human beings.[79]

Abravanel

Isaac Abravanel (1437–1508) served, in succession, Afonso V of Portugal, Ferdinand and Isabella of Spain (with whom he interceded in vain to revoke the edict expelling the Jews from Spain in 1492), Ferrante I and Alfonso II of Naples, and latterly the Council of Venice. This background, combined with vast erudition, led him to incorporate in his biblical commentaries observations relating to the European society of his time and formulating political notions such as his preference for republican government over monarchy.

He comments on Deuteronomy 20:10, "When you approach a city to make war against it, you shall proclaim peace." (The paragraph continues to state that if the city accepts the terms offered it shall become tributary, but that if it resists and is conquered the women and children should be spared.)

> The offer of peace is desirable for three reasons. (a) It is proper to follow the ways of God, Who does not desire [people's] death and the destruction of the world, but forgives the penitent; (b) peaceful conquest denotes the power and magnanimity of the ruler; (c) the outcome of war is at best uncertain and at worst catastrophic.
>
> Should the offer of peace be rejected war is justified since it is proper that the more perfect should dominate the less perfect. ("Perfect" here is understood as possessing the true religion: Abravanel appears to offer the same justification for conquest as the Conquistadores themselves!)
>
> The women and children should be spared since they are by nature non-combatants.[80]

Abravanel completed his commentary on Deuteronomy in 1496, well before men such as Victoria and Suarez rejected the idea of "holy war" for the sake of religion.

His remarks on war should moreover be read in the context of his rejection of monarchy as an extreme form of domination of one person by another.[81] In an ideal world there would be no kings – Messiah will not rule forcefully with an army and officers like an ordinary king, but "will smite the earth with the rod of his mouth, and with the breath of his lips" (Isaiah 11:4). But once a king has been established legitimately it is wrong to rebel against him even if he acts unjustly, contrary to the position taken by John of Salisbury.[82] Abravanel's position is that in these pre-Messianic times we have to accommodate ourselves to the essentially undesirable phenomena of autocracy and its concomitant, warfare; this being so, both have to be restrained within the limits imposed by Torah.

His contention that the Torah spares women and children because they are non-combatants[83] opens the way to a full-scale doctrine of non-combatant immunity. However, he also states that they are exempt because they are weak and incapable of fighting; apart from the fact that many individual women are stronger than many individual men, this reason would not apply nowadays when success in battle depends on skilful use of technology rather than on brute strength.

The modern period

Wars of the West

Western attitudes to war have undergone four major transformations in the modern period. First, in reaction to the Wars of Religion, a consensus emerged that wars should not be fought to spread "true" religion.

Second, the industrial revolution led to the invention of more effective weapons and communications, and made possible the deployment of large armies over great areas. The French Revolution and the Napoleonic wars (1789–1815) were perhaps the first "total" wars of modern times, involving whole populations in determining their way of life. The new concepts of war were articulated by the nineteenth-century Prussian military strategist Carl von Clausewitz (1780–1831), whose *Vom Krieg* first appeared in 1832/4. Clausewitz regarded war as an instrument of policy, designed to disarm the opponent and hence impose one's own political will on him. War is "only a part of political intercourse, therefore by no means an independent thing in itself".[84] The conduct of war must be strictly controlled by attainable political objectives. Clausewitz could almost be Samuel rebuking Saul when he writes:

> in such dangerous things as War, the errors which proceed from bene-
> volence are the worst . . . it is even against one's own interest, to turn away
> from consideration of the real nature of the affair because the horror of its
> elements excites repugnance.[85]

Third, the development of international law from Grotius onwards, and its institutionalization through the League of Nations and subsequently the United

Nations, has established the position that the only permitted wars are defensive wars, including wars for the defence of an injured third party and arguably also pre-emptive strikes.

Finally, the principle that all nations have a right to self-government has been accepted, and imperialism has been discredited.

Special factors affecting Jewish attitudes

The piecemeal and often tenuous emancipation of Jews in the West from the eighteenth century onwards resulted in three trends in the interpretation of Judaism:

1   The traditionalists (eventually known as "Orthodox") continued to teach on the basis of rabbinic texts, though their interpretations were often coloured by the ambient culture.
2   Religious Reformers stressed the ethical and universal dimension of Jewish teaching; this led them to modify or even abandon *halakha* (traditional Jewish law) in favour of what they took to be the purely ethical monotheism of the prophets.
3   Secularists accorded primacy to "Jewish culture", again stressing its ethical dimension in contrast to *halakha*. Many of them, rebuffed when they attempted to gain acceptance within the new European nations, articulated their own, Jewish nationalism, since 1892 termed Zionism. It was this third group who until recently dominated Zionism and Israeli society, and who determined the doctrine of the Israel Defence Forces.

None of the positions has been rigid, nor have the dividing lines always been clear. The recent dynamic of Jewish war ethics has involved all three trends in inter-reaction against the background of evolving Western political theory.

From mercenary to patriot

The Babylonian Talmud seems to approve the presence of Jews at a siege, since this might put them in a position to save other Jews who are in the town, "provided they are not reckoned amongst them". Later authorities speculate whether this reservation means "provided they do not support the siege" [e.g. with supplies], or "provided they are not part of the besieging army".[86] Either way, it would seem that the Talmud forbids Jews to serve as mercenaries in wars in which there is no clear Jewish interest, though in practice many ignored this ban, and as we have seen there are occasional reports of Jewish mercenaries throughout the centuries.

As Jews in the Western world gained rights as citizens of the countries in which they lived, they assumed the responsibility of participating in the armed struggles of those countries, not as mercenaries, but as citizens, or would-be citizens. When Joseph II introduced conscription of Jews in Austria-Hungary in 1787 many regarded it as a privilege of citizenship.

Czar Nicholas I introduced, in 1827, the Cantonist system which conscripted Jewish youths aged from 12 to 25 years into military service; those aged under 18 were sent to special military schools also attended by the children of soldiers. So intolerable was this that it was a major factor in stimulating Jewish emigration to the United States and elsewhere. Alexander II abolished the seizure of Jewish children for military service, reduced the maximum period of service to 15 years, and in 1874 enacted a law obliging all Russian citizens to report for military service at the age of 21, so placing Jews on an equal footing with others.

Jews fought on both sides in the American Civil War (1861–65) and in the First World War. In the Second World War well over a million Jews served in the Allied armies, almost half a million of them, including more than 100 generals, in the Soviet army; over 100 Jews were awarded the title Hero of the Soviet Union. Some 150,000 US Jews saw service in the Korean war and nearly 30,000 fought in Vietnam, though Jews were also active in the anti-war movement.

But how have the *religious* authorities looked on such activity? And how has it come about that whereas the religious authorities forbade or at least discouraged active Jewish involvement in international wars well into early modern times, by the nineteenth century in the West they condoned it and in the twentieth frequently encouraged young Jews to volunteer?

The answer to this lies in the changing collective self-perception of Western Jews. Throughout the Middle Ages Jews lived in autonomous communities and saw themselves as a separate nation in exile; with the Emancipation they learned to look on themselves as citizens of the new European nation-states. Defence became defence of the nation-state, or of civilization itself, rather than of Jews collectively, and ideas on warfare were strongly influenced by those of the surrounding nations; Clausewitz rather than Maimonides determined Jewish public policy.

Central European Orthodoxy

By the end of the eighteenth century Orthodox rabbis were forced to address the issues of whether Jews might participate in the armed conflicts of the new states, of how they should conduct themselves if they did participate, and of what was the attitude of Torah to the conflicts themselves. It is not certain to what extent the few comments that were committed to writing reflect the actual views of the rabbis; the situation was delicate, and they had to express themselves circumspectly.

Moses Schreiber ('*Hatam Sofer*' 1762–1839), who as Rabbi of Pressburg (Bratislava) lived in proximity to the seat of Austro-Hungarian government, forbade those under his authority to engage in aggressive war, though conceding that land acquired through war was legitimately retained;[87] he objected to voluntary enlistment.[88]

Naftali Zevi Yehuda Berlin (1817–93), head of the Yeshiva of Volozhin (Belarus) for some 40 years, exerted a powerful influence over the secular as well religious leadership of late nineteenth-century non-hasidic Jewry. He argued that non-Jews "and even Jews" were permitted to engage in war. Genesis 9:5 forbids Noah, and by implication all humanity, to murder: "From man also shall I require satisfaction for the death of his brother." Berlin, whose commentary on the Pentateuch was first published in 1879/80, seized on the word "brother":

> When is man punished? When it is appropriate to treat [the other] as brother. But this is not so in wartime, ". . . a time to hate . . ." (Ecclesiastes 3:8),[89] a time to kill, and there is no punishment at all for this, since this is the way the world was set up, as we find in the Talmud (Shavu'ot 35) "A government that kills one in six is not punished", and this applies even to an Israelite king, who may engage in milhemet reshut even though many Israelites would be slain as a result.[90]

In a footnote Berlin struggles to reconcile this with the Talmud's sharp condemnation of David for sending Uriah on what was in effect a suicide mission. One might ask what drives Berlin to such a questionable reading of Talmud (no authority cites the passage in a legal context), and to ignore the severe restraints *halakha* imposes on the initiation of *milhemet reshut*; he evidently thought the matter sufficiently important to reiterate in his comments on Deuteronomy 20:8. Possibly he was anxious to set at rest the minds of his students, many of whom would be recruited into the Russian army. He may also have felt it prudent to promote a view which would satisfy the secular (Russian) authorities that Jews were loyal to the regime. His assertion that "this is the way the world was set up" reads as a sigh of resignation from a man who cannot envisage a purely human, pre-Messianic, progress to universal peace, and who regards war as an unavoidable evil of nature on a par with disease and earthquakes.

Israel Meir Hacohen (1838–1933), better known as the Hafetz Haim, was a leading Polish halakhist who combined outstanding spirituality with a reactionary outlook. He published his legal commentary, *Mishna Berura*, between 1894 and 1907, when the more lenient conscription introduced by Alexander II was still in force. He rules that Jews must allow themselves to be conscripted in accordance with the "law of the land": "Know that nowadays when nations from beyond our borders come to despoil us we are obliged to confront them with arms, even if [they come only to rob]."[91] Hafetz Haim is probably concerned more with Jewish defence ("if we do not play our part the citizens will be angry and kill us" – it was after all a period of pogroms) than with any theory of *jus ad bellum*, but even from this perspective the implication is clear that armed combat is only appropriate for defence. Like other Orthodox rabbis, he was concerned that Jews should as far as possible without endangering life be able to observe religious requirements such as the Sabbath and food laws; he had in 1881 compiled *Mahane Yisrael*, a code of practical laws for Jewish conscripts, and endeavoured to ensure that when stationed near Jewish communities kosher food was provided for them.

Menahem Zemba (1883–1943) argued that the Torah forbade Jews to engage in aggressive war.[92] Zemba was one of the last Warsaw rabbis to remain in the ghetto after the first wave of extermination. On the eve of the Warsaw Ghetto Uprising, Catholic circles offered their assistance to save the three remaining rabbis of Warsaw, but Zemba declined the offer and died a martyr's death in the ghetto. At a meeting of its surviving leaders on 14 January 1943, he gave rabbinic approval for the uprising, stating:

> Of necessity, we must resist the enemy on all fronts . . . We shall no longer heed his instructions . . . Sanctification of the Divine Name manifests itself in varied ways. During the First Crusade, at the end of the 11th century, the Halakhah . . . determined one way of reacting to the distress of the Franco-German Jews, whereas in the middle of the 20th century, during the liquidation of the Jews in Poland, it prompts us to react in an entirely different manner. In the past, during religious persecution, we were required by the law "to give up our lives even for the least essential practice". In the present, however, when we are faced by an arch foe, whose unparalleled ruthlessness and program of total annihilation know no bounds, the Halakhah demands that we fight and resist to the very end with unequaled determination and valor for the sake of Sanctification of the Divine Name.[93]

West European Orthodoxy

Rabbis and scholars in the West were more strongly influenced than their Eastern colleagues by Enlightenment culture, and generally more broadly educated. In Germany, the neo-Orthodox Samson Raphael Hirsch (1808–88) strove to interpret Torah in terms of "modern culture", and stressed its ethical content as strongly as did his Reform opponents. The struggle for emancipation was more successful than in Eastern Europe, though its achievements were insecure; consequently, Western Jews tended to assert to excess their loyalty and their readiness to fulfil civic obligations including military service. Moses Mendelssohn (1729–86), for instance, in a caustic response to J. D. Michaelis's argument that Jews should not be granted full civic rights since their religion rendered them incapable *inter alia* of becoming soldiers, points out that no religion, Christianity included, has the task of making men soldiers. Church and State ought to be rigorously separated;[94] in no way did Jews lag behind other in civic conduct, and they were as committed as anyone to the defence of the fatherland.[95] Mendelssohn was at the time reacting positively to Joseph II's *Toleranzpatent* of 1782.

Samuel David Luzzatto (1800–65), in his posthumously published Hebrew commentary on the Pentateuch, comments on Deuteronomy 20:10–11:

> The text does not specify the cause for a permitted war or [say] whether Israel may wage war without cause, merely to despoil and take booty. [But] it seems to me that in the beginning of this section [20:1], in saying "When you go forth to battle against your enemy," scripture indicates that

we should make war only against our enemies. The term "enemy" refers only to one who seeks to harm us; so scripture is speaking only of an invader who would enter our territory to take our land and despoil us. Then we are to go out to war against him, and make him an offer of peace. The [nature of the] peace is that he should make a treaty with us not to enter our territory any more, but on the contrary in restitution of the damage he has done to us, and having obliged us to go to war, he should render us tribute.[96]

Luzzatto has read Philo,[97] who limited the application of the verse in like vein. But he is also aware of contemporary political discussion, and is clearly trying to accommodate his interpretation of Deuteronomy to the international standards of his time.

The Slovakian born, American trained, J. H. Hertz (1872–1946), who from 1913 until his death was Chief Rabbi of the United Hebrew Congregations of the British Commonwealth, preached an intercession sermon, "Through Darkness to Light", at the Great Synagogue, London, on 1 January 1916:[98]

None could have foretold that civilized mankind would rush back to savagery with such dreadful fervour . . .

The men who fought and died at Gallipoli have not fought and died in vain. They have created new standards of human courage. Their dead lie on the abandoned cliffs, but the memory of all they did and tried to do will never fade . . .

Is there nothing for which to bless God . . . the readiness for unbounded sacrifice, as soon as it was realized that we were confronted by a powerful foe who desired nothing less than England's annihilation. Nobly have also the sons of Anglo-Jewry rallied round England in the hour of her need. And our Honour Record will be rendered longer and more luminous now that the large number of our brethren who are naturalized British subjects, or the children of such naturalized British subjects, have been admitted to the glorious privilege of fighting for their country . . .

Can anyone say that Prussian militarism, or the snarling of the nations at one another during the last decade, was religion?

With the victory of Great Britain, the old Egyptian idols and heathen ideals – the worship of brute force – will be shattered . . . Let us prayerfully resolve that the new order be a better order, rooted in righteousness, broad-based on the liberty of and reverence for each and every nationality, and culminating in a harmony of peoples. Amen.

In 1917 Hertz published, in easily portable format, *A Book of Jewish Thoughts*, designed to give solace and inspiration to soldiers on the front; it is a far cry from the anxious ritual manuals produced by his continental co-religionists.

Hertz, like Luzzatto, is very much a child of the Enlightenment. War is no longer, to him, an issue of Israel versus the world of idolatry, but of enlightened civilization versus barbarism and superstition. With this hermeneutic key he interprets Bible and tradition to allow identification of his Jews with the British – equals civilized, equals Torah-true – cause.

Precisely this hermeneutic enables Jews to rally to the defence of democracy, liberal values and even, for those who think it is justified, the "War Against Terrorism".

Pacifism

There is no clear tradition of pacifism in Judaism. To the contrary, to stand idly by when someone is threatened with violence by a third party is a sin if one is in the position to rescue the victim by violent means, though the violence should be kept to a minimum.

Niditch argues that there is "a biblical war ideology that is critical of war itself and of people's participation in the taking of life that is a part of war". She discovers this ideology in Hosea 1:4, in Judges 9, in the plea for fair treatment of prisoners in 2 Kings 6:20–23, in the attempts at moral justification or rationalization for bans of extermination, the need for subsequent purification rituals, and again in Genesis 49:5–7 and Amos 1–2; she notes how the author of Chronicles both omits many of the atrocities attributed to David in the Books of Samuel and explains that David's bloodshed disqualified him from building the Temple. She rightly observes that "the implicit war ideology of 2 Chronicles", namely that God, not people, will destroy the enemy, is "a step towards containment of war-making".[99] A distaste for war cannot, however, be equated with pacifism; Clausewitz thought war was horrible, but he was no pacifist!

Wilcock reviews the activities of an impressive array of Jewish pacifists. The American Reform rabbi Judah Magnes (1877–1948), who eventually became chancellor and first president of the Hebrew University of Jerusalem, jeopardized his public career by pacifist-based opposition to US entry into the First World War in 1917[100] In the 1920s there was a Jewish Peace Society in England, and the American Reform rabbinate affiliated with peace organizations in the USA.[101] The Prague-born Hans Köhn (1891–1971) and the Italian Enzo Sereni (1905–44) both attempted to espouse pacifism in Mandatory Palestine.[102] The Second World War, and in particular the Holocaust, gravely undermined pacifism as a practical option, but the impetus is still felt in Jewish (as well as general) opposition to American intervention in Vietnam and more recent conflicts; the Conservative rabbi Abraham Heschel (1907–72) exercised leadership not only in the Civil Rights movement but in the campaign against the Vietnam war.[103]

Many refused to serve in the Vietnam war not because they objected to war on principle but because they regarded that particular war as objectionable; the United States Supreme Court ruled, however, that "selective conscientious objection" could have no legal standing in American society. Many Jews contested this ruling, but Maurice Lamm compared it to the situation that might have arisen had a properly constituted Sanhedrin, with full authority, mandated a war; their moral authority, he maintained, would override the individual conscience. He finds radical pacifism contrary to Judaism: "Judaism, unlike Buddhism and fundamentalist Christianity, would not counsel the application of perfectionism to this imperfect world and so it cannot accept pacifism as a way of life."[104]

In Israel female conscientious objectors have a statutory right under a 1959 law to exemption, but males are exempted from military service only at the discretion of the Minister of Defence. The issue of "selective conscientious objection" arose in the 1980s when some men petitioned the High Court for exemption from service in Southern Lebanon even though they were not pacifists in principle. The petitions were dismissed in a judgement that incorporated reference to halakhic precedents.[105]

The Jewish state

Secularism and early Zionism

Anita Shapira, following the 1982 Israeli invasion of Lebanon, wrote:

> The past century witnessed a fundamental transformation in what were assumed to be abiding and genuine Jewish characteristics . . . [This study] explores how concepts derived from Jewish antiquity gained new vitality and were translated from the lofty plane of abstraction to the sphere of practical action. It also examines how concepts, incorporated from a European ambience, were internalized by a new generation confronting the reality of Palestine.[106]

The story of Zionism is the story of the transformation of an ancient religious ideal into a version of European nationalist politics; Jews were to become a *Volk*, a political entity, "like the nations round about".[107]

Jewish emancipation in Europe stimulated the desire for "normality". Secularists were embarrassed by the narrowness of Jewish occupations; surely Jews should be farmers, soldiers and so on – again, "like the nations round about".

Saul Ascher (1767–1822), a Berlin-born author, philosopher and pioneer of religious reform, preached this kind of assimilation. His first work, *Bemerkungen ueber die buergerliche Verbesserung der Juden, veranlasst durch die Frage: Soll der Jude Soldat werden* (1788), was a critical response to Joseph II's conscription of Jews the previous year; even so, he calls on his fellow Jews to relinquish their way of life and prejudices in order to obtain civic emancipation.

The call is echoed in Russia almost a century later by the Hebrew poet Judah Leib Gordon, in his poem "Awake, my People", written about 1862:

> . . . raise your head high, stand up straight
> Look at [your fellow-Europeans] with loving eyes,
> Open your hearts to wisdom and reason
> Become an enlightened nation, speaking their tongue.
> Everyone capable of learning should study
> Laborers and artisans should take to a craft
> The strong and the brave should be soldiers
> Farmers should buy fields and ploughs.[108]

The religious proto-Zionist, Rabbi Zevi Hirsch Kalischer (1795–1874), witnessing the armed independence struggles of several European nations, proposed a militarily trained home guard to protect settlements in the Land of Israel,[109] but the early secular Zionists paid little attention to the possibility of war, even defensive. Theodor Herzl , for instance, in his vision of a future Jewish state (not necessarily in Palestine), "allotted far more space to describing how steam engines were changing the face of the earth than to the topic of the defence of the proposed state".[110] As their naive slogan "The land without a people for the people without a land" indicates, they were but dimly aware of the Arab population of Palestine, even though Ahad Ha-'am, the great proponent of "cultural Zionism", who spent some months in Palestine in 1891, had trenchantly pointed out that there were few desolate fields awaiting Jewish cultivation, and that the "natives" were not uncivilized simpletons nor would they welcome wholesale Jewish immigration.[111]

Two factors, however, impelled some Zionists at the Sixth Zionist Congress (Basle, Switzerland, 1903) to envisage a more proactive military role. Reaction to the Kishinev pogrom of 1903 had stimulated the creation of trained Jewish defence groups in the Pale of Settlement;[112] and there was increasing acceptance of Ahad Ha-'am's assessment that not only was the land populated, but its population was likely to be hostile towards Jewish settlement. Though the majority demurred, some of the younger delegates including Vladimir Jabotinsky (1880–1940) called for military preparedness. Jabotinsky fought with the Jewish units under Allied command in the First World War, and after the war insisted on the need to maintain the Jewish Legion in Palestine as a guarantee against the outbreak of Arab hostility; this led to the formation in 1920 of the Haganah, later to become the Israel Defence Forces.

These secular developments were anxiously watched by the religious. Rabbi Abraham Isaac Kook (1865–1935), Ashkenazic Chief Rabbi of pre-state Palestine, urged that Jewish settlement of the land should proceed by peaceful means only; he nevertheless refused a compromise, acceptable to the secular Zionist leadership, that might have acknowledged Muslim title to the Western Wall.[113] Even a Jewish king, Kook reasoned, would need to consult the High Court before embarking on war, for no war (other than purely defensive) might be pursued against those who observe the Seven Commandments, and if the enemy were idolaters (this would exclude Muslims and Christians) it would still be necessary for the Court to examine their moral condition before declaring the war justified.[114] (For Kook it was axiomatic that no such Court existed in the present day.) Later, a similar position prohibiting offensive war was taken by the ultra-Orthodox Yeshayahu Karelitz (the *Hazon Ish* 1878–1953).[115]

There was, however, an inherent inconsistency in Kook's stance that became evident as time went on. On the one hand, there were those who shared or further developed the irenic aspect of his teaching, and who are represented in Israel today by the religious peace movements. Kook's younger contemporary, Moshe Avigdor Amiel (1883–1946), illustrates this trend. On 25 August 1938[116] Amiel wrote to the editor of a Jewish journal in Prague. Amiel, who was at that time Chief Rabbi of Tel Aviv, felt that his criticism of the Zionist policy of restraint (see below) had been misunderstood. He makes clear in his letter that what he had objected to was not restraint, but the impression given by the secular Zionists that military restraint was an act of generosity towards the Arabs. Far from it, it was an *absolute* demand of Torah law, for "Thou shalt not kill" applied irrespective of whether the victim was Arab or Jew, and was the basis of Jewish ethics.

> In my opinion, even if we knew for certain that we could bring about the Final Redemption [by killing Arabs] we should reject such a "Redemption" with all our strength, and not be redeemed through blood. Moreover, even if we were to apprehend several Arab murderers, if there was the slightest possibility that one of them was innocent we should not touch them, lest the innocent suffer.[117]

On the other hand Kook's own son Tzvi Yehuda (1891–1982) focused on his father's irredendist concept of Redemption through return to the Land: "the establishment of Jewish sovereignty over Eretz Yisrael is a commandment of the Torah."[118] He cites with approval a remark attributed to the Hafetz Haim, who as we saw above, encouraged or at least acquiesced in the recruitment of Jews into the Russian army, that serving in gentile armies was good since "In a short time the Mashiach will come, and we will have a State, and a State needs an army. Will you wait until then to learn how to be soldiers?"[119] Tzvi Yehuda demanded that no land within the Biblical boundaries of Israel be given up voluntarily once settled by Jews, though he did not advocate aggressive conquest. His followers are found today amongst the religious in the "settler" movement.

The Israel Defence Forces

Until the mid-1930s the Zionist leadership in Palestine permitted defensive action only; the policy of *havlaga*, or restraint, was maintained even in the face of the Arab riots of 1920, 1921, 1929 and 1936, and only slightly modified when the British Captain Orde Wingate insisted on the need to take action to prevent further massacres of Jews. It is in the 1930s that the concept of *tohar ha-nesheq* "purity of arms" emerges, demanding minimum force in the attainment of military objectives, and discrimination between combatants and non-combatants.[120] Despite doubts in the face of indiscriminate terrorism *tohar ha-nesheq* remains the guiding rule for the Israeli forces.

Neither *havlaga* nor *tohar ha-nesheq* figures in the traditional sources. But that is not to say that they lack firm foundation within Judaism. They arise out of:

- The secular, reformist and neo-Orthodox stress on the ethical and moral values of Judaism.
- Extrapolation from the *halakha* on personal relationships to that on international relationships.
- The desire for moral approval and hence political support from the world community, combined with the naive belief that military restraint would attain these objectives.

These foundations have sustained a fair degree of consensus among Jews, both religious and secular.

Some extracts from the Israel Defence Forces' (IDF) official Doctrine Statement will amplify these comments.[121] The IDF Mission is:

- To defend the existence, territorial integrity and sovereignty of the state of Israel.
- To protect the inhabitants of Israel and to combat all forms of terrorism which threaten the daily life.

Basic Points in the Security Doctrine stem from the notion that "Israel cannot afford to lose a single war". The IDF stance is "defensive on the strategic level, no territorial ambitions"; war should be avoided by political means, but a credible deterrent posture maintained.

At the Operational Level "the IDF is subordinate to the directions of the democratic civilian authorities and the laws of the state. Its Basic Values include: "Human Dignity – The IDF and its soldiers are obligated to protect human dignity. Every human being is of value regardless of his or her origin, religion, nationality, gender, status or position." The values are defined as:

- Human Life – The IDF servicemen and women will act in a judicious and safe manner in all they do, out of recognition of the supreme value of human life. During combat they will endanger themselves and their comrades only to the extent required to carry out their mission.
- Purity of Arms – The IDF servicemen and women will use their weapons and force only for the purpose of their mission, only to the necessary extent and will maintain their humanity even during combat. IDF soldiers will not use their weapons and force to harm human beings who are not combatants or prisoners

of war, and will do all in their power to avoid causing harm to their lives, bodies, dignity and property.
• Discipline . . . IDF soldiers will be meticulous in giving only lawful orders, and shall refrain from obeying blatantly illegal orders.

The IDF Doctrine Statement is not, of course, a religious document. Nevertheless, it commands broad acceptance among the religious, and that is because of the modern reading of traditional sources which, partly through Zionism, has absorbed both secular and universal ethical elements.

Rabbinic debates in modern Israel

Israel's need for military defence has generated considerable debate among the religious, and this is reflected in the large number of rabbinic responsa, addressed mainly to individual enquirers, on the conduct of war. Three trends may be discerned:

1 Some of the ultra-Orthodox refuse to serve in the armed forces. This may be because (a) they are de facto pacifists, believing that God will defend the faithful, (b) they believe they are "doing their bit" for the country by praying and studying Torah, or (c) they are afraid of "contamination" by the non-Orthodox, in which case they particularly object to the conscription of women.
2 The mainstream Orthodox serve in the regular forces, and consider it their religious duty to defend the land.
3 The Orthodox "settlers"[122] (by no means all settlers are Orthodox or even religious) believe they have a religious duty to maintain a Jewish presence wherever possible throughout the biblical "Land of Israel", though few if any believe there is a religious duty actively to conquer it.

Shlomo Goren (1917–94), Ashkenazi Chief Rabbi of Israel from 1972–83, was not only a distinguished Talmudic scholar and for several years chief chaplain of the Israeli forces, but a qualified paratrooper who rose to the rank of brigadier-general and was commended for his bravery in the field. He set the tone for Jewish discussion on *jus in bello*:

> Human life is undoubtedly a supreme value in Judaism, as expressed both in the *Halacha* and the prophetic ethic. This refers not only to Jews, but to all men created in the image of God.[123]

> We see that God has compassion for the life of idolators and finds it difficult to destroy them. Since we are enjoined to imitate the moral qualities of God, we too should not rejoice over the destruction of the enemies of Israel.[124]

The following are typical of the matters discussed in the responsa and allied literature.

Nahmanides listed "conquest of the land"[125] as a divine commandment. Nahum Rabbinowitz, presumably targeting the religious "hawks", writes that this does not afford "any basis for concluding that war is permitted [in the present era] for the sake of conquest of the Land. What is worse, such a reading entails indifference towards bloodshed. Such indifference undermines the very foundations of society and endangers the entire enterprise of the beginning of our redemption."[126]

Related to this is the religious status of the Israel-controlled areas of the West Bank, and the question of whether it is permissible to risk life in holding on to them. Chaim David Halevi (b. 1925), then Sefardi Chief Rabbi of Tel Aviv/Jaffa, argued that there was a religious duty to settle in these areas, but not to conquer them by force.[127] He takes issue with some rabbis who had maintained that those territories should be defended at all costs as part of the "land of Israel", and urges a more pragmatic view on political negotiation.[128]

Several, including the late British Chief Rabbi Lord Jakobovits, have asked: Can land be traded for peace? The land they are talking about is land occupied by Israel as a result of the 1967 war, not land within the internationally recognized borders of Israel. Most, in line with the powerful advocacy of Sefardi Chief Rabbi Ovadya Yosef and Ashkenazi Rabbi Shilo Refael,[129] answered positively, but no Arab offer of peace has been elicited that has been sufficiently reassuring to put the matter to the test.

Is there a prima facie religious duty to serve in the army?[130] If so, does it apply to yeshiva students, who are engaged full-time in the study of Torah?[131] Halevi, like others, addresses these questions; but he also speculates on theological matters. Several of his responsa in the aftermath of the Yom Kippur war of 1973, in which Israel had suffered substantial losses, attempt to reconcile the events with divine providence.[132]

Avraham Sherman, writing in 1988 in the aftermath of Arab attacks on West Bank settlements, seeks Torah guidance on how the fully armed Israel Defence Forces should respond to an enemy that includes unarmed, non-combatant men, women and children.[133] Restraint, he argues, arises from the Torah's prohibition to wantonly destroy fruit trees in the course of war (see below); if we are forbidden to destroy fruit trees, we are certainly forbidden to destroy the lives of non-combatants. However, Nahmanides permits destruction [of trees] if it materially contributes to undermining the enemy, and Maimonides probably agrees (cf. 2 Kings 3:19). Provided the intention is not to vent anger, as in terrorism, but actually to undermine the enemy, hostile non-combatants may also be targeted, just as injury may be caused by a doctor who intends to heal, or pressure may be brought to bear on the widow and the orphan for their own good.

Yehuda Shaviv, an editor of the journal to which this argument was submitted, was shocked, and in his rejoinder attacks Sherman for suggesting the "dangerous principle" that "the end justifies the means", namely means that are intrinsically evil. The examples of permitted injury Sherman cites, he points out, are for the benefit of the victim, not the attacker; a surgeon operates (i.e. injures) to benefit the patient, not himself, and pressure may be brought to bear on the widow and the orphan only for their own good. Moreover, Jacob was afraid that he might have to kill in self-defence, which indicates that he thought it was still evil, even if necessary.

Sherman, perhaps chastened, defended himself by arguing that the "end" that justified the course of action he advocates was an ethical end, as defined by the Torah itself, namely defensive war, which is an extension of the Talmudic category of *ha-ba l'horg'kha hashkem l'horgo* "If someone intends to kill you, kill him first".[134]

Though Sherman is at pains to claim that his ethics is defined by the Torah, it does seem that both he and his opponent implicitly acknowledge an ethical standard beyond that of the explicit rules of *halakha*, if in accordance with Jewish tradition. Indeed, much of the halakhic discussion on war issues presupposes an extra-halakhic ethical stance that drives the interpretation of the sources.[135]

Conclusion

We must now consider how all these traditions and interpretations lead us to address the harsh realities of contemporary international conflict. Several Jewish religious thinkers, for instance Irving Greenberg among the Orthodox, and Marc Ellis among the liberals, have taken the line that Jewish "empowerment" brings a new responsibility. They exaggerate the degree of Jewish empowerment; Israel is small among the nations of the world, and under constant threat, while the Jewish communities of the United States and other democracies have no power per se and only limited influence on the world scene.

Nevertheless, the point is well taken; to the extent that people have power, they have responsibility to use it wisely and justly. Unfortunately, this moral stance does not get us very far. It stirs our consciences, but does not advance clear thinking about either *jus ad bellum* or *jus in bello*.

For Jews today the question of involvement in war arises in two contexts, namely Israel, and participation in wars of countries of which Jews are citizens. Their religious traditions, as we have seen, afford ample resources to guide them, but must be read within a modern context markedly different from that in which the traditional sources were compiled. Differences include:

* There is general recognition of the principle of national self-rule (i.e. imperial-ism is rejected), though it is not always clear what constitutes a nation.
* At a global level, and in most instances even at the national level, religious pluralism is accepted (i.e. individual religious freedom must be guaranteed, and it is not acceptable to impose religion by force).
* International communications are better than ever before, and there is at least a semblance of international law and order independent of religious authority.
* Modern armaments are capable of inflicting large-scale damage, but not of discriminating effectively between combatants and non-combatants.

These differences set the parameters within which a Jewish theologian has to re-evaluate traditional sources. On this basis s/he might reasonably conclude:

- Every attempt should be made to settle international disputes by negotiation, not by war nor by the threat of war.
- The only possible just wars are defensive, "defence" being understood as defence of national territorial integrity and/or the physical safety of citizens. In extreme cases attempted "cultural genocide" might afford grounds for defensive war.
- Such wars are not only permissible but mandatory; in appropriate circumstances there is a duty to assist other nations in their defence.
- The extent to which perceived threat rather than the actual onset of hostilities justifies pre-emptive warfare is a matter for judgement in particular cases. Deterrent (preventive) wars, aiming to stop a potential enemy getting to the point at which he might threaten, are less justifiable.
- Territorial or religious expansion does not justify war.

As to the conduct of war:

- Minimum casualties should be inflicted to attain legitimate objectives. This is not the same as minimum force. The threat, or even the use, of maximum force may shorten a conflict and minimize casualties.
- If at all possible non-combatants should be spared. The difficulty of exercising such discrimination with modern weapons of mass destruction means that it is not always possible to spare non-combatants; but on the other hand it would be absurd for a country to surrender to an aggressor simply to save the life of one non-combatant hostage.
- If at all possible there should be no recourse to nuclear, biological and chemical weapons, or other weapons destructive of the environment.
- Hostages should not be taken; prisoners' rights should be respected.

As the phrase "if at all possible" indicates there are few if any absolutes in the conduct of war. A document such as the 1949 Geneva Convention IV Relative to the Protection of Civilian Persons in Time of War,[136] and its subsequent Protocols, may attempt to define categories of non-combatants, or may recommend that hospitals be sited as far as possible from military objectives (Article 18), but this is of little help where opposing combatants are targeting hospitals or deliberately siting their own military units in hospitals in order to use the sick as hostages.

Standards can be adopted unilaterally, or set by international agreement, but the moral dilemma arises of whether a party that ignores the standards can be allowed through its perpetration of evil to gain ascendancy over the moral side. Article 7 #1 of the 1981 UN Weapons Convention candidly states "When one of the parties to a conflict is not bound by an annexed Protocol, the parties bound by this Convention and that annexed Protocol shall remain bound by them in their mutual relations".[137] But they are not bound by them in their relations with the unbound party.

The legal formulation by no means determines the moral position. However, only a "party" with overwhelming military superiority can afford to be generous towards an unscrupulous foe.

Other interesting questions remain: What constitutes "competent authority" to declare war? Traditional Judaism, we have seen, requires a Great Court of 71 justices, as well as divine approval through the oracle of the High Priest, for a "voluntary" war. But as the only allowable wars (in the present world order) are defensive, this unattainable requirement need not be invoked. Is the United Nations the competent authority? In the case of defensive wars, it is unrealistic to expect a country under attack to await authorization from the UN before defending itself, just as it would be unrealistic to expect a citizen who is about to be mugged to await police authorization before defending himself. That is why Article 51 of the UN Charter permits self-defence: "Nothing in the present Charter shall impair the inherent right of individual or collective self-defence if an armed attack occurs against a Member of the United Nations, until the Security Council has taken measures necessary to maintain international peace and security."[138] The only competent authority is therefore the legitimate national government of the defending state.

Terrorism is difficult to fit into any of the traditional categories. If it is state-sponsored, or permitted by a host state, it can be classified as an act of war. Alternatively, it could be viewed as a form of hostage taking.

The taking of hostages is clearly forbidden by the Jewish sources, since it involves both depriving non-combatants of their freedom and the credible threat of violence against them. On the other hand, traditional sources seem unanimous that one should not yield to an enemy who *has* taken hostages, even though refusal to concede to the hostage-taker's demands may result in harm to innocent hostages.[139]

What constitutes "territorial expansion"? Where there is a territorial dispute between two nations, as between Israelis and Palestinians, what appears to one side as expansion appears to the other side as recovery of the homeland.

Though the religious principles for engagement in and the conduct of war seem clear, their application in practice is hard to determine. The acute questions that arise in modern warfare tend to be about the assessment of particular situations. For instance, if Iraq posed a serious (how serious?) threat to the security of the United States or any of its allies, and if the threat could not be averted by diplomatic means, *jus ad bellum* would permit the United States to wage war against Iraq. What is questionable is not the principle, but the assessment of the situation.

Likewise, if it was clear that either the Israeli assessment of the Palestinian threat was objectively correct, or that Palestinian accounts of Israel's actions and intentions were objectively correct, it would not be hard to know what to do. The doubts arise through the lack of consensus as to salient facts including the aims of the other side, through subjectivity of judgement, through different perceptions of history, and through the adoption of conflicting value systems.

Again, *jus in bello* demands that non-combatants be spared. But this does not help us to define who is a combatant, nor does it define what degree of sacrifice is necessary to save non-combatants from harm, or what degree of restraint is appropriate to avoid "collateral damage" when using powerful and indiscriminate weaponry.

In sum, it seems that many exponents of contemporary Judaism read the traditional texts in close conformity with secular ethics and international law. This convergence is hardly surprising in view of the interaction between secular ethics, international law and Jewish texts, including those later than the Bible. A minority of fundamentalist rabbis, however, differ on specific issues rather than general principles, in particular with regard to definition of the borders of Israel and the acceptability of relinquishing control of areas of "historic" Israel once conquered.

All share the ideal of peace, and so we close with two Jewish texts extolling its virtue. The first is a rabbinic comment on a verse from the "military oration" of Deuteronomy:

"You shall proclaim peace to it". Great is peace, for even the dead need peace. Great is peace; even in war Israel needs peace. Great is peace, for even those who dwell on high[140] need peace, as it is said, "He makes peace in His high places" (Job 25:2). Great is peace, for the priestly blessing concludes with it. Moses too loved peace, as it is said, "And I sent messengers from the desert of Qedemot . . . [with] words of peace. (Deuteronomy 2:26)."[141]

The second is one of the most famous of prophetic visions:

And they shall beat their swords into ploughshares,
And their spears into pruning-hooks
Nation shall not lift up sword against nation,
Neither shall they learn war anymore.
(Isaiah 2:4; Micah 4:3)

Notes

1 Goren, Shlomo (1987) "Combat morality and the Halakha" in *Crossroads* I: 211–231, pp. 223–6.
2 Weinfeld, Moshe (1972) *Deuteronomy and the Deuteronomic School*, Oxford: Clarendon Press: 45.
3 On this distinction see Johnson, J. T. (1977) *Ideology, Reason and the Limitation of War: Religious and Secular Concepts 1200–1749*, Princeton, NJ: Princeton University Press: 53.
4 Compare Deuteronomy 9:5. The novelist Dan Jacobson explored the Bible's ambivalence about the conquest in (1982) *The Story of the Stories: The Chosen People and its God*, New York: Harper & Row. Michael Walzer aptly observes that no biblical author "undertakes to construct an argument on behalf of the seven Canaanite nations comparable to Abraham's argument on behalf of the Canaanite cities of Sodom and Gomorrah". Walzer, Michael (1992) "The Idea of Holy War in Ancient Israel", in *Journal of Religious Ethics* 20(2): 215.

5 Jerusalem Talmud *Shevi'it* 6:1.
6 "For the sin of the Amorites will not be total until then" (Genesis 15:16) is a justification of the Israelite conquest on the grounds that God would not have permitted the Canaanites to be destroyed unless and until their evil justified it.
7 Those outside the rabbinic tradition, as Alexander Yannai (see below), may have taken a different view.
8 David's rather limited "expansionist" wars were not religiously motivated.
9 Victoria, Franciscus de (1917) *De Indis et De Jure Bellis Relectiones*. Classics of International Law, ed. Ernest Nys. Washington: Carnegie Institute. Sect. II, 16, cited by Johnson (1977): 156–157. (He is known in Spanish as Francisco de Vitoria.)
10 Weinfeld (1972) compares Deuteronomy's military orations with those to be found in Herodotus and Thucydides; they are "literary programmatic creations and do not convey the actual content of speeches delivered in concrete circumstances" (51). He attributes them to the scribes of Josiah's Reform (158f.).
11 1 Samuel 15; 1 Kings 20. Whether the extant Deuteronomy was in existence at that time is irrelevant.
12 Theoretically it is possible that Amos nevertheless held that Israel had an exceptional covenantal obligation to "cleanse" the land of idolaters; perhaps he hints at that in 2:9, though the "destroying" is there attributed to God.
13 Some English translations have "lay in wait".
14 The Hebrew *nahal* may be translated "valley" or "inheritance"; Rabbi Mani interprets the verse as hinting that Saul was troubled about the means by which he was to secure possession of the land for Israel.
15 The allusion is to the atonement ceremony to be performed by representatives of the town nearest to where a slain person was found (Deuteronomy 21:1–9, immediately following the section on war).
16 Babylonian Talmud *Yoma* 22b. *Midrash Rabba* Deuteronomy 5:12 ascribes to Moses the initiative, confirmed and praised by God, to seek peace with Sihon; Midrash Tehillim on Psalm 120:7 ascribes a similar initiative to the Messiah.
17 The last of these was the revolt at Sepphoris in 351 against Gallus Caesar, the tyrannical emperor Constantinus II. It was suppressed by the Roman general Ursicinus. In 614 Jews of Palestine made a short-lived alliance with the Persians in the hope of regaining Jerusalem.
18 Josephus *Antiquities* 13:15. Whiston's note on his translation at the end of the chapter, notwithstanding his derogation of the Pharisees, is a salutary warning against wars of religion, presumably directed against British imperial aggression in the early nineteenth century.
19 Vermes, G. (1997) *The Complete Dead Sea Scrolls in English*, London: Penguin Press: 161–189.
20 Mishna *Shabbat* 6:4.
21 Other diagnoses are of course possible.
22 Babylonian Talmud *Sota* 10a.
23 For an example of this application see *Crossroads* 199.
24 Altogether ten nations are named in various verses, but they are conventionally referred to as seven.
25 Joshua's example concerned a self-proclaimed "Ammonite proselyte" who if not for Joshua's ruling would have been forbidden to marry a native-born Jewish woman. See Mishna *Yadayim* 4:4.
26 Rabbi Nathan in *Sifré* on Numbers 31:7. Perhaps he wants to explain how despite the annihilation of the Midianites alleged in Numbers, Midianite raids are reported in Judges 6. Meir Simcha Ha-Kohen of Dvinsk (Daugaupils, Latvia) (1843–1926), in his commentary *Meshekh Hokhma* (1927), notes that whereas Nahmanides understands

the requirement of an escape route as motivated by compassion, Maimonides regards it as merely tactical.

27 That is, Esau, the twin of Jacob (Genesis 25:25).

28 At a still earlier stage, reflected in the Dead Sea Scrolls, it may simply be a convenient ellipsis to avoid the political consequences of openly criticizing Rome.

29 A condensed translation of his commentary *Sefat Emet* on the Pentateuch has been produced in Green, Arthur (tr.) (1988) *The Language of Truth: The Torah Commentary of the Sefat Emet, Rabbi Yehudah Leib Alter of Ger*, Philadelphia, PA: The Jewish Publication Society.

30 Ravitsky, Aviezer (1996) *Messianism, Zionism and Jewish Religious Radicalism*, tr. M. Zwirsky and J. Chipman, Chicago, IL: University of Chicago Press gives a penetrating analysis of Messianic Religious Zionism, in particular of the problematic resulting from Rav Kook's teaching as interpreted by his son, Zvi Yehuda Kook.

31 Cohen-Almagor describes the legal process involved in this unprecedented step in Cohen-Almagor, Raphael (1994) *The Boundaries of Liberty and Tolerance: The Struggle against Kahanism in Israel*, Gainesville: University Press of Florida. On the ideology of the movement see Ravitsky, Aviezer (1986) "The Roots of Kahanism", in *Jerusalem Quarterly* 39: 98–118. There is an extensive bibliography of the movement and reaction to it at http://users.skynet.be/terrorism/html/israel_kahane.htm, and the Kach movement maintains an active website.

32 Babylonian Talmud *Sota* 44b.

33 The Puritan Henry Ainsworth, leader of the Separatist congregation in Amsterdam, in his *Annotations upon the Five Books of Moses* (London: John Bellarmine, 1627), leaning upon Maimonides, makes the same distinction. Johnson (1977) footnote p. 131, comments that "this distinction overrides any that might be attempted between offensive and defensive war"; he is incorrect.

34 Inbar, Efraim (1987) "War in the Jewish Tradition", in *Jerusalem Journal of International Relations* 9: 2, 83–99: 86, and n. 6 on 98, points to the distinction between pre-emptive and preventive war. He cites *Lehem Mishneh* who interprets Maimonides' expression "war to enlarge the borders of Israel" (*Mishneh Torah: Melakhim* 5:1) as preventive war, to deter potential aggressors. (Inbar wrongly attributes *Lehem Mishneh* to Joseph Karo; the author was the Salonika-born rabbi Abraham ben Moses di Boton, 1545?–1588.)

35 That the rabbinic tradition is not entirely anti-imperialist is demonstrated by a midrash such as *Targum Sheni* on Esther (probably eighth century) that wildly exaggerates the extent of the dominions of Solomon and Ahab.

36 The Urim and Tumim (Exodus 28:30), the precise nature of which is a matter of debate. The oracular function assumed by the rabbis is hinted at in Ezra 2:62; Nehemiah 7:65. Compare the Roman practice of seeking guidance from auguries through the fetial priests.

37 Mishna *Sanhedrin* 1:5.

38 Johnson (1977): 104, and 117f., especially the section on Alexander Leighton 125f.

39 Inbar (1987): 94 refers only to the later comments of Rashi (*Gittin* 8b and *Avoda Zara* 20b) and Maimonides (*Terumot* 1:2) for the consensus requirement.

40 *Genesis Rabba* 76:2.

41 Babylonian Talmud *Sanhedrin* 72a.

42 Babylonian Talmud *Sanhedrin* 74a.

43 Ambrose, *De Officiis* 1.41.201. Augustine Letter 185 (to Boniface) and *Contra Faustum* 22.74, 78.

44 Mishna *Avot* 3:2. The statement is attributed to Hanina the Deputy High Priest (first century CE).

45 Midrash Rabbah *ad loc*. Nothing is known of Rabbi Onia. "Bar Koziba" is (the

archaeologically attested correct name of) Bar Kochba; could Shutelah ben Ephraim be Patricius, leader of the revolt of Sepphoris?

46 Midrashic attributions are uncertain, and this Midrash may well reflect attitudes under Islamic rather than Byzantine rule.

47 Ravitsky (1996): Appendix 211–234 "The Impact of the Three Oaths in Jewish History" (some versions have three rather than four oaths) argues that "the wall placed by the oaths between the people and its land was far higher than the historians suggest".

48 Philo: 219–223. (Philo of Alexandria (Philo Judaeus), *The Special Laws*, in Vol. VII of the Complete Works, tr. and ed. F. H. Colson and G. H. Whitaker, in the Loeb series (1953–63).

49 Ibid.: 224.

50 *Sefer ha-Hinukh* No. 527. The work is of unknown authorship, and wrongly ascribed to Aaron ha-Levi of Barcelona (*c*.1235–1300).

51 Tosefta *Sota* 7:14. (Tosefta is conventionally thought to be a third-century supplement to Mishna.)

52 Mishna *Avoda Zara* 1:7.

53 Babylonian Talmud *Avoda Zara* 16a.

54 Halevi Vol. 1 #19. (Halevi, Chaim David, *'Asé l'kha Rav* (Hebrew), 4 vols., Jerusalem: Mosad Harav Kook. Vol. 1 5736 (1975/6) and Vol. 3, second edition, Tel Aviv 5739 (1978/9)). See also *Shulhan 'Arukh: Yore De'a* 151 and *Hoshen Mishpat* 409. Some more recent responsa are reviewed in Bleich, David J. (1982) "Sale of Arms", in *Tradition* 20: 358–359.

55 *Encyclopaedia Judaica* s.v. Samuel Ibn 'Adiya.

56 The matter is enshrouded in legend, unknown from Jewish sources, and there is doubt as to Kahina's Jewishness. See Hirschberg, in *Tarbiz* (Hebrew), 26 (1956/57): 370–383.

57 The Khazars constituted an independent Turkic nation centred on what is now Southern Ukraine between the seventh and tenth centuries CE. During part of this time the leading Khazars professed Judaism.

58 Ravitsky (1996): 122 gives references for armed resistance to marauding Crusaders in the Rhineland.

59 See his letter informing the Exilarch Hezekiah in Jerusalem of his victory over Seville in 1055 (Weinberger, Leon J. (1973) *Jewish Prince in Moslem Spain: Selected Poems of Samuel Ibn Nagrela*, Alabama: University of Alabama Press: 8 and references).

60 Weinberger (1973): 118.

61 Ibid.: 40.

62 The debate as to whether to engage even in defensive warfare on the Sabbath goes back at least to Hasmonean times; the rabbinic view was unambiguously that saving life has priority over Sabbath observance. Amongst the questions addressed by Hisdai Ibn Shaprut to the Jewish Khazar king *c*.960 was whether war abrogates the Sabbath; Hisdai was not in doubt about the law, but interested to know Khazar practice.

63 The distinction derives from the Mutazilite Abu-l-Hudyl-al-Alaf. See Schreiner *Der Kalam in der Jüdischen Literatur*, 26.

64 Levine, D. (ed.) (1966) *The Bustan al-Ukul by Natanaël Ibn al-Fayyumi*, with an English translation, *The Garden of Wisdom*, New York 1908; repr.: English 40 Arabic 24. Netanel's first group of laws would be shared by Muslims; the second group consists of specifically Jewish rituals. Bahya's list in the *Introduction* to his *Kitab al-Hidaya ila Faraid al-Qulub* reads, in Mansoor's version "prayer, fasting, alms-giving, learning His book and spreading the knowledge of it, fulfilling his commandments concerning the tabernacle, the palm-branch, the fringes, the doorpost, the railing on the roof and the like." Bahya (1973) *The Book of Direction to the Duties of the Heart*, introduction, translation and notes by Menahem Mansoor, London: Routledge & Kegan Paul: 89. Evidently ibn Fayyumi's inclusion of *jihad* is no accident.

65 Maimonides, Moses (1949) *The Code of Maimonides (Mishneh Torah) Book 14: The Book of Judges*, Newhaven, CT: Yale University Press: Melakhim 7:15. Radbaz, who traces Maimonides' rulings to their sources, comments laconically, "Some of this is in midrashim, and some the Master compiled on the basis of biblical verses".

66 For Maimonides' opinion of Al-Farabi see the letter cited by Pines in Maimonides, Moses (1963) *The Guide of the Perplexed*, tr. Shlomo Pines, 2 vols, Chicago, IL and London: University of Chicago Press: lx. For Al-Farabi's views on leadership and war see Butterworth, Charles E. (1990) "al-Farabi's Statecraft: War and the Well-Ordered Regime", in J. Kelsay and J. T. Johnson (eds.) *Cross, Crescent, and Sword: The Justification and Limitation of War in Western and Islamic tradition*, New York: Greenwood: 79–100.

67 Numbers 18:20, 23; Deuteronomy 18:1, 2.

68 Maimonides (1949): *Shemita v'Yovel* 13:12, 13.

69 Thomas Aquinas Summa Theologica 2:2 40:2; *Corpus Juris Canonici: Decretum* Quaest. VIII, Cans. IV, XIX.

70 This treatise, like the "Peace of God" declared at the Council of Chanoux in 988, is concerned with the sacredness of the lives of Christians, that is with internecine Christian warfare; there is no evidence that immunity was applicable to clergy and non-combatants of idolaters or heretics.

71 The original Arabic is *al-haqq*, which could be a term for God.

72 Maimonides (1963): 1:54. The point is made even more briefly in 1:36. The emphases are the translator's (Shlomo Pines); they indicate Hebrew words within the Arabic text.

73 Thomas Aquinas *Summa Theologica* 2:2 40:1: *requiritur ut sit intentio bellantium recta*. Thomas was acquainted with the *Guide* in Latin translation, and occasionally acknowledges a debt to it, but in this case his model was Gratian (his citation from Augustine is unidentifiable).

74 The most controversial instance is his interpretation of the sacrificial system (*Guide* 3:32).

75 Deuteronomy 21:10–14. Babylonian Talmud *Qiddushin* 21b "The Torah spoke in response to [man's] evil inclination".

76 No. 3 of the supplementary list of Positive Commandments in his Notes on Maimonides' *Sefer ha-Mitzvot*.

77 Ralbag on Deuteronomy 7:9. Jerusalem: Mosad Rav Kook edition, 5760 (2000) Vol. 5, 54.

78 Arama *Aqedat Isaac* #74 and #81 on Numbers. See Munk, Eliyahu (tr.) (1986) *Akeydat Yitzchak: The Commentary of Isaac Arama on the Torah* (condensed version), 2 vols, Jerusalem: Rubin Mass: 726f. and 791f.

79 Ibid. # 81, cited by Ravitsky, Aviezer (1996) "Prohibited Wars in the Jewish Tradition", in Terry Nardin (ed.) *The Ethics of War and Peace: Religious and Secular Perspectives*, Princeton, NJ: Princeton University Press: 115–127, pp. 121/2.

80 Summary is necessary on account of his prolix style. The Commentary on Deuteronomy has not, so far as I know, been translated into English.

81 His anarchism (all human government is bad, since it involves the domination of one person by another) is expounded in his Commentary on Genesis 2, and was clearly influenced by Seneca's 90th Epistle.

82 *Polycraticus* 8:10.

83 Commentary on Deuteronomy 20. Philo (see above) held the same view, but Abravanel was unacquainted with his writings.

84 Clausewitz, Carl von (1982) *On War*, edited with an Introduction by Anatol Rapoport, London: Penguin Books: Book 5, Chapter 6, p. 402. See also Book 1, Chapter 24 on War as a continuation of policy by other means.

85 Ibid.: Book 1, Chapter 1, p. 102.

86 Tosafot *Avoda Zara* 18b s.v. *lo yithashev immahem*.
87 Bleich, David J. (1983) *Contemporary Halakhic Problems* II, New York: Ktav: 165, citing Chatam Sofer *Yore De'ah* 19.
88 Ibid.: 166, citing *Hatam Sofer* 6:29.
89 Berlin expects the reader to be familiar with the whole verse: "A time to love and a time to hate; a time for war and a time for peace."
90 *Ha'ameq Davar* on Genesis 9:5.
91 *Mishna Berura* 329:17.
92 Bleich (1983): 165, citing *Zera' Abraham* 24.
93 *Encyclopaedia Judaica* s.v. Zemba.
94 This is the theme of Mendelssohn's well-known and frequently translated *Jerusalem*.
95 Mendelssohn, Moses (1843) *Anmerkungen zu des Ritters Michaelis Beurteilung des ersten Theils von Dohm, über die bürgeliche Verbesserung der Juden*, in *Moses Mendelssohn's gesammelte Schritften*, Leipzig, Vol. 3: 365–367.
96 Luzzatto, Samuel Davide (1876) *Il Pentateuco: volgarizzato e commentato da Samuel Davide Luzzatto*, Vol. 5, Padova: F. Sacchetto: 157. Walzer, Michael (1996) "War and Peace in the Jewish Tradition", in Terry Nardin (ed.) *The Ethics of War and Peace: Religious and Secular Perspectives*, Princeton, NJ: Princeton University Press: 95–112, p. 101. Walzer citing this at second hand unfortunately lacks the final sentence of this passage.
97 He cites him later in the chapter, though not on this point.
98 Hertz, J. H. (1938) *Sermons, Addresses and Studies*, Vol. 1, London: Soncino Press: 25–29.
99 Niditch, Susan (1993) *War in the Hebrew Bible: A Study in the Ethics of Violence*, New York and Oxford: Oxford University Press: 136f.
100 Wilcock, Evelyn (1994) *Pacifism and the Jews*, Stroud: Hawthorn Press: chapter 2.
101 Ibid.: 52.
102 Ibid.: chapter 3.
103 Brown, Robert McAfee, Abraham Heschel and David Novak (1967) *Vietnam: Crisis of Conscience*, New York: Association Press.
104 Lamm, Maurice (1978) "After the War – Another Look at Pacifism and Selective Conscientious Objection", in Menachem Kellner (ed.) *Contemporary Jewish Ethics*, New York: HPC: 221–238, p. 227.
105 Shein *et al.* v. Minister of Defence *et al.*, H.C. 734/83, *P.D.* 38(3) 393, discussed by Sinclair, Daniel B. (1988) "Conscientious Objection", in *Jewish Law Annual* IX, Chur: Harwood Academic: 262–265. (Summarizes Israel High Court decision 734 / 83).
106 Shapira, Anita (1999) *Land and Power: The Zionist Resort to Force, 1881–1948*, tr. William Templer, Stanford, CA: Stanford University Press: Introduction, viii.
107 Solomon, Norman (2000) "Zionism and Religion: The Transformation of an Idea", in *Annual of Rabbinic Judaism* Vol. III: 145–174. For the general background of Zionist ideology see Shimoni, Gideon (1995) *The Zionist Ideology*, Hanover, MA and London: Brandeis University Press.
108 Translation Stanislawski, Michael (1988) *For Whom Do I Toil? Judah Leib Gordon and the Crisis of Russian Jewry*, New York: Oxford University Press: 49–50. The original Hebrew *Haqitza 'Ami* is in *Kitve Yehuda Leib Gordon: Shira*, Tel Aviv, 1956: 17–18.
109 According to Shapira (1999): 16, the proposal is in Kalischer's *Derishat Zion* (1862). I have not located it there, and Shapira's footnote cites only Moses Hess's *Rome and Jerusalem*, New York edition, 1956: 106.
110 Shapira (1999): 10.
111 Ahad Ha-'am ("one of the people") was the pseudonym adopted by Asher Hirsch Ginsberg (1856–1927). His composed his essay *Emet me-Erets Israel* (the first of two with that title) on 21 Iyar 5651 (1891) on board ship en route from Jaffa to Odessa and it was published later that year in the Hebrew journal *Ha-Melits* 13–24 Sivan 5651.

112 That is, the areas under Russian domination where Jews were permitted to live.

113 Samson, David and Tzvi Fishman (1996) *Eretz Yisrael: Lights on Orot: The Teachings of HaRav Avraham Yitzhak HaCohen Kook*, Jeruslaem: Torat Eretz Yisrael Publications, 5756: xv–xvi.

114 Ravitsky (1996): 116, based on Kook *Igrot R'ayah* (Jerusalem 1966) 1:140.

115 Ravitsky (1996): 116, based on Karelitz's notes on Maimonides' Code *Melakhim* 5:1 in the Jerusalem, 1957 edition.

116 It is dated 25 Ab 5698.

117 The letter (in Hebrew) was republished in Tehumin X: 148.

118 *Torat Eretz Yisrael*, 165.

119 Ibid.: 169–170, citing Kook's *Netivot Israel* 2:6.

120 See Flliot Dorff's remarks in Landes, Daniel (ed.) (1991) *Confronting Omnicide: Jewish Reflections on Weapons of Mass Destruction*, Northvale, NJ and London: Jason Aronson: 177–179.

121 The extracts are excerpted from the English text on http://www.idf.il

122 "Settlers" does not capture the religious dimension of the Hebrew term *mitnahalim*, "those who take possession of a rightful inheritance".

123 Goren (1987): 211. Goren is at some pains to establish that the correct text of Mishna Sanhedrin is "Therefore man was created singly, to teach us that one who causes the loss of a single life is considered by the Torah as though he has caused the loss of an entire world" and not as in some copies "one who causes the loss of a single *Jewish* life"; his reading has strong manuscript support.

124 Ibid.: 215.

125 We remarked above that he probably meant no more than "living in".

126 Rabbinowitz in *Tehumin* 5 (1984), 184, cited by Ravitsky (1996): 118.

127 Halevi Vol. 3 #60: 366–367.

128 Halevi Vol. 3 #61, and also his *Dat u-Medina*, 49. There is a fuller discussion by Saul Israeli, Halevi and Mordecai Breuer in the Hebrew publication *Af Sha'al*.

129 Their papers were published in 1980 by the religious peace movement, *Oz v'Shalom*, for whom they had been written. They were republished in *Tehumin* 10 (5749/1989).

130 Halevi Vol. 3: #58.

131 Halevi Vol. 1 #21.

132 Ibid.: ##7–9.

133 *Tehumin* 9 (1988), 231f.

134 Babylonian Talmud *Sanhedrin* 72a. See above.

135 For two contrasting views on the relationship between law and ethics in Judaism see the essays Borowitz, Eugene B. (1990) *Exploring Jewish Ethics: Papers on Covenant Responsibility*, Detroit, MI: Wayne State University Press; and Lichtenstein, Aharon (1975) "Does Jewish Tradition Recognize an Ethic Independent of Halacha?", in Marvin Fox (ed.) *Modern Jewish Ethics: Theory and Practice*, Columbus, OH: Ohio State University Press: 102–123. Kellner, Menachem (ed.) (1978) *Contemporary Jewish Ethics*, New York: HPC: 102–123, reprints the Lichtenstein essay, and in addition carries interesting material by Jacobs, Zieman, Fackenheim and Samuelson.

136 Roberts, Adam and Richard Guelff (eds.) (1989) *Documents on the Laws of War*, revised edition, Oxford: Clarendon Press: 271ff.

137 UN Convention on Prohibitions or Restriction on the Use of Certain Conventional Weapons Which May be Deemed to be Excessively Injurious or to Have Indiscriminate Effects. Roberts and Guelff (1989): 473ff.

138 Chapter VII Article 51 of the Charter of the United Nations. The text is available on the United Nations website. International lawyers have argued that this permission extends to pre-emptive strikes.

139 Mishna *Terumot* 8:12, and Daube.

140 Angels.
141 *Sifré* Deuteronomy 199.

Bibliography

Ambrose of Milan, *De Officiis*.

Aquinas, Thomas, *Summa Theologica* II / II, Quest. XL.

Artson, Bradley Shavit (1988) *Love Peace and Pursue Peace: A Jewish Response to War and Nuclear Annihilation*, New York: United Synagogue of America.

Augustine of Hippo, *Contra Faustum*.

Augustine of Hippo, Letter 185, to Boniface.

Bahya (1973) *The Book of Direction to the Duties of the Heart*, introduction, translation and notes by Menahem Mansoor, London: Routledge & Kegan Paul.

Bleich, David J. (1982) "Sale of Arms," *Tradition* 20: 358–59.

Bleich, David J. (1983) *Contemporary Halakhic Problems* II, New York: Ktav: 159–66 (War and Non-Jews); 169–88 ("The Sanctity of the Liberated Territories"); 189–221 ("Judea and Samaria: Settlement and Return").

Bleich, David J. (1989) *Contemporary Halakhic Problems* III, New York: Ktav: 251–92 ("Preemptive War in Jewish Law") and 293–305 ("Of Land, Peace and Divine Command").

Borowitz, Eugene B. (1990) *Exploring Jewish Ethics: Papers on Covenant Responsibility*, Detroit, MI: Wayne State University Press.

Brown, Robert McAfee, Abraham Heschel and David Novak (1967) *Vietnam: Crisis of Conscience*, New York: Association Press.

B'Tselem (Hebrew) Journal devoted to the critique of Israeli, especially settlers', behaviour in the occupied territories.

Butterworth, Charles E. (1990) "al-Farabi's Statecraft: War and the Well-Ordered Regime," in J. Kelsay and J. T. Johnson (eds.) *Cross, Crescent, and Sword: The Justification and Limitation of War in Western and Islamic Tradition*, New York: Greenwood: 79–100.

Clausewitz, Carl von (1982) *On War*, edited with an introduction by Anatol Rapoport, London: Penguin Books.

Cohen-Almagor, Raphael (1994) *The Boundaries of Liberty and Tolerance: The Struggle against Kahanism in Israel*, Gainesville: University Press of Florida.

Crossroads: Halakha and the Modern World. Zomet: Jerusalem 1987/5747. (See below *Tehumin*.)

Daube, David (1965) *Collaboration with Tyranny in Rabbinic Law*, London: Oxford University Press.

Gendler, Everett E. (1978) "War and the Jewish Tradition," in Menachem Kellner (ed.) *Contemporary Jewish Ethics*, New York: HPC: 189–210.

Goren, Shlomo (1987) "Combat morality and the Halakha" *Crossroads* I: 211–31.

Green, Arthur (tr.) (1988) *The Language of Truth: The Torah Commentary of the Sefat Emet, Rabbi Yehudah Leib Alter of Ger*, Philadelphia, PA: The Jewish Publication Society.

Greenberg, Irving (n.d.) "Judaism and the Dilemmas of War," in *Judaism and World Peace: Focus Viet Nam*, New York: Synagogue Council of America.

Habermann, A. M. (1947) *Kol Shire Rabbi Shmuel ha-Nagid* (Hebrew), Tel Aviv: Mahbarot l'Sifrut, 5707.

Halevi, Chaim David, *'Asé l'kha Rav* (Hebrew), 4 vols., Jerusalem: Mosad Harav Kook. Vol. 1 5736 (1975/6) and Vol. 3, second edition, Tel Aviv 5739 (1978/9).

Hertz, J. H. (1938) *Sermons, Addresses and Studies*, Vol. 1, London: Soncino Press.

Inbar, Efraim (1987) "War in the Jewish Tradition," *Jerusalem Journal of International Relations* 9(2): 83–99.

Jakobovits, I. (1990) *Territory for Peace?* London: Office of the Chief Rabbi.

Johnson, J. T. (1977) *Ideology, Reason and the Limitation of War: Religious and Secular Concepts 1200–1749*, Princeton, NJ: Princeton University Press.

Johnson, J. T. (1981) *The Just War Tradition and the Restraint of War*, Princeton, NJ: Princeton University Press.

Kelsay, J. (1990) "Islam and the Distinction between Combatants and Noncombatants," in J. Kelsay and J. T. Johnson (eds.) *Cross, Crescent, and Sword*, New York: Greenwood: 197–220.

Kelsay, J. and J. T. Johnson (eds.) (1990) *Cross, Crescent, and Sword: The Justification and Limitation of War in Western and Islamic Tradition*, New York: Greenwood.

Kelsay, J. and J. T. Johnson (eds.) (1991) *Just War and Jihad: Historical and Theoretical Perspectives on War and Peace in Western and Islamic Traditions*, New York and London: Greenwood.

Kook, T. Y. (1991) *Torat Eretz Yisrael: The Teachings of HaRav Tzvi Yehuda HaCohen Kook*, with commentary by David Samson, Jerusalem: Torah Eretz Yisrael Publications.

Lamm, Maurice (1978) "After the War – Another Look at Pacifism and Selective Conscientious Objection," in Menachem Kellner (ed.) *Contemporary Jewish Ethics*, New York: HPC: 221–38.

Landes, Daniel (ed.) (1991) *Confronting Omnicide: Jewish Reflections on Weapons of Mass Destruction*, Northvale, NJ and London: Jason Aronson.

Levine, D. (ed.) (1966) *The Bustan al-Ukul by Natanaël Ibn al-Fayyumi*, with an English translation, *The Garden of Wisdom*, reprint, New York: Columbia University Press, 1908.

Lichtenstein, Aharon (1975) "Does Jewish Tradition Recognize an Ethic Independent of Halacha?", in Marvin Fox (ed.) *Modern Jewish Ethics: Theory and Practice*, Columbus: Ohio State University Press: 102–23.

Luzzatto, Samuel Davide (1876) *Il Pentateuco: volgarizzato e commentato da Samuel Davide Luzzatto*, Vol. 5, Padova: F. Sacchetto.

Maimonides, Moses (1949) *The Code of Maimonides (Mishneh Torah) Book 14: The Book of Judges*, Newhaven, CT: Yale University Press.

Maimonides, Moses (1963) *The Guide of the Perplexed*, tr. Shlomo Pines, 2 vols, Chicago, IL and London: University of Chicago Press.

Marx, Tzvi (n.d.) *Ethics Within the Reality of War*, Jerusalem: Shalom Hartman Institute, undated, after 1982.

Mendelssohn, Moses (1843) *Anmerkungen zu des Ritters Michaelis Beurteilung des ersten Theils von Dohm, über die bürgeliche Verbesserung der Juden, in Moses Mendelssohn's gesammelte Schritften*, Leipzig, Vol. 3.

Munk, Eliyahu (tr.) (1986) *Akeydat Yitzchak: The Commentary of Isaac Arama on the Torah* (condensed version), 2 vols, Jerusalem: Rubin Mass.

Nardin, Terry (ed.) (1996) *The Ethics of War and Peace: Religious and Secular Perspectives*, Princeton, NJ: Princeton University Press.

Niditch, Susan (1993) *War in the Hebrew Bible: A Study in the Ethics of Violence*, New York and Oxford: Oxford University Press.

Novak, David (1974) *Law and Theology in Judaism*, New York: Ktav.

Peli, Pinchas (1982–83) "The Possession and Use of Nuclear Weapons in the Light of the Torah," *Ecumenical Institute for Theological Research*: 151–62.

Philo of Alexandria (Philo Judaeus), *The Special Laws*, in Vol. VII of the Complete Works, tr. and ed. F. H. Colson and G. H. Whitaker, in the Loeb series (1953–63).

Piron, Mordechai (1979) "War and Peace in Jewish Thought," *Revue Internationale d'Histoire Militaire* 42: 16–24.

Ramsey, Paul (1968) *The Just War: Force and Political Responsibility*, New York: Charles Scribner's Sons.

Ravitsky, Aviezer (1986) "The Roots of Kahanism," *Jerusalem Quarterly* 39: 98–118.

Ravitsky, Aviezer (1996) *Messianism, Zionism and Jewish Religious Radicalism*, tr. M. Zwirsky and J. Chipman, Chicago, IL: University of Chicago Press.

Ravitsky, Aviezer (1996) "Prohibited Wars in the Jewish Tradition," in Terry Nardin (ed.) *The Ethics of War and Peace: Religious and Secular Perspectives*, Princeton, NJ: Princeton University Press: 115–27.

Roberts, Adam and Richard Guelff (eds.) (1989) *Documents on the Laws of War*, revised edition, Oxford: Clarendon Press.

Samson, David and Tzvi Fishman (1996) *Eretz Yisrael: Lights on Orot: The Teachings of HaRav Avraham Yitzhak HaCohen Kook*, Jeruslaem: Torat Eretz Yisrael Publications, 5756.

Shapira, Anita (1999) *Land and Power: The Zionist Resort to Force, 1881–1948*, tr. William Templer, Stanford, CA: Stanford University Press (reprint of the 1992 Oxford University Press publication).

Sinclair, Daniel B. (1988) "Conscientious Objection," in *Jewish Law Annual* IX, Chur: Harwood Academic: 262–5. (Summarises Israel High Court decision 734 / 83.)

Sherman, A. (1988) "Halakhic Foundations for Ethics in War," *Tehumin* 9, Alon Shvut (Israel): *Zomet* (Hebrew): 231–40.

Shimoni, Gideon (1995) *The Zionist Ideology*, Hanover, MA and London: Brandeis University Press.

Solomon, Norman (2000) "Zionism and Religion: The Transformation of an Idea," *Annual of Rabbinic Judaism*, Vol. III: 145–74.

Stanislawski, Michael (1988) *For Whom Do I Toil? Judah Leib Gordon and the Crisis of Russian Jewry*, New York: Oxford University Press.

Tehumin is an Israeli journal devoted to halakhic matters. It is published at Alon Shvut, on the West Bank, and its editorial committee consists largely of rabbis among the "settlers". Several volumes carry articles on military and personal defence, and volume X (5749/1989) has a useful index. Select material has been published in English under the title *Crossroads*.

Vermes, G. (1997) *The Complete Dead Sea Scrolls in English*, London: Penguin Press.

Victoria, Franciscus de (1917) *De Indis et De Jure Bellis Relectiones*, Classics of International Law, ed. Ernest Nys, Washington: Carnegie Institute.

Wald, Marcus (1944) *Jewish Teaching on Peace*, New York: Bloch.

Walzer, Michael (1977) *Just and Unjust Wars: A Moral Argument with Historical Illustrations*, New York: Basic Books.

Walzer, Michael (1992) "The Idea of Holy War in Ancient Israel," *Journal of Religious Ethics* 20(2) (note exchange with Yoder).

Walzer, Michael (1996) "War and Peace in the Jewish Tradition," in Terry Nardin (ed.) *The Ethics of War and Peace: Religious and Secular Perspectives*, Princeton, NJ: Princeton University Press: 95–112.

Weber, Max (1952) *Ancient Judaism* tr. and ed. Hans H. Gerth and Don Martindale, Glencoe, IL: The Free Press, chapters IV and V.

Weinberger, Leon J. (1973) *Jewish Prince in Moslem Spain: Selected Poems of Samuel Ibn Nagrela*, Tuscaloosa, AL: University of Alabama Press.

Weinfeld, Moshe (1972) *Deuteronomy and the Deuteronomic School*, Oxford: Clarendon Press.

Wilcock, Evelyn (1994) *Pacifism and the Jews*, Stroud: Hawthorn Press.

2

ISLAMIC TRADITION AND THE JUSTICE OF WAR

John Kelsay

Anne Lambton once remarked that any survey of Islamic political thought should deal with at least three types of literature: philosophical treatises, in which such noteworthies as al-Farabi and Ibn Sina (Avicenna) provided an Islamic expression of the analyses offered by Plato and Aristotle; mirrors of princes, where one reads the wisdom of courtly advisors, now presented for the education of Muslim rulers; and the opinions of scholars of the Shari'a, the "sacred law."[1] As with political thought generally, so with discussions of the justice of war; a full survey of the topic requires attention to a variety of modes of Muslim reflection. Within this diversity, however, there can be no doubt that the inquiry surrounding the Shari'a has pride of place. In terms of a long and consistent history it is preeminent. It is also the form of discourse that exercises the strongest influence among contemporary Muslims.

In this chapter, the focus will be on discussion surrounding the law, or as I will henceforth put it, the practice of Shari'a reasoning. I begin with a description of what this phrase entails, providing a brief survey of the history of the emergence of consensus regarding the sources of and rules governing Shari'a reasoning. As will become plain, the practice points to a transgenerational conversation among Muslims regarding the right and wrong, good and evil, of specific actions.

In such an extended conversation, one must listen, or read, with an eye toward the shifting contexts of participants. Thus a second section of this chapter will provide an overview of the changing emphases in Shari'a reasoning about war through the centuries. This will bring us to the present day, when the adherents of al-Qa'ida and other groups of irregular fighters offer public justifications of their actions in terms familiar to Shari'a reasoning. Their arguments, and the responses of others devoted to the tradition, constitute the most recent point in this long and richly variegated conversation. I conclude with some observations about the relationships between Shari'a reasoning and the just war tradition.

The practice of Shari'a reasoning

The term Shari'a is usually translated as Islamic "law" or Islamic "religious law." While this translation is not wrong, it is slightly misleading. This is particularly so whenever "law" is taken to imply a list of settled judgments or "legislation."

The term Shari'a refers less to such a list, and more to the notion that there is an ideal way to live. Quite literally, Arabic dictionaries speak of "the path" or "the way that leads to refreshment," namely Paradise.[2] The notion, or if one likes, the faith that there is such a way is a presupposition of the discussion I shall be tracking in this chapter.

Quickly joined with the proposition that there is an ideal way to live is faith in the possibility that human beings can know or, in a more literal translation of related Arabic terms, "comprehend" the Shari'a. Al-Shafi'i (d. 820) gave expression to this faith when he wrote that "No misfortune will ever descend upon any of the followers of God's religion for which there is no guidance in the Book of God to indicate the right way" and that God "made clear [to Muhammad's people] what God permitted . . . and what God prohibited, as God knows best what pertains to their felicity by avoidance of it in this world and in the hereafter."[3] One may, in the manner of some schools of Islamic theology, hold that there is a native human capacity to ascertain the first principles of practical judgment. One may also hold that this capacity can only be awakened through the hearing of God's Word. In either case, the faith of Islam is that comprehension is possible. For al-Shafi'i, as for most scholars participating in the tradition of Shari'a reasoning, such comprehension is a matter of interpreting God's "signs." Theoretically, "signs" is a category coextensive with all creation. So the Qur'an speaks of the lessons of history, the stories of holy people, or the course of nature as "signs" intended to bring about reflection or to provide guidance to human beings. As the passages from al-Shafi'i indicate, however, the best signs, because the clearest, are the ones specially given by God as a "mercy" to humanity. These sources are those referred to in the "theory of Islamic jurisprudence" or "the roots of comprehension" (usul al-fiqh) of the Shari'a.[4]

A serious survey of this theory is beyond the scope of the current chapter. It is important to grasp certain notions, however. Thus, as al-Shafi'i indicates, the first "root" of comprehension is the Book of God or the Qur'an. One who reads al-Shafi'i's *Risala* or "epistle," which is devoted to these matters, will learn quickly of his interest in the requirements for reading "God's Book." Interpretation is not an easy task for al-Shafi'i or other scholars engaged in the attempt to comprehend the Shari'a. In particular it requires a mastery of Arabic, with special reference to the use of terms characteristic of Arabs at the time of revelation. Some verses must be understood as "particular," meaning they provide very specific guidance for Muhammad and his companions. Others are "general," meaning they refer to "the human condition" or to all humanity. Discriminating between these is again not an easy task. Sometimes grammatical clues are the key; sometimes a knowledge of the biography of Muhammad is important, as it may provide information regarding the "occasions of revelation" as a factor in interpretation. This is most obviously the case in association with the category of verses al-Shafi'i and others refer to as "the abrogating and the abrogated." Here, the basic reference is to Qur'an 2:100:

> We do not abrogate any signs
> Or cause them to be forgotten
> Without substituting for them
> Something better or similar.
> Do you not know that God's decree
> Governs all things?[5]

This text, which is ambiguous, to say the least, was taken by many exegetes to indicate a phenomenon important to their task. In the divine economy, one should say, God may command a particular course of action at one time, then at a later time "reverse course." If that is the case, then the latter verse abrogates the former, and this is for the good of humanity.

Textual reasoning, required in order to comprehend divine guidance, is no task for the faint of heart (or the weak of mind)! It demands the best learning available, so that God's guidance may become available to humanity.

If this is so with respect to the Qur'an, it is also the case for other signs designated as roots of comprehension for Shari'a reasoning. All the books on the topic tell us, for example, that Shari'a reasoning refers to the *sunna* of the Prophet, along with the verses of the Qur'an. But establishing the *sunna* or "exemplary practice" of Muhammad is no easy matter, nor is interpreting it. In al-Shafi'i's time, the collection of *ahadith* or "reports" of Muhammad's practice was well under way. Within a century, most of the standard collections utilized by Sunni scholars were in place. In these collections, scholars focused on "*hadith* criticism" sorted various reports as "sound," "weak," or something in between, as well as according to the various topics of interest in Shari'a reasoning ("The book of [reports concerning] *jihad*," for example.) Judgments concerning the "soundness" of reports typically rested on the identification of the chain of transmitters by which a *hadith* came to a scholar compiling a collection. One engaged in Shari'a reasoning could accept the judgment of a collector. In some cases, however, collectors admitted the chain was incomplete, or had one weak link, while others were sound. In such cases, utilization of the report could be difficult. A conservative scholar might err on the side of restriction, and not make use of such reports. Others employed greater latitude, typically citing the need to address a wide range of cases before them.

As al-Shafi'i's *Risala* shows, even the interpretation of a well-attested report required linguistic and other forms of training analogous to those necessary for exegesis of the Qur'an. Some of the same difficulties emerge with respect to the particular or general meanings of a text, or in terms of the possibilities that a report from later in the career of the Prophet might abrogate one based in earlier circumstances. Then, too, while al-Shafi'i, and with him a number of other scholars engaged in Shari'a reasoning, held that only the practice of Muhammad himself should be considered among the roots of comprehension, other scholars held that sound reports of the practice of Muhammad's companions, especially those who held the office of caliph in the early period (632–61) should count.

If the notion that emerges thus far is that Shari'a reasoning is a complicated matter, that is correct. The point is that we are dealing with a text-based theory of reasoning, in which scholars recur again and again to certain agreed-upon sources. Certain parts of the tradition are clear. Everyone agrees that the Qur'an and the example of the Prophet (or in some cases, of the Prophet and his companions) are a means by which God provides guidance to humanity.[6] At the same time, everyone agrees that interpreting these texts is not a simple matter. Training in language, inclusive of the way the meanings of terms and grammatical forms change over time, is important, as is knowledge of the life of Muhammad and the early history of Islam.

Given this set of notions, it is hardly strange that Shari'a reasoning came to be associated with the work of a certain class of people. The "*ulama*," as they came to be known, were recognized as those "learned" in the interpretation of the Qur'an and authoritative reports of prophetic practice. Admission to the class involved the recognition of those already established as "*ulama*." Eventually this would entail completion of a set course of study at one of several centers of Islamic learning. Even in the early period, it involved study in a center organized around the work of a great scholar. Thus the disciples of al-Shafi'i, eventually recognized as the "founder" of an independent scholarly tradition, wrote biographies of the master in which he is said to master the learning of the leading centers of his time: the school of Medina, where scholars trained according to the style of Malik b. 'Anas (d. 797); the school of Syria (Damascus), where the name of Awza'i was revered; and, above all, the school of Iraq, where Abu Hanifa (d. 767), Abu Yusuf (d. 795), and al-Shaybani (d. 804) were regarded as masters of Shari'a reasoning.

In all of this, the point is that the interpretive work in the various schools itself came to constitute a third "root" for Shari'a reasoning. In effect, members of the learned class won their credentials by mastering the approach characteristic of a particular school. Take a question about practice, for example concerning the proper distribution of booty captured by Muslim fighters. On this, for instance, we find the following reported in an early compendium used by students in the Iraqi or Hanafi school.

Abu Yusuf said: I asked Abu Hanifa concerning the food and fodder that may be found in the spoil and whether a warrior in need may take from that spoil any of the food for himself and fodder for his mount.
Abu Hanifa replied: There is no harm in all that.[7]

As we are given to understand, the question follows from the Hanafi school's characteristic insistence that booty should only be divided when the fighters had returned to territory governed by Muslims. A variety of reasons are given for this, the simplest of which have to do with attaining the level of discipline characteristic of a professional army. As a little reading in military history tells us, the development of such a force was under way during the caliphate of Harun al-Rashid, which provides the context for a number of the judgments attributed to the early Hanafi scholars.[8]

For subsequent generations of scholars trained in the Hanafi *madhdhab* or "way" of interpretation, compendia of such judgments provided a set of precedents by which to measure their own answers to questions of their day. The problem, in a sense, is that comprehending the ideal way of life involves aiming at a moving target. The questions change as the social and political conditions of human beings develop. One generation of scholars engaged in the practice of Shari'a reasoning learns from its predecessors – not, one hopes, for the sake of sheer imitation, but for the sake of continuing an extended conversation concerning the path that leads to refreshment. Thus, the Qur'an, the example of the Prophet, and the "consensus" of the scholars in a recognized *madhdhab* constitute a series of references to which a scholar must recur in responding to the questions of people about right and wrong, good and evil, in a particular time and place. These texts may bind scholarly judgment, as in matters upon which the Qur'an pronounces clearly and in "general" terms. More often, they instruct or direct scholarly inquiry, in the sense that they correlate with dispositions to judge cases in a particular way. In connection with the latter, we learn that the fourth and final root of comprehension is scholarly reasoning, characteristically presented in terms of *al-qiyas* or "analogy." The idea is that a present-day scholar, posed a question about practice, attempts to discern the underlying principles by which particular precedents may be compared with contemporary cases. In a sense, the judgment of such a scholar *is* the Shari'a regarding the question raised, though this is qualified by the fact of scholarly "review." Other contemporary scholars may revisit the judgment of their colleague, and subsequent generations will certainly do so. In this way, the practice of Shari'a reasoning keeps its connection with the questions facing contemporary Muslims, and the Shari'a itself retains a dynamic or living character. The point, as we are told in numerous scholarly texts, is the effort (*jihad* or the related *ijtihad*) to comprehend the guidance of God for God's people.[9] Merit is less a matter of "getting it right," than of righteous intention signified by a conscientious effort to interpret the signs provided by God.

Shari'a reasoning and issues of war

Given the foregoing remarks on Shari'a reasoning, one should expect that Islamic thought regarding war will be characterized by a combination of continuity and change. The former is particularly present in certain overarching patterns of reasoning: the sources one cites, the notion of precedent as that to which one must respond, the presentation of the task of the scholar as providing guidance for the questions of a given person or group in a particular place and time – all these are consistent aspects of the tradition, which builds and grows into a veritable library of texts, created in particular historical contexts yet waiting to participate in a contemporary conversation. Change is implied in the way the conversation begins, with reference to questions raised by the Muslims of a given epoch. And indeed, the career of Shari'a reasoning with respect to war provides a good example of the continuity and change built into the system.

For example, one of the most influential pieces of Shari'a reasoning about war points to conversations that took place among scholars of the Iraqi or Hanafi school c.750–804. One must say, "points to," because the text reporting these conversations comes to us in connection with the work of an eleventh-century scholar, al-Sarakhsi. As a scholar trained in the Hanafi *madhdhab*, Sarakhsi's interest in the work of the early masters of the school is not only understandable; given the nature of Shari'a reasoning, it was obligatory. Sarakhsi's extended commentary on a book called *Kitab al-Asl* ("Book of the Foundation"), and in particular on the chapters on *siyar* ("movements") are noteworthy contributions in themselves. More relevant at this point in our discussion, however, is the text he reproduces, the subject of his commentary.[10]

Al-Sarakhsi and his contemporaries understood the Book of the Foundation to be the work of the great Muhammad ibn al-Hasan al-Shaybani (d. 804), the third in the succession of the early masters of the Hanafi school. Throughout the ninth and tenth centuries, various scholars interested in the *siyar* spoke about the work, in particular its chapters on *siyar*, as exemplary of the earliest Hanafi judgments about issues of war. While these occasionally quote from the text, al-Sarakhsi provides our earliest example of a "copy." We do not know, of course, how much was added to or taken away from this account of early Hanafi reasoning in the intervening centuries. For that matter, we do not know how much of the thinking of al-Shaybani and his predecessors may have been left out of the text in its original. We do know that subsequent generations of scholars, up to and then beyond al-Sarakhsi, took the work as a starting point for their deliberations. We can read it that way, as an illustration of Shari'a reasoning in a particular time and place, all the while understanding that our placement and interpretation of the text has the quality of "probable."

From the moment we open al-Shaybani's text, we understand that he and his colleagues approached the question of war in connection with broader issues of political ethics. The term *siyar*, for example, means "movements," as noted above. The movements in question are those between and within two broadly defined political-territorial associations, namely the "territory of Islam" and the "territory of war." The first of these terms indicates the area within which Islam is the dominant political reality. The second is a generic term for political-territorial associations not governed by Islam. In the territory of Islam, the ruler is a Muslim, the system of government is organized to serve the expansion of Islam, and the people within the territory are identified according to their participation in various groups, each of these defined by its relation to Islam. The primary group is Muslims, but there are also "protected peoples" (*dhimmis*, mainly Christians and Jews, though other groups could come under this category), "rebels" (*bughat*, indicating groups of Muslims dissenting from the policy of the established leadership), "apostates" (*murtadd*, meaning those who were once Muslims but have in some way dissociated themselves from the true faith), and "brigands" (*muharibun*, indicating criminals who prey off ordinary people and live as "highwaymen"). In the territory of war, the overarching category is *harbi* (roughly, "war person"). Subcategories, for example "women," "children," the elderly, or in some cases, Muslims residing in the territory of war, are identified primarily with discussions of the means of war. Al-Shaybani and his colleagues are concerned with the justification and conduct of war in the context of this political-territorial arrangement. Thus their judgments are developed in response to questions like "What is the proper behavior for Muslim fighters who cross into the territory of war?" or "What is the appropriate way to respond to Muslim rebels?"

War is thus a means to a political end, which has to do with the establishment and governance of a political-territorial association governed by Islam. If one wishes, one can take this further: the establishment of an Islamic state is itself a means by which the Muslim community can carry out its divinely mandated mission of calling humanity to the relationship with God signified by "submission" (*al-islam*). In this connection, one might say that war is a means to a political end (establishing an Islamic state), which is itself a means to an overarching religious goal (calling humanity to Islam.) In this way, one sees that there is nothing particularly good or bad about war in itself. It is a means to an end, and should be viewed as such. Resort to war is thus a matter of estimating its likely effectiveness in attaining certain goals. Notions of just conduct in war are similarly suggested by the desire to gain particular objectives.

Perhaps the simplest way to illustrate this is to cite a report with which al-Shaybani's text begins. Here, the Prophet Muhammad is depicted as giving directions to Muslim fighting forces – first, to those in command and, through them, to all members of the army. The text establishes precedents to which everyone who will subsequently engage in the practice of Shari'a reasoning about war will recur.

> Whenever God's Messenger sent forth an army or a detachment, he charged its commander personally to fear God, the Most High, and he enjoined the Muslims who were with him to do good.

He said:

> Fight in the name of God and in the path of God. Fight the *mukaffirun* ["ingrates," "unbelievers"]. Do not cheat or commit treachery, and do not mutilate anyone or kill children. Whenever you meet the *mushrikun* [idolaters], invite them to accept Islam. If they do, accept it and let them alone. You should then invite them to move from their territory to the territory of the émigrés. If they do so, accept it and leave them alone. Otherwise, they should be informed that they will be in the same condition as the Muslim nomads in that they are subject to God's orders as Muslims, but will receive no share of the spoil of war. If they

refuse, then call upon them to pay tribute. If they do, accept it and leave them alone. If you besiege the inhabitants of a fortress or a town and they try to get you to let them surrender on the basis of God's judgment, do not do so, since you do not know what God's judgment is, but make them surrender to your judgment and then decide their case according to your own views. But if the besieged inhabitants of a fortress or a town ask you to give them a pledge in God's name or in the name of God's Messenger, you should not do so, but give the pledge in your names or the names of your fathers. For if you should ever break it, it would be an easier matter if it were in the names of you or your fathers.[11]

There is much to learn from this text, which is basic to all Shari'a reasoning on the topic of war. In it, for example, al-Shaybani and others found precedent for limiting the right of war to the head of state. Muhammad, as W. M. Watt's biographical study suggests, was both "prophet" and "statesman."[12] Scholars in the Shari'a tradition saw in this report an example of his statesmanship, which was then to be followed by those who succeeded him or walked in his footsteps (the literal referent of the term "caliph").

Resort to war requires the order of a legitimate authority. It also requires a just cause and righteous intention. So scholars in the Shari'a tradition understood, as the words attributed to the Prophet echoed in their minds: "Fight in the name of God and in the path of God. Fight the *mukaffirun*." The purpose of war, as already mentioned, is the establishment and governance of an Islamic state. That state, in turn, finds its purpose in connection with the Muslim community's mission of calling human beings to Islam. A just war must be tied to these purposes. And those authorizing it show that their intention is consistent in this regard by carrying out a specific protocol, namely the issuing of an invitation to the enemy.

One might well ask what identifies the "enemy." The Prophet's statements point to *mukaffirun*, which quite literally indicates "ingrates," and is typically translated "unbelievers." Staying strictly with the terms of this report, one would say that such people are identified by their response to the invitation proffered by Muslim fighters.

One might suggest that the mention of *mushrikun* a few sentences later provides further specification. Signifying "idolaters" or perhaps more literally "associationists," the term often bears the meaning of "polytheists." That would constitute a considerable limitation regarding resort to war, since the category specifically does not include Jews and Christians. For al-Shaybani and his colleagues, however, Jews and Christians are clearly among those to whom an invitation should be issued, unless and until they pay tribute and thus come under the sway of Islam as *dhimmis* or "protected" peoples. Thus practitioners of Shari'a reasoning would find just cause for war in the fact that a given people refused the invitation of the Muslims to accept Islam or to pay tribute and thus come under the protection of the Islamic state.

The procedures outlined in this report thus establish a notion of war as a means of pursuing goals considered legitimate. One should note, given the character of the invitation, that war is not the first or primary means recommended. Fighting is only prescribed when other means fail. If such is not precisely the equivalent of the just war criterion of "last resort," it is nevertheless an indication that resort to war must follow an attempt to pursue legitimate goals by non-lethal means. Thus the tradition of Shari'a reasoning already provides an equivalent to the *jus ad bellum* criteria of legitimate authority, just cause, righteous intention, and "timely" resort.[13] One might see in the overarching purpose of establishing and maintaining an Islamic state something equivalent to the just war criterion of "aim of peace" as well. Proportionality and reasonable hope of success do not show up, at least in this report.

The preoccupation of the report is of course with those who are not already under the protection of the Islamic state. As we read al-Shaybani's text, we come to understand that fighting against residents of the territory of Islam is also possible, though justified for somewhat different reasons. Governance of the non-Muslim "protected" peoples, for example, is set in terms of obligations established by treaties. If the protected peoples violate their obligations, for example by initiating fighting against the armies of the Muslim state, then the ruler of the Muslims is justified in disciplining them.[14] Again, if rebels rise up against the state, fighting can be justified.[15] In either case, the overarching purpose of fighting is to restore peace, order, and justice to the territory of Islam. Protected peoples are to be returned to their rightful status; rebels are to be reconciled, which implies that war is not only a means of discipline, but is to be conducted in such a way that any legitimate grievances on the part of the rebels may be redressed. In the case of apostates, the point is to return those who have turned away back to the way of Islam or, failing success in the matter, to prevent injustice by killing them.[16] Similarly in the case of highwaymen, the point is the security of the territory of Islam and its residents, and the ruler is justified in undertaking those measures necessary to protect it.[17] Interestingly enough, for reasons that will become clear below, al-Shaybani and his colleagues do not address the question of fighting in response to an enemy invasion. The text seems quite confident in that regard.

Jus ad bellum criteria are not the only measures of justice in war, of course. And thus it is noteworthy that the prophetic dicta include matters related to the *jus in bello* or conduct of war. In particular, the saying of the Prophet includes prohibitions of cheating, treachery, mutilation, and the killing of children. As I shall indicate in a moment, this, along with other reports of the Prophet's practice, gave rise to more extensive restrictions on targeting that should be seen as analogous to the just war tradition's concern for "discrimination" or the "immunity of noncombatants" from direct and intentional attack. Other considerations have to do with fair dealing in the distribution of booty and prudence in making agreements. As mediated by al-Shaybani and his colleagues, the report does not contain any references to weapons that may or may not be used – the typical concern associated in the just war tradition with *jus in bello* proportionality.

Al-Shaybani and his colleagues built on this and other reports of the practice of Muhammad and his companions, providing answers to specific questions raised in their own day. In reading their collected judgments, it is important to remember their role as advisors at the Abbasid court, which explains their preoccupation with matters of administration. The following account of an exchange between two of the early masters of al-Shaybani's school is typical:

> Abu Yusuf said: I asked Abu Hanifa concerning the food and fodder that may be found in the spoil and whether a warrior in need may take from that spoil any of the food for himself and fodder for his mount.
> Abu Hanifa replied: No harm in all that.[18]

Such questions have little to do with the concerns of modern just war tradition. They are connected with the questions of the early Hanafi jurists, however, because of their focus on movements between the territories of Islam and of war, and probably also because of movements in Muslim military organization in the direction of a professional army.[19]

The question emerges in connection with the repeated consensus of the school that booty should only be divided after its return to the territory of Islam. Such judgments attempt to ensure a just distribution of the booty, and also to keep the troops focused on their military task.

In dealing with the conduct of Muslim fighters in enemy territory, however, al-Shaybani and others dealt with a number of questions of direct relevance to our concerns. Thus we read the following:

> If the army attacks the territory of war and it is a territory that has received an invitation to accept Islam, it is commendable if the army renews the invitation, but if it fails to do so it is not wrong. The army may launch the attack by night or by day and it is permissible to burn fortifications with fire or to inundate them with water.[20]

The first sentence is reminiscent of the Prophet's directives to fighters. As I have suggested, the requirement of an invitation is critical for the establishment of just cause and righteous intention. It also reveals much regarding the overarching religious and political purposes which war is supposed to serve, and to place war within a hierarchy of means to be deployed in pursuit of those purposes. Here, we are to envision a case in which hostilities have begun. An invitation having been given and refused, the enemy is tasting the steel of the Muslims. Should the Muslims now renew the invitation, giving the enemy a second chance to submit, or should fighting be carried to a conclusion – as al-Shaybani seems to assume, a conclusion that involves decisive victory for the Muslims? The judgment is in the nature of a recommendation: renewal of the invitation would be good, but is not required. Commanders in the field have discretion in this matter. One might imagine cases in which they or the fighters under their command judge it best to renew the invitation. One can also imagine cases in which this would not seem an appropriate or advisable option.

The second sentence, however, moves in a direction not covered by the Prophet's statements. Here, scholars directly address the question of military means. And, in this case, they do so in ways that give a great deal of latitude to the fighters. The army may fight by night or by day – the former likely involving a greater risk of injury or death to the Muslim fighters, as well as to certain people on the enemy side who fall into the category of noncombatants. Similarly, the army may utilize tactics that increase the potential for injury, specifically burning fortifications with fire or inundating them with water.

Throughout the text, one discerns a strong inclination toward a position one might characterize as "military realism." Given that requirements associated with the *jus ad bellum* are satisfied, and Muslim troops are thus engaged in a legitimate war, al-Shaybani and his colleagues are willing to grant wide latitude to commanders in the determination of appropriate means. Such latitude is not total, of course. The Prophet's dicta are clear regarding cheating, treachery, mutilation, and the direct targeting of children. With respect to the last, in particular, al-Shaybani and his colleagues demonstrate respect for early Muslim practice in classifying a number of enemy persons as, in effect, immune from direct attack. In addition to children, we read of prohibitions against the direct and intentional targeting of slaves, women, old people, the lame, the blind, and the helpless insane – all these are immune from direct attack.[21] In addition, the text indicates a concern regarding the presence, or even the possible presence, of Muslims in enemy territory – a condition that must have been particularly ubiquitous along the "frontier," where Muslim and Byzantine forces often took turns conquering and reconquering particular towns and regions along the border between their respective territories.[22] If any persons in enemy territory are presumed "innocent," and thus immune from direct attack, then Muslims in the midst of the enemy would be among them. For the life and property of Muslims were considered inviolable from the earliest times. Direct and intentional targeting of any of those mentioned violates an express directive of the Prophet, or a legitimate extension of that directive. It also involves dishonor to fighters, who win their reputation in direct engagement with other fighters. As the Qur'an has it:

> Fight in the path of God
> Those who are fighting you;
> But do not exceed the bounds.
> God does not approve the transgressors.[23]

"Do not exceed the bounds"; even in the revealed text, the reference is to a warriors' code. Now, al-Shaybani and his colleagues, guided by the example of the Prophet and his companions, must elaborate such a code for their day.

As they do so, their judgments indicate their adherence to precedent, while at the same time furthering the impression of a disposition toward military realism. Thus we read:

> Would it be permissible to inundate a city in the territory of war with water, to burn it with fire, or to attack with hurling machines even though there may be slaves, women, old men, and children in it?
>
> Yes, I would approve of doing all of that to them.
>
> Would the same be true if those people have among them Muslim prisoners of war or Muslim merchants?
>
> Yes, even if they had Muslims among them, there would be no harm to do all of that to them.
>
> Why?
>
> If the Muslims stopped attacking the inhabitants of the territory of war for any of the reasons that you have stated, they would be unable to go to war at all, for there is no city in the territory of war in which there is no one at all of these you have mentioned.[24]

One who fights should employ the means necessary to win – or so it would seem, given the final statement in this sequence of judgments.

That is not all there is to it, however. In just war tradition, one should recall that military policy can be highly realistic, while at the same time adhering faithfully to the guidelines indicated by the *jus in bello* criterion of discrimination or non-combatant immunity. As more than one interpreter suggests, the idea is that noncombatants are immune from attacks that are direct and intentional. They cannot be immune from any harm whatsoever. An attack that is legitimate, in the sense of directly intended as a strike against the enemy's ability to fight, may at the same time result in the deaths of noncombatants. This may be purely accidental, for example in cases where a child happens to wander by a military target and is caught in the crossfire. It may also be a matter of something foreseeable but unavoidable, as in cases where an enemy's military resources are deployed in the midst of a civilian population. In the latter case, in particular, the deaths of civilians are foreseen but unintended. To put it another way, these deaths are the indirect or secondary (in the sense of "unintended") consequence of the deployment of means necessary to accomplish a legitimate military purpose. Soldiers whose actions take place under such conditions are said to be excused from the guilt associated with unjust killing. Alternatively, the actions undertaken may be described as justified, though with some regrettable (secondary) effects. This holds so long as the incidence of unintended, collateral damage is proportionate with the military objective.

Given this, it is not surprising that we read:

If the Muslims besieged a city and its people positioned behind the walls shielded themselves with Muslim children, would it be permissible for the Muslim fighters to attack them with arrows and hurling machines?

Yes, but the warriors should aim at the inhabitants of the territory of war and not the Muslim children.

Would it be permissible for the Muslims to attack them with swords and lances if the children were not intentionally aimed at?

Yes.

If the Muslim warriors attack with hurling machines and arrows, flood cities with water or burn them with fire, thereby killing Muslim children or men, or enemy women, old men, blind, crippled, or lunatic persons, would the warriors be liable for blood money or acts of expiation?

They would be liable neither for blood money nor for acts of expiation.[25]

The reasoning is quite reminiscent of just war tradition and its approach to collateral damage. One would be quite wrong, in the case of just war or of Shari'a reasoning, to read such a passage as negating respect for the immunity of noncombatants. The point is that the attacks are not directly and intentionally aimed at noncombatants. Without this overarching categorization, the military acts described would be unjust, and those engaging in them would need to make restitution. As it is, al-Shaybani and his colleagues are best read as trying to combine military realism with respect for rules that measure just conduct in the midst of war. In so doing, they mean to establish norms appropriate to the conduct of a professional army.

The judgments advanced by al-Shaybani become part of a historical deposit with which subsequent generations will have to deal. Not that later practitioners of Shari'a reasoning will always agree with al-Shaybani! Even the title of a text like that written by the great al-Tabari (d. 923) indicates the conversational nature of the discipline: *Kitab al-Ikhtilaf al-Fuqaha fi al-jihad wa 'l-jizya'*, that is "The Book of the Disagreement of the Practitioners of *fiqh* on the *jihad* and the tax (imposed on conquered peoples)." As al-Tabari's book shows, Shari'a reasoning about war constituted a lively discourse, in which there could be considerable disagreement about the administrative matters so important to al-Shaybani and his colleagues. For that matter, there could even be disagreement over whether soldiers who participated in an action by which noncombatants were unintentionally killed should perform acts of expiation, or even over the precise classes of persons who belonged to the class of noncombatants (though one should make clear on this point that all of the scholars included in al-Tabari's book admit that at least some enemy persons fall into this category).[26]

In Shari'a reasoning, one does best to think of judgments like those of al-Shaybani as "precedent." Those familiar with debates over the status of precedent in American constitutional or British common law will know that this is itself a contentious notion. That seems the case with Shari'a reasoning as well, with some opting for a stronger, some a weaker, notion of precedent. This is a matter that needs further study, and I am not prepared to issue a strong opinion at present. However, I am sure that the notion of Shari'a reasoning requires the possibility of independent judgment (*ijtihad*), in the sense of judgment that is informed yet not bound by precedent. Even more, all the evidence shows that scholars of one generation are often preoccupied with a different set of questions than those of another.

Thus by the time of al-Mawardi (d. 1058), the preoccupation of Shari'a reasoning appears to shift from the details of administrative law to the superstructure of right authority. Consider, for example, the following:

> When the Caliph appoints a governor of a province or city, the latter's jurisdiction may be either general and unrestricted or special and restricted. General governorship is of two kinds: regular (by recruitment), in which appointment is made by the sovereign's free choice; and usurped, in which the appointment is made through coercion . . .
>
> Governorship by usurpation is coercion in the sense that its holder acquires by force certain districts over which the Caliph gives him a decree of appointment, assigning him their management and the maintenance of public order therein. By seizing power, the governor becomes an independent and exclusive controller of political matters and administration, while the Caliph, by his permission, becomes the implementer of the dictates of religion, thus transforming unlawfulness into legality, and the forbidden into the legitimate. Although by doing so he does not adhere closely to the conventions of appointment in respect of conditions and procedures, his action upholds the canon law and its provisions in ways that are too important to be disregarded. Thus, decisions that would normally be unacceptable in regular appointment based on choice are permissible under usurpation and necessity, owing to the difference between ability and incapacity.[27]

As al-Mawardi's text makes clear, he presumes that designation of a ruler is a requirement of Shari'a; that the office must be singular (that is, there cannot be two legitimate rulers, even if they reside in different cities); and that the person holding leadership must meet certain qualifications, most notably descent from the Quraysh, the clan into which the Prophet Muhammad was born. It is noteworthy, given other trends in the Muslim community of his day, that al-Mawardi does not require that the ruler be "of the Prophet's household" or "of the family of the Prophet (or of 'Ali)"; this was the slogan of the various Shi'i groups. Al-Mawardi further stipulates that the ruler may be designated by his predecessor or chosen by electors. The latter may be any of the number of Muslims who are truthful, possess knowledge of the required characteristics of the ruler, and whose prudence and wisdom make it likely that they will choose the right person. As a matter of custom, he writes, this role usually falls to the leading citizens of the capitol of the territory of Islam.

Thus far, there is nothing particularly controversial about al-Mawardi's argument. Indeed, it reflects the standard presentation of Abbasid imperial practice. Similarly, when al-Mawardi comments on the ministry (*al-wizara*), noting that appointment to this office is the right of the sovereign ruler and that appointment may constitute the minister's authority as "delegated" or "executive," he seems to reflect the standing practice of the Abbasid court. No ruler is able to administer the day-to-day affairs of a far-flung empire; the Abbasid caliphs tended to assign many of these tasks to court advisors, the most authoritative of which held the position of ministers. If the authority of a minister is "delegated," al-Mawardi says, this suggests greater independence. If it is "executive," this indicates the ruler is setting policy, and restricting ministerial practice to carrying out his orders.

It is in the comments on "governors" that al-Mawardi's reasoning becomes creative. Many, perhaps most, commentators read his notion of a governor "appointed" by coercion as a pure example of *realpolitik*.[28] It was in fact the case from c.935 that no Abbasid ruler really exercised power in the style of the High Caliphate. Instead, power was concentrated in the provinces of the empire, whose governors commanded armies, collected taxes, and generally carried out the duties of statecraft. Among these, the more powerful carved out larger territorial units than Abbasid practice allowed. Powerless to remove such "usurpers," what was the Caliph to do? By al-Mawardi's lights, the Caliph should do his duty, namely maintain the unity of the territory of Islam by authorizing such governors to rule as agents of the Abbasid court. If that seems a bit irregular, he writes, it is nevertheless true that a Caliph who acts in this way "upholds the Shari'a and its provisions in ways that are too important to be disregarded." In effect, the ruler "delegates" authority to the usurping governor. The latter thereby achieves legitimation, and the former hopes to preserve the unity of Islam, as is his charge. Governors must therefore "uphold the office of the sovereign [the Caliph] as a vicar of prophecy and manager of religious affairs, in order to fulfill the legal requirement of ensuring its existence and preserving the rights arising therefrom."[29] Insofar as the usurper is lacking in formal qualifications, "it is up to the Caliph to sanction his appointment as a means of winning him over and putting an end to his disobedience and intransigence."[30] In certain conditions, this may even lead to an arrangement whereby the Caliph appoints a minister to work with the usurper, and to exercise executive power.

With respect to war, al-Mawardi's judgment legitimating governorship by usurpation should be read as a critical modification in the notion of right authority. "General" governorship, in particular, comes with full power to make war.[31] There is a sense in which one who seizes power becomes the Caliph's designated minister for political and military affairs. Subsequent to al-Mawardi (even, to some extent, during his lifetime), leaders of the Seljuq Turks played such a role, *wazir* (minister) or perhaps better, *al-sultan* (the power) in concert with the Abbasid Caliphs' role as guardian of Islam.[32]

If general governorship comes with the full power to make war, it also imposes duties. Al-Mawardi's comments in this regard are a subject for study in themselves.

As commander, the general governor sees to the formation, equipping, and *esprit* of a fighting force. He manages fighting against "the idolaters in enemy territory," as well as against apostates, rebels, and brigands within the territory of Islam. With respect to the first group, al-Mawardi suggests there are two classes: (1) "those who have received the call to Islam but rejected it and turned away from it," and (2) "those whom the call to Islam has not reached."[33] Group (1) is subject to attack or the threat of attack at any time, depending on the commander's sense of what is best. Group (2), of which al-Mawardi writes that such people would be "very few today on account of the victory the Almighty has accorded His Prophet's mission, unless there be nations unknown to us beyond the Turks and Greeks we meet in eastern deserts and remote western areas" cannot be subjected to a surprise attack.[34] The invitation indicated in the saying of the Prophet (above) is required, prior to fighting. For al-Mawardi, this includes the presentation of material intended to persuade the unbelievers of the truth of Islam: "making the Prophet's miracles known to them, and informing them of such arguments as would make them to respond favorably."[35] In a style indicative of the conversational nature of Shari'a reasoning, he notes that, should a commander (improperly) initiate fighting without making an attempt to persuade such an uninformed enemy about the truth of Islam,

> he will owe them blood-money, which, according to the more correct view in the Shafi'i school, is equal to that due to Muslims, although it has been suggested that it should be the same as the various amounts of compensation paid to the heathens according to their different beliefs. Abu Hanifa has, on the other hand, said: "There is no compensation for killing them, and their lives are to be taken freely."[36]

One must cite precedents, in the sense of judgments characteristic of the various practitioners of Shari'a reasoning; one need not follow each and all.

"Killing women and children is not permitted in war or otherwise so long as they do not fight, owing to the Prophet's injunction against killing them . . . God's Prophet . . . has also forbidden the killing of servants and slaves."[37] Here, al-Mawardi acknowledges the authority of the Prophet's directives delimiting the range of legitimate targets. He also moves toward the identification of a general principle one might see as "behind" the listing of groups that fighters are not supposed to target for direct attack. The point is not, in other words, simply that the Prophet identified women, children, and others as protected groups. Rather, these persons are listed because, as a general matter, they "do not fight." Indeed, as he goes on to write, if women or children do take up arms, they "should be fought and killed," albeit in ways that maintain honor.[38] Indeed, in some ways al-Mawardi's account of the limits placed on just killing is more stringent than that of al-Shaybani and his colleagues (above), since al-Mawardi argues that Muslim fighters faced with an enemy which shields itself with Muslims should stop killing. That is, if the Muslim fighters find it impossible to continue without killing the "Muslim shields," they should stop attacking. Should the enemy take advantage of this, surrounding the Muslim army while still protecting itself with Muslim shields, the Muslim fighters should defend themselves, trying all the while to avoid killing their co-religionists; if one of the shields is killed, the killer must pay blood money and/or make expiation, depending on whether he actually knew the religious identity of the one killed.[39]

Al-Mawardi shows both the continuity and change characteristic of Shari'a reasoning about war. Subsequent writers provide further illustration. Shortly after al-Mawardi's death in 1058, for example, we find the *Kitab al-Jihad* of al-Sulami of Damascus (d. 1106). One should note here that al-Sulami was not and is not particularly known for his practice of Shari'a reasoning; he was evidently an instructor in Arabic language and letters at the Grand Mosque in his home city. And much of his book on *jihad* has to do with language intended to evoke action on the part of Muslims, especially those in positions of authority, in response to incursions into the territory of Islam by *al-faranj*, "the Franks" or the crusader armies. Nevertheless, al-Sulami's mode of reasoning and above all his indication of the formal duty to fight indicates participation in the practice of Shari'a reasoning.[40]

For our interests, it is particularly striking that al-Sulami's preoccupation is with defensive war. Al-Shaybani and other early Hanafi jurists seem entirely unconcerned about this topic, namely fighting in a context defined by the success of an external, non-Muslim enemy in occupying Muslim territory. For al-Shaybani and his colleagues, the focus of war with non-Muslims had to do, as indicated above, with the ways Muslim fighters should conduct themselves during an incursion into enemy territory. Similarly, al-Mawardi's preoccupation is with the rights and wrongs of war aimed at expanding the territory in which Islam is established. A brief mention of the right of a governor "with limited powers" whose province is located on the border between the territory of Islam and the territory of war to fight non-Muslims if they strike first, and without obtaining the Caliph's authorization, is an exception within his general focus.[41]

With al-Sulami, we have a different idea. His context is the crusades, as mentioned. Specifically, he writes in response to the First Crusade, which by 1099 yielded Christian control of Jerusalem, as well as significant portions of greater Syria.[42] Al-Sulami argues that the duty to extend the territory of Islam, expressed at least through an annual expedition organized and led by the ruler, was established by the Prophet and the early Caliphs. Subsequent rulers followed in this way, until a particular caliph (unnamed in the text) failed to carry through, either for reason of neglect or for reasons of state. From this point, others failed for similar reasons. The incursions of Franks into Islamic territory are a judgment of God, executed due to this sin of omission. And now, al-Sulami says, Muslims find themselves in a distinctive situation, which affects the construal of the duty to struggle for justice. Citing al-Shafi'i, al-Sulami notes that the raising of an army for purposes of carrying out expeditions into enemy territory is the minimum obligation of the Muslim ruler, and that if sufficient forces are not raised, it becomes the duty of those "in the rear" to fulfill God's command. This shows, according to al-Sulami, that the duty of fighting (he uses the term *ghazw*, "raiding") is, in cases of necessity, incumbent upon all the members of the community. The current situation, in which enemy forces are making inroads into the territory of Islam, constitutes such a case. With further citations from al-Ghazali (d. 1111), the greatest scholar of his day, al-Sulami goes on to stipulate that this means, for example, that if a town in Syria is attacked by the Franks, and cannot defend itself, all the other (Muslim) cities of the region are obligated to come to its aid. Supporting and extending his argument with further Shari'a references, he concludes with the judgment that "the book [the Qur'an], the example of the Prophet, and the consensus [of representative practitioners of Shari'a reasoning] with respect to the community's obligation to fight makes clear that in cases of necessity, this duty becomes one of the individual duties."[43] As the last reference makes clear, al-Sulami's judgment is that in the type of context he describes, the duty to fight is like the duty of fasting. Only those unable by reason of sickness or other incapacity may be excused from its performance.

Was al-Sulami the first to argue in this way? That would be unlikely, since reasoning about the necessity for every Muslim to contribute according to ability in situations of defense seems a rather obvious move. At the same time, the precedents he cites do not say precisely that fighting becomes an "individual duty." Rather, as indicated, they suggest that those who are "distant" from the affected area are called to step forward and give aid. Just how much distance there is between this and al-Sulami's judgment that the incursions of the Franks make fighting an individual duty is a matter in need of further exploration.

In any case, by the time one gets to Ibn Taymiyya (d. 1328), reference to fighting as an individual duty in circumstances of emergency seems to come easily. If, he writes, the enemy attacks the Muslims, then the duty to fight becomes a personal or individual duty both for "those against whom the attack was made and those not directly affected by it."[44] Citing the Qur'an and the example of the Prophet, this scholar, much of whose career was spent in the prisons of those ruling in Damascus and in Cairo, writes that every Muslim must provide assistance, even if he is not a professional soldier. In the battle of the Trench (627), when the Muslims in Medina came under siege, "God permitted none to abandon the jihad." Once the siege was broken, and fighting involved pursuit of the enemy, a different set of judgments prevailed. Ibn Taymiyya writes that the defense of Medina "was a war to defend the religion, the family honour and the lives [of community members]; an obligatory fighting . . . [Pursuit of the enemy following the siege] was voluntary fighting to increase the prestige of the religion and frighten the enemy."[45] Different circumstances suggest distinctive judgments about the nature of the duty to fight.

Do they suggest distinctive rules? The answer, it seems, is "no." Those who "do not constitute a defensive or offensive power, like the women, the children, the monks, old people, the blind and the permanently disabled should not be fought."[46] This general rule is supported as the consensus of the Muslims, the example of the Prophet, and Qur'an 2:190: "fight in the way of God against those who fight against you, but do not commit aggression. Truly, God does not love those who commit aggression." Ibn Taymiyya comments that "we should only fight those who fight us, if we really want the Religion of Allah to be victorious."[47]

Ibn Taymiyya does suggest that noncombatants may forfeit their protected status if they "carry on a kind of fighting with words" or serve as spies, provide transport for munitions, or in other ways participate more directly in the enemy war effort. Earlier writers, as noted, typically stipulated that women, children, and others move to combatant status if and when they take up arms. The principle, in either case, seems to be that those who do not, or may be presumed not to participate in the enemy's war effort are not to be the target of direct attack by the Muslim forces.[48]

This brings us, however, to an emphasis that many commentators view as a special focus of Ibn Taymiyya's judgments about war. As he writes, the "heaviest jihad should be directed against the unbelievers and those who refuse to abide by certain precepts, like the abstainers from paying zakat-alms and the Kharijites."[49] The latter case has drawn attention from many students of Ibn Taymiyya's work. Here, I offer only a few comments.

The wording of Ibn Taymiyya's sentence suggests the notion of fighting against apostates (al-murtadd) and rebels (al-bughat). Discussion of the rules governing fighting against these groups was an established practice of Shari'a reasoning. Al-Shaybani and his colleagues discussed the matter, for example. Apostates were understood along the lines of the precedent attributed to Abu Bakr (d. 634), the first to follow the Prophet as Caliph of the Muslim community. Having received a communication from a particular group regarding its intention to maintain faith in God and God's Prophet, but to forego payment of al-zakat to the common treasury, Abu Bakr declared his intention to fight in order to compel obedience. Al-zakat, he said, is not optional for Muslims. Believers must contribute to the common treasury, administered by a legitimate authority. Those who refuse to do so have "turned" (the literal meaning of al-murtadd) away from the faith, even if they continue to recite the basic creed and to perform obligatory prayers. Ibn Taymiyya is quite consistent with his predecessors on this matter, even in his discussion of "the preacher of heresy contrary to the teachings of the Book and the Sunna."[50] In either case, the wrong has to do with public departure from Islam, as established and protected by a legitimate authority. Such wrongs are connected with Qur'an 2:214 and other texts that stipulate that fitna or "civil strife" is more blameworthy than the shedding of blood.

Similarly with rebels. The Kharijites, whom Ibn Taymiyya mentions explicitly, were an early group understood as "secessionists" (the literal meaning of the name al-khawarij, anglicized as "kharijites"). According to traditions consistently cited by practitioners of Shari'a reasoning, the group seceded from the rightful leadership of 'Ali ibn Abi Talib (d. 661), the fourth successor to the Prophet. Their secession was motivated by an objection to 'Ali's approach to conflict with Mu'awiya, governor of Syria and an opponent of 'Ali. In justifying their actions, the Kharijites cited Qur'anic texts. They understood themselves as advocates for justice, and saw others as moral slackers, in need of encouragement or, in some cases, of punishment. 'Ali responded with a mixture of persuasion and force, the goal being to limit the damage done by this group of "irregular fighters" while at the same time hoping for reconciliation. Over time, the Kharijites became a standard reference for those who, while well motivated, committed acts that did more harm than good. In justifying fighting against such persons, Ibn Taymiyya again was consistent with Shari'a precedent. It is the duty of a Muslim ruler to establish and protect the practice of Islam. Such a ruler does not use military force to make new converts. Rather, the ruler fights to extend or protect the hegemony of Islamic values in a what one might call "geopolitical space." Even within that space, fighting is not authorized to force conversion. As Ibn Taymiyya writes, the protected peoples (ahl al-dhimma), for example Jews and Christians living under Muslim rule, may only be fought if they violate the terms of their treaty with the Muslim ruler. Their difference in religion is not itself a justification for fighting.[51]

Force is authorized, however, to protect the establishment of Islam. So apostates and rebels are seen as a greater threat than those unbelievers who live outside the boundaries of the Islamic state. A legitimate ruler is authorized, even required, to use force to limit the ability of such groups to "spread corruption in the earth."[52]

Thus far, Ibn Taymiyya seems consistent with his predecessors in the practice of Shari'a reasoning. He does write as one intent on purifying the practice of Islam; his treatise on the institution of al-hisba, or the public exhortation of Muslims to fulfill their duties, is indicative of this concern, as are numerous tracts and formal Shari'a opinions about the dangers practices that depart from true Islam.[53] For Ibn Taymiyya, any Muslim refusing to perform those duties or to observe those prohibitions established by Shari'a reasoning is subject to punishment. If such refusal is a matter of performance only, the miscreant may be considered an unbeliever, an apostate, or a "half Muslim" – this, Ibn Taymiyya writes, is a matter on which Shari'a authorities disagree. If refusal is accompanied by explicit statements to the effect that regulations established by Shari'a reasoning do not hold, the person is simply an unbeliever. In any case, however, "punishment" does not rise to the level of "fighting" unless departure from duty is accompanied by armed resistance. If such resistance is present, then punishment with fighting is necessary. Depending on the circumstance, participation in fighting to discipline those who have departed from their duties may be a matter for the standing army, or it may be an individual duty incumbent on each and every Muslim.[54]

Ibn Taymiyya's zeal for purity in Islamic practice may or may not involve an expansion of the typical concerns of Shari'a reasoning. Where he does seem a bit different from his predecessors is in his construal of the relations between rulers and subjects. For Ibn Taymiyya, these are reciprocal. Rulers owe it to their subjects to provide leadership; to govern wisely; to establish those institutions that will ensure that subjects understand their duties and are encouraged to fulfill them.

Subjects owe obedience; this is a standard judgment of Shari'a reasoning. There are times and places when subjects must "omit to obey," as for example when a ruler commands something contrary to the Qur'an and the example of the Prophet. This again is standard. Ibn Taymiyya seems to take this further, however, in the sense that it is a duty of subjects to remind rulers of the demands of obedience to God's law. Indeed, it appears that Ibn Taymiyya presumes that "commanding right and forbidding wrong" is a task in which all Muslims have a part. Not that they are all public officials with rights and duties associated with enforcement of the Shari'a. But all Muslims do have a share in the task of commanding good and forbidding evil, and this might be understood in ways that expand the rights of subjects in relation to rulers. For rulers, as well as subjects, may be negligent in their duties. Rulers, as well as subjects, may depart from Islam in ways suggestive of apostasy, rebellion, or unbelief. When this holds, who has the duty, and with it the right of punishing the ruler? The establishment of legitimate authority, Ibn Taymiyya holds, is a requirement of the Shari'a. Who will establish such authority if and when those who hold the reigns of power are themselves corrupt?

It is difficult to see Ibn Taymiyya as a full-blown advocate of just revolution. He wrote in a time when the unified caliphate presumed by his predecessors no longer existed. With the invasion of the Mongols, the Abbasid caliphate proved unsustainable, even in the special role envisioned by al-Mawardi. The Muslim state was in a time of transition, with competition between various claimants to power. The Mamluk sultanate in Cairo held pride of place. The Mongols themselves were in transition; having conquered large portions of the territory of Islam, they appeared to be quintessential unbelievers. They were, however, in the process of converting to Islam, and by the time of Ibn Taymiyya governed their portion of the territory of Islam by a kind of mixed legal regime. Judgments associated with the Shari'a were set alongside those characteristic of the Mongol code of honor. In this context, Ibn Taymiyya's concerns for pure Islamic practice seemed to suggest the necessity of fighting against the Mongols, and in certain opinions he appears to say that such fighting is a duty for Muslims. Such judgments are put forth with care, however; much depends on the trajectory of the Mongol state with respect to adherence to Shari'a norms. The transitional nature of authority in Ibn Taymiyya's time, in other words, makes it difficult to read his judgments as constitutive of a theory of just revolution.[55]

Ibn Taymiyya's reasoning on such matters is worthy of much attention because of the role his opinions play in contemporary Islam. One who turns to the various statements issued by al-Qa'ida, for example, will find him cited as *shaykh al-islam*, implying that he is "first among equals" when it comes to the practice of Shari'a reasoning. The February 1998 *Declaration on Jihad against Jews and Crusaders*, for example, cites Ibn Taymiyya: "As for fighting to repulse [an enemy], it is aimed at defending sanctity and religion, and it is a duty as agreed [by consensus]. Nothing is more sacred than belief, except repulsing an enemy who is attacking religion and life."[56] Similarly, Ibn Taymiyya is cited by the author of *The Neglected Duty* as setting precedent for the notion that an ostensibly Muslim ruler may be classified as an apostate whenever he or she fails to make the Shari'a the law of the land. In such a case, the author argues, it falls to individual members of the Muslim community to enforce God's law by executing the ruler and instituting an alternative regime.[57]

In both of these cases, the citation of Ibn Taymiyya is problematic. The *Declaration*, for example, goes on to stipulate that the "ruling to fight the Americans and their allies, civilians and military, is an individual duty for every Muslim who is able, in any country where it is possible."[58] As indicated above, Ibn Taymiyya's discussion of the rules of fighting maintains a distinction between civilians or noncombatants and combatants. Only the latter may be the direct target of military action. On this point, as others, Ibn Taymiyya's judgment is consistent with the precedents set by al-Mawardi, al-Shaybani, and indeed, the Prophet Muhammad. It is not clear how one reasoning in the framework of the Shari'a would arrive at the conclusion set forth by the authors of the *Declaration*. The document itself assesses the condition of contemporary Muslims in terms of an emergency: "a time in which nations are attacking Muslims like people fighting over a plate of food . . . [a] grave situation."[59] For Ibn Taymiyya and others, this is the kind of situation that indicates that fighting is an individual, rather than a collective duty. It does not justify indiscriminate war, however. In other places, Usama bin Ladin has defended the judgment in the *Declaration* on grounds of reciprocity. The United States and its allies, he says, fight without regard for the civilian/soldier distinction, and this means that others can respond in kind. Alternatively, bin Ladin argues that civilians in the United States benefit from the unjust policies set by their leaders, and are thus guilty by association.[60] In either case, bin Ladin does not cite Shari'a precedents for such judgments. If one follows the lead of the *Declaration* and examines the precedents established by Ibn Taymiyya, it seems clear that bin Ladin's judgments depart from the practice of the one spoken of as *shaykh al-islam*.

The Neglected Duty, by contrast, is problematic in its attempt to appropriate Ibn Taymiyya's reasoning on a case in which he was unclear. As noted above, the demise of the Abbasid caliphate in 1258 created a situation in which the assignment of legitimate authority was contested. The question of who should lead the Muslim community was more or less open. Ibn Taymiyya worried about the case of the Mongols, but his thoughts on that matter provide only an ambiguous precedent. Similarly, his notion that power might be held in a complex relationship of reciprocity between rulers and subjects does not provide a clear guide for action. Most problematic is the citation in *The Neglected Duty* of passages from Ibn Taymiyya's books regarding the fighting of apostates and rebels. Their "punishment," as noted, is "heavier than the punishment of an unbeliever . . . Any group of people that rebels against any single precept of the clear and reliably transmitted precepts of Islam must be fought."[61] In this connection, the cited text makes clear that such fighting is to be guided by an established public authority. One who would turn this text into a justification for irregular or revolutionary violence will have to do a bit more work than the author of *The Neglected Duty*.

Nevertheless, these contemporary documents do illustrate the character of Shari'a reasoning in one very important respect. As I argued throughout this chapter, Shari'a reasoning is best understood as transgenerational conversation about the rights and wrongs of human acts. Such a conversation is governed by settled practices involving the reading and interpreting of texts, namely the Qur'an and reports of the practice of the Prophet. As one generation reads and interprets with respect to questions of its day, it establishes precedents to which subsequent generations must recur. In so doing, they need not view each and every precedent as binding. Circumstances, in the sense of the "facts relevant to a situation" may well suggest the need to move in new directions. When one does depart, however, one must provide reasons. And, ultimately, those reasons, or indeed the entire process of Shari'a reasoning, gives honor to God whose will is to instruct human beings in the art of living.

Conclusions

Does the Islamic tradition exhibit ways of thinking about war that resonate with the just war tradition? I think the answer is clearly yes, and I have tried to make that clear through a presentation of a number of standard practitioners of the art of Shari'a reasoning. For war to be just, there must be a legitimate authority, a just cause, and right intention. The last, in particular, is demonstrated through the process of invitation established by the practice of the Prophet Muhammad, which, while not precisely the same as the just war tradition's criterion of last resort, provides an approximation of that tradition's concerns. The ruler or commander of armies must consider issues of proportionality and reasonable hope of success. The entire structure of Shari'a reasoning regarding war is motivated by the concern to build a just and stable order, as in the just war criterion of aim of peace. And war must be conducted with honor, as indicated by the consistent affirmation that there are noncombatants among the enemy, and that these are not to be the direct and intentional target of attack or by the discussion of weapons that might cause disproportionate harm. All these are characteristic concerns of historic Shari'a reasoning, with the result that Muslims may find a rich deposit of precedent to guide considerations of war in the circumstances of contemporary life.

Why, then, one may ask, does it appear that this tradition is in such disarray? Why, for example, do we find statements like *The Neglected Duty* or the *Declaration on Jihad against Jews and Crusaders*, the authors of which clearly see themselves as participants in the transgenerational conversation about the Shari'a, yet whose own contributions can only be described as highly problematic?

One way to answer such questions must focus on the changing nature of authority in Islam. Richard Bulliett points to the importance of new print technology during the nineteenth and twentieth century in this regard.[62] By increasing the availability of historically significant works, such technical advances made possible an increase in the numbers of Muslims able to read and contribute to conversations relative to the Shari'a. More recently, the availability of internet access fosters conversations among far-flung groups of Muslims. Add to this increased literacy and the growth of a professional class in many Muslim communities, and one has a recipe for increased participation – a good thing, by most lights – but also a means by which people can bypass the question of credentials – a less good thing, as it turns out.

Historically speaking, Shari'a reasoning was the preserve of a learned class, the *ulama*. One generation learned from its predecessors regarding which texts to read, how to read them, and how to reason from them with respect to new types of questions. Only those who completed the most advanced course of training, coupled with a record of published judgments reviewed and discussed by peers, had the right to issue independent opinions. The vast majority of practitioners was limited to repeating and applying established judgments, and was to refer questions calling for more creativity to their more learned colleagues.

The changes outlined by Bulliett provide a partial explanation for the current crisis in Shari'a reasoning; that is people who are not qualified nevertheless feel free to issue independent judgments on questions of the day. None of the signers of the *Declaration* possessed traditional credentials. The author of *The Neglected Duty* was similarly unqualified.

In such a context, one would expect members of the class of *ulama* to respond. And so they have. Johannes J. G. Jansen's translation of *The Neglected Duty* includes a number of responses from Muslim authorities, including a long assessment by the Shaykh al-Azhar.[63] The opinions of those who hold this office carry great weight among the learned, and indeed in popular Islam as well. In this case, the Shaykh warned that the author of *Duty* and his comrades risked committing the mistake of the Kharijites. Well-intentioned Muslims can nevertheless do more harm than good, he wrote, and those following the logic of *Duty* were likely to shed the blood of innocent people. One can ask many questions about the legitimacy of established governments; one might even reach the conclusion that a given regime is unjust. One must still ask whether, in taking action to depose such a regime, one will cause more harm than good.

Similarly, a more recent holder of the Azhar office joined his voice with others who condemned the *Declaration* and other acts undertaken by al-Qa'ida as unjust. No one can justify indiscriminate attacks on Shari'a grounds, he argued. Any direct and intentional killing of noncombatants is ruled out by the Qur'an, the example of the Prophet, and the consensus of prior generations.[64]

What, then, is the nature of the current problem? Is it that the tradition is in disarray? Is it that the opinions that receive widest coverage do not present very good examples of Shari'a reasoning? The answers to these questions must be "yes." It is also true, however, that the conversational nature of Shari'a reasoning makes it a difficult phenomenon to track. One cannot simply point to a statement by a particular group, or by a particular scholar, and know with certainty that the statement in question represents the Shari'a point of view. For that kind of certainty, one must allow time, and the forging of a consensus among a variety of practitioners. Even then, the conversational character of the tradition lends a certain openness or air of an unfinished task to practical judgment. Consider the following case, with which I close.

Since the middle 1990s, the figure of the Palestinian martyr or, as some would have it, "suicide bomber" has been a feature of the confrontation between Palestinians and Israelis. Among the many questions one might ask about this matter, surely the question of how Shari'a reasoning judges the legitimacy of this kind of action. Muslim groups (Hamas and Islamic Jihad) are more often than not the sponsors of "martyrdom operations." Within such groups, those who carry out such operations are hailed as heroes and heroines, and their actions are viewed as an important tactic in the struggle against Israeli injustice.

It thus caused much consternation when, in the Spring of 2001, a leading Saudi scholar issued a *fatwa* suggesting that martyrdom operations may lack the support of precedent. Indeed, since those who carry them out are in effect taking their own lives, it would seem that they commit suicide, which from the standpoint of Shari'a reasoning is prohibited.

Reactions were not long in coming. From Yusuf al-Qaradhawi (a scholar associated with the Muslim Brethren) to the Shaykh al-Azhar, the Saudi scholar's reasoning was criticized as a misunderstanding of the facts. Those who carry out martyrdom operations do not commit suicide, in the sense that the Shari'a condemns. For their intention is not to end their lives, but to sacrifice for justice. They are not sinners, but heroes, and as such are deserving of praise.

In his response, however, the Shaykh al-Azhar made an important and interesting qualification regarding his judgment that such acts are praiseworthy. Noting that the consensus of *ulama* always requires that military action avoid the direct and intentional targeting of civilians, he suggested that those planning and carrying out martyrdom operations must take care about the targets of their attacks. The attacks should not take place in Israel, said the Shaykh; martyrdom operations should be limited to territory where it is clear that Israeli forces are an occupying power. And a martyr must be careful about his or her intention, so that the deaths of any children or other noncombatants are not at the front of his mind in planning or carrying out the mission.

As stated, the Shaykh al-Azhar's reasoning suggested some important limitations on martyrdom operations. One might still say, however, that the notion of intention seems very "mentalistic," whereas the historic patterns of Shari'a reasoning seem to suggest something more objective, along the lines of taking care to avoid harm to civilians.

In any case, Shaykh Qaradhawi and others responded with the argument that the militarized state of Israeli society made it impossible to discriminate between soldiers and civilians. One must imagine, it seems, that every Israeli of a certain age is either in the armed forces, or likely to be. This makes them, prima facie, legitimate targets. One who gives his or her body as a "human bomb" in order to blow up a bus thus kills a number of fighters or potential fighters, and is engaged in a legitimate military attack. If children or the very old or disabled people are killed, that is regrettable, but justified by military necessity. And for scholars associated with

Hamas and Islamic Jihad, such attacks are legitimate in Israel proper, as well as in the West Bank and Gaza, because all the land is occupied, and Muslims must fight to regain all of their lost territory.[65]

Is that the final word by practitioners of Shari'a reasoning on the matter of martyrdom operations? One hopes not. And beginning with Summer 2002, one heard some scholars beginning to question the practice again, this time on the grounds of its effectiveness as a tactic of fighting.[66] The argument thus far appears to be grounded on an appeal to issues of utility, rather than on matters of discrimination or proportionality. What will emerge, we shall have to see.

Notes

1 Lambton, A. K. S. (1981) *State and Government in Medieval Islam*, Oxford: Oxford University Press.
2 Cf. Lane, Edward (1865) *An Arabic–English Lexicon*, London: Williams and Norgate, I/4: 1534–36.
3 Muhammad ibn Idris al-Shafi'i, as translated by M. Khadduri (1961) in *Islamic Jurisprudence: Shafi'i's Risala*, Baltimore, MD: Johns Hopkins University Press: 11.
4 Standard introductions to *usul al-fiqh* are Schacht, Joseph (1964) *An Introduction to Islamic Law*, Oxford: Clarendon Press; and Coulson, N. J. (1964) *A History of Islamic Law*, Edinburgh: Edinburgh University Press. These should be supplemented by Hallaq, Wael B. (1997) *A History of Islamic Legal Theories*, Cambridge: Cambridge University Press, which indicates necessary revisions of Schacht and Coulson at a number of points.
5 Following Yusuf 'Ali's translation, modified according to my sense of the Arabic text.
6 In the case of Shi'i reasoning, where one of the principles of religion is that God appoints one leader or Imam for every generation, the authoritative reports must be confirmed by the inclusion of one or more of the designated imams. Cf. Sachedina, Abdulaziz (1988) *The Just Ruler in Sh'iite Islam*, Oxford: Oxford University Press; idem (1981) *Islamic Messianism*, Albany: State University of New York Press. Note, for reasons of space, I will not deal with Shi'i interpretations of the law of war in this chapter. The doctrinal emphasis on the designated Imam as *ma'sum*, "elevated" or protected from the commission of injustice, and the correlative insistence that the types of war to be identified with the term *jihad* can only be authorized by the Imam of the age, leads to important variations in practical judgment. I hope to deal with this matter in a future publication. Sachedina's *Just Ruler* contains important comments at 105–18.
7 From M. Khadduri's translation in (1966) *The Islamic Law of Nations: Shaybani's Siyar*, Baltimore, MD: Johns Hopkins University Press: 96.
8 On this period of Islamic history, cf. Hodgson, Marshall G. S. (1974) *The Venture of Islam*, Chicago, IL: University of Chicago Press, vol. 1.
9 *Ijtihad* is typically translated as "independent judgment," which indicates a capacity for creativity reserved to the most advanced scholars. More generally, however, it indicates "effort" in reasoning about the sources of Shari'a.
10 On the history of the text, cf. Khadduri's introduction in (1966): 1–74. Also cf. comments on the dating of the text and its redactional history in Calder, N. (1993) *Studies in Muslim Jurisprudence*, Oxford: Clarendon Press: 39–66; more briefly, but suggestively, the comments in El Fadl, Khaled Abou (2001) *Rebellion and Violence in Islamic Law*, Cambridge: Cambridge University Press: 144–47, and in particular 145, at notes 167 and 168.

11 Khadduri (1966): 75–77.

12 Watt, W. M. (1961) *Muhammad: Prophet and Statesman*, London: Oxford University Press, which summarizes the more detailed presentations in (1953) *Muhammad at Mecca*, Oxford: Clarendon Press and (1956) *Muhammad at Medina*, Oxford: Clarendon Press.

13 According to an interpreter like Paul Ramsey, "timely resort" is actually the import of the last resort criterion in any case. Cf. (1988) *Speak Up for Just War or Pacifism*, University Park and London: Pennsylvania State University Press: 85. On just war tradition generally, cf. Johnson, James Turner (1999) *Morality and Contemporary Warfare*, New Haven, CT: Yale University Press. For formal comparisons of just war tradition and Islamic thought, cf. Kelsay, John (1993) *Islam and War: A Study in Comparative Ethics*, Louisville, KY: Westminster/John Knox Press; Kelsay, John (1990) "Religion, Morality, and the Governance of War: The Case of Classical Islam," in *Journal of Religious Ethics* 18(2): 123–39; Kelsay, John (1996) "Bosnia and the Muslim Critique of Modernity," in G. Scott Davis (ed.) *Religion and Justice in the War over Bosnia*, New York and London: Routledge, 117–42; Kelsay, John with James Turner Johnson (eds.) (1991) *Just War and Jihad*, Westport, CT: Greenwood Press; Johnson, James Turner with John Kelsay (eds.) (1990) *Cross, Crescent, and Sword*, Westport, CT: Greenwood Press; James Turner Johnson (1997) *The Holy War Idea in Western and Islamic Traditions*, University Park: Pennsylvania State University Press; Firestone, Reuven (1999) *Jihad: The Origin of Holy War in Islam*, Oxford: Oxford University Press; Tibi, Bassam (1996) "War and Peace in Islam," in T. Nardin (ed.) *The Ethics of War and Peace: Religious and Secular Perspectives*, Princeton, NJ: Princeton University Press, 128–45; Hashmi, Sohail (1996) "Interpreting the Islamic Ethics of War and Peace," in Nardin, 146–68.

14 As at Khadduri (1966): 218–22.

15 Ibid.: 230–46 and 250–53.

16 Ibid.: 195–218 and 222–29.

17 Ibid.: 247–50.

18 Ibid.: 96.

19 Cf. Kelsay, John (2003) "Al-Shaybani and the Islamic Law of War," in *Journal of Military Ethics* 2(1): 63–75; also V. J. Parry (1970) "Warfare," in P. M. Holt, A. Lambton, and B. Lewis (eds.) *The Cambridge History of Islam*, Cambridge: Cambridge University Press, 2: 824–50.

20 Khadduri (1966): 95.

21 Ibid.: 86–7, 101–02.

22 Ibid.

23 2:190, Yusuf 'Ali translation, with modifications.

24 Khadduri (1966): 101–02.

25 Ibid.: 102.

26 Portions of al-Tabari's text are translated by Ibrahim, Yasir S. in *A Translation of al-Tabari's Book of the Disagreement among Muslim Jurists: The Book of Jihad (sections 1–49)* Tallahassee, FL: MA thesis, 1998.

27 Using the translation of *Ahkam al-Sultaniyya wa al-Wilayat al-Diniyya* prepared in Wahba, Wafaa H. (1996) *The Ordinances of Government*, Reading, UK: Garnet Publishing: 32, 36.

28 For example, cf. Lambton (1981); also Rosenthal, E. I. J. (1958) *Medieval Islamic Political Thought*, Cambridge: Cambridge University Press.

29 Wahba (1996): 36.

30 Ibid.: 37.

31 Ibid.: 38–59.

32 On these matters, cf. Hodgson, vol. 2.

33 Wahba (1996): 40.
34 Ibid.
35 Ibid.
36 Ibid.: 41.
37 Ibid.: 45.
38 Ibid.
39 Ibid.
40 For portions of the Arabic text, as well as a translation and comments, see Sivan, E. (1966) "La Genese de la Contre-Croisade: Un Traite Damasquin du Debut du XII Siecle," *Journal Asiatique* 254: 197–224.
41 Wahba (1996): 35.
42 In general, cf. Jane I. Smith, "Islam and Christendom," in Esposito, John L. (ed.) (1999) *The Oxford History of Islam*, Oxford and New York: Oxford University Press, esp. 337–41.
43 From Arabic text given in Sivan (1966). My translation.
44 From his *Siyasat al-Shar'iyya*, citing the translation by Omar A. Farrukh, *Ibn Taimiya on Public and Private Law in Islam*, Beirut: Khayats: 146. For a short account of Ibn Taymiyya's life and thought, see Henri Laoust's entry on him in the *Encyclopedia of Islam*, second edition, Leiden: Brill, 1986, III: 951–55.
45 Ibid.: 147.
46 Ibid.: 140.
47 Ibid.: 141.
48 Ibid.
49 Ibid.: 146. On rebels, cf. El Fadl (2001), who discusses Ibn Taymiyya at 271–79.
50 Ubid.: 141.
51 Ibid.: 142.
52 As per Qur'an 5:33.
53 On *al-hisba*, cf. the translation by M. Holland in *Public Duties in Islam*, Leicester, UK: The Islamic Foundation, 1982. On the more general duty with which this treatise is concerned, i.e., "commanding right and forbidding wrong," cf. Michael Cook (2000) *Commanding Right and Forbidding Wrong in Islamic Thought*, Cambridge: Cambridge University Press.
54 Farrukh, *Ibn Taimiya*, 145–48.
55 On these matters, cf. M. Holland, *Public Duties*, and Cook (2000), esp. 151–57.
56 There are several translations of the *Declaration* available; for this one, see http://www.fas.org/irp/world/para/docs/980223-fatwa.htm For analysis, cf. Kelsay, "Bin Laden's Reasons," *The Christian Century* 119/5 (February 27–March 6, 2001): 26–29.
57 For a translation of this text, see Jansen, Johannes J. G. (1986) *The Neglected Duty: The Creed of Sadat's Assassins and the Resurgence of Islamic Militance in the Middle East*, New York: Macmillan; for analysis, cf. Kelsay, *Islam and War*, 100–06.
58 See above, note 56.
59 Above, note 56.
60 See, for example, the May 1998 interview with ABC correspondent John Miller. Text is available through www.pbs.org
61 Farrukh, *Ibn Taimiya*, 60.
62 Bulliett, Richard W. (2002) "The Crisis within Islam," *Wilson Quarterly* 26(1) (Winter, 2002): 11–19.
63 As cited above, note 57.
64 Opinion published in *Al-Quds*, August 17, 1998; selections translated at www.memri.org from May 2, 2001, Inquiry and Analysis Series No. 53.
65 For translations of portions of the relevant materials, and also for places of publication in Arabic, see www.memri.org, Inquiry and Analysis Series Nos. 53, 54, 65, and 66.

For a brief analysis, cf. Kelsay, John (2002) "Suicide Bombers," *The Christian Century* 119(17) (August 14–27): 22–25.
66 Kelsay, "Suicide Bombers."

Bibliography

Bulliett, Richard W. (2002) "The Crisis within Islam," *Wilson Quarterly* 26(1) (Winter): 11–19.

Calder, N. (1993) *Studies in Muslim Jurisprudence*, Oxford: Clarendon Press.

Cook, Michael (2000) *Commanding Right and Forbidding Wrong in Islamic Thought*, Cambridge: Cambridge University Press.

Coulson, N. J. (1964) *A History of Islamic Law*, Edinburgh: Edinburgh University Press.

El Fadl, Khaled Abou (2001) *Rebellion and Violence in Islamic Law*, Cambridge: Cambridge University Press.

Esposito, John L. (ed.) (1999) *The Oxford History of Islam*, Oxford and New York: Oxford University Press.

Firestone, Reuven (1999) *Jihad: The Origin of Holy War in Islam*, Oxford: Oxford University Press.

Hallaq, Wael B. (1997) *A History of Islamic Legal Theories*, Cambridge: Cambridge University Press.

Hashmi, Sohail (1996) "Interpreting the Islamic Ethics of War and Peace," in T. Nardin (ed.), *The Ethics of War and Peace*, Princeton, NJ: Princeton University Press: 146–68.

Hodgson, Marshall G. S. (1974) *The Venture of Islam*, Chicago, IL: University of Chicago Press.

Ibrahim, Yasir S. (1998) *A Translation of al-Tabari's Book of the Disagreement among Muslim Jurists: The Book of Jihad (sections 1–49)*, Tallahassee, FL: MA thesis.

Jansen, Johannes J. G. (1986) *The Neglected Duty: The Creed of Sadat's Assassins and the Resurgence of Islamic Militance in the Middle East*, New York: Macmillan.

Johnson, James Turner (1997) *The Holy War Idea in Western and Islamic Traditions*, University Park: Pennsylvania State University Press.

Johnson, James Turner (1999) *Morality and Contemporary Warfare*, New Haven, CT: Yale University Press.

Johnson, James Turner with John Kelsay (eds.) (1990) *Cross, Crescent, and Sword*, Westport, CT: Greenwood Press.

Kelsay, John with James Turner Johnson (eds.) (1991) *Just War and Jihad*, Westport, CT: Greenwood Press.

Kelsay, John (1990) "Religion, Morality, and the Governance of War: The Case of Classical Islam," *Journal of Religious Ethics* 18(2): 123–39.

Kelsay, John (1993) *Islam and War: A Study in Comparative Ethics*, Louisville, KY: Westminster/John Knox Press.

Kelsay, John (1996) "Bosnia and the Muslim Critique of Modernity," in G. Scott Davis (ed.) *Religion and Justice in the War over Bosnia*, New York and London: Routledge: 117–42.

Kelsay, John (2001) "Bin Laden's Reasons," *The Christian Century* 119/5 (February 27–March 6): 26–29.

Kelsay, John (2002) "Suicide Bombers," *The Christian Century*, 119(17) (August 14–27): 22–25.

Kelsay, John (2003) "Al-Shaybani and the Islamic Law of War," *Journal of Military Ethics* 2(1): 63–75.

Khadduri, Majid (1961) *Islamic Jurisprudence: Shafi'i's Risala*, Baltimore, MD: Johns Hopkins University Press.

Khadduri, Majid (1966) *The Islamic Law of Nations: Shaybani's Siyar*, Baltimore, MD: Johns Hopkins University Press.

Lambton, A. K. S. (1981) *State and Government in Medieval Islam*, Oxford: Oxford University Press.

Lane, Edward (1865) *An Arabic-English Lexicon*, London: Williams and Norgate.

Ramsey, Paul (1988) *Speak Up for Just War or Pacifism*, University Park and London: Pennsylvania State University Press.

Rosenthal, E. I. J. (1958) *Medieval Islamic Political Thought*, Cambridge: Cambridge University Press.

Sachedina, Abdulaziz (1981) *Islamic Messianism*, Albany: State University of New York Press.

Sachedina, Abdulaziz (1988) *The Just Ruler in Sh'iite Islam*, Oxford: Oxford University Press.

Schacht, Joseph (1964) *An Introduction to Islamic Law*, Oxford: Clarendon Press.

Sivan, E. (1966) "La Genese de la Contre-Croisade: Un Traite Damasquin du Debut du XII Siecle," in *Journal Asiatique* 254: 197–224.

Tibi, Bassam (1996) "War and Peace in Islam," in T. Nardin (ed.) *The Ethics of War and Peace: Religious and Secular Perspectives*, Princeton, NJ: Princeton University Press: 128–45.

Wahba, Wafaa H. (1996) *The Ordinances of Government*, Reading, UK: Garnet Publishing.

Watt, W. M. (1953) *Muhammad at Mecca*, Oxford: Clarendon Press.

Watt, W. M. (1956) *Muhammad at Medina*, Oxford: Clarendon Press.

Watt, W. M. (1961) *Muhammad: Prophet and Statesman*, London: Oxford University Press.

Part II

SOUTH ASIA

3

BETWEEN PRUDENCE
AND HEROISM

Ethics of war in the Hindu tradition

Torkel Brekke

In this chapter I intend to explore the Hindu ideology of war and warfare in order to find out whether classical India has produced something comparable to the Christian tradition of just war. The central idea of this chapter is that there is a lasting tension in the Hindu tradition between heroism and prudence. On one hand, there is the heroic ideal espoused by the great epics, the *Mahabharata* and the *Ramayana*. On the other hand, there is the ideal of prudence espoused by the tradition of statecraft, the *arthashastra*. These two ideals, and the traditions that convey them, make for fundamentally different ideas about the ideology and ethics of war in Hindu India.

In a study of classical Hindu ideas of war the two great epics, the *Mahabharata* and the *Ramayana*, must have a central position. In addition to these epic sources, there are a number of works belonging to the *dharmashastra* literature, i.e. the tradition about the duties and privileges of the different classes of people according to factors such as social class, age and gender, and to the *arthashastra* literature, i.e. the literature about "worldly gains", or the science of statecraft. Although these sources sometimes refer to the epic tradition to illustrate their views on aspects of war, these texts are written as manuals to assist rulers in their business. Therefore, they are not only far shorter and more concise than the epics, but belong to a completely different tradition in terms of how they see man's relation to the divine. This does not mean that the authors are not religious, but religion, as well as ethics, has been objectified and relativized by them often to a surprising degree. One could, perhaps, say that their relation to the Hindu myths and legends of the epics is akin to the relationship between Machiavelli's works and the Bible. Just like Machiavelli, the *arthashastra* authors are interested in myth and religion mainly as a source to understand the psychology of human social behaviour, which is considered to be indispensible knowledge to the sovereign.[1]

There are several texts dealing specifically with war and warfare, such as certain chapters of the *Kautiliya Arthashastra* and the much later *Nitisara* of Kamandaki.

According to one tradition, the author of the *Kautiliya Arthashastra* was the adviser and mentor of the great king Chandragupta Maurya, who ruled a great North Indian empire from the end of the third century BC. There is also a tradition saying that Kamandaki was the disciple of the infamous Kautilya, which is obviously wrong.[2] In the *arthashastra* tradition we should also mention the *Barhaspatya Sutra*, although this is probably of secondary importance. Kautilya refers to this work but there does not seem to be any connection between the present *Barhaspatya Sutra* and the work to which Kautilya refers.[3] In the following I will look at these and other Hindu sources, as well as the available secondary material, in order to establish a more balanced picture of ideas of war in Hinduism than the one advanced through the ideas of *karmayoga*. I will also touch on questions about war and ethics in other Indian traditions, like Buddhism and Jainism.

Heroism, *karmayoga* and the ritual of battle

The study of just war in world religions already has a long history in the Christian tradition and the literature on war in Islam is growing. It has been pointed out that classical Islam gives criteria for just war which are similar to those found in the Christian tradition.[4] Hinduism, on the other hand, has been seen as completely alien in its theoretical treatment of war and warfare. The sociologist James Aho, for instance, has divided the religious symbolism surrounding war into two broad categories where Hinduism comes out as radically different from the Judeo–Christian–Islamic family of religions.[5]

In a recent chapter on the ethics of war in Hinduism, Francis X. Clooney points out that sacrificial violence is generally justified because it is required by the Veda, whereas killing for mundane goals is always forbidden, according to the dominant ethical traditions of Hinduism.[6] From the sacrificial violence of the Brahmins, the priests, Clooney goes on to discuss the use of violence by the Kshatriyas, the warriors. He looks at the duty of the king to use violence to maintain order and he observes that in the literature describing these duties "causing pain is conceded a due place in the exercise of royal power; indeed, exerting force and causing pain lessens the overall amount of pain in the long run".[7]

Still, although the instrumental aspects of military means is evident in classical Indian literature, Hindu ideas on war have often been seen as following a completely different type of rationality from other world religions. This alien rationality has been summed up in one word: *karmayoga*. To support this view one can point to the famous verse of the *Bhagavadgita* in which Krishna tells Arjuna to see the fighting itself as the end and not the fruits of the battle.[8] One can find other passages in the great epic *Mahabharata* that will corroborate the traditional view of Hindu ethics as completely different. For instance in verse 12.99 – the subsection about the duties of the king, i.e. *Rajadharmaparvan* of the *Shantiparvan* to which I shall return frequently in this chapter – Yudhishthira asks his teacher Bhishma to what worlds (*loka*) the heroes go when they die in battle.[9] In the preceeding verse Yudhishthira has pointed out that in the business of war the king kills large numbers of people. There is in fact no profession or duty which is more sinful than that of the Kshatriya (*kshatradharma*) he maintains.[10] *Karmayoga* is the solution. Bhishma explains that battle itself is a great sacrifice. Every soldier who advances against the enemy in battle takes part in the sacrifice of battle (*yuddhayajña*).[11] Then follows a long exposition by Bhishma about the details of the battle and their respective parallels in the conventional sacrifice. Thus, the flesh and the blood of the dead become oblations, and mutilated bodies, bones, hair, severed heads, weapons, elephants and even the sounds of cutting and piercing have precise functions in the sacrifice of battle, according to Bhishma. Such references have made scholars conclude that the *Mahabharata* war really is a sacrifice.[12]

The *Mahabharata* is the great epic about the conflict in the Kuru lineage culminating in the war between the hundred sons of Dhritarashtra and the five sons of Pandu and their armies. In the subsection of the Shantiparvan of the *Mahabharata* devoted to the duties of the king, *rajadharma*, we find an important collection of rules for war.[13] Typically these rules are taught Yudhishthira, who represents the ideal Hindu king, by Bhishma, the wise teacher of the five brothers. In the epic literature there is a lack of rules for just war. In the literature on the duties of the king we will not find clear statements about the right authority to initiate war or what constitutes a just cause for war. That does not mean that the Hindu tradition did not care about justifications of war. The fact is that in the world view of the *Rajadharma* questions of just war were so fundamental that they were seldom spelled out. They were implicit in any debate on the rights and duties of kings and the question of justification does not seem to arise in the same way as it did for Christian theologians from Thomas Aquinas onwards. From the point of view of the *karmayoga* it is possible to explain this omission. Warfare is part of the duties of kingship, part of the *rajadharma*, and the battle becomes a great sacrifice where the king ensures a rebirth in heaven for himself. These ideas of *dharma* and *karmayoga* are closely connected to the view of kingship as a divine institution. According to an important strand of political theory kingship is instituted by the gods. Even a boy-king deserves unconditional respect for he is a god in human form, says Manu.[14] Only a king can challenge a king and somebody who is not a king must never attack a king.[15] According to the myth of king Vena in the Vishnu Purana 1.13.16–18, even the most wicked king cannot be attacked without punishment of cosmic proportions. The problem of the king's divine authority and tyrannicide was a serious topic in ancient India.[16]

On the surface, this reminds us of the discussion of the authority of kings in Europe that was sparked by the Reformation and the religious conflicts between Catholics and different strands of Protestants during the sixteenth and seventeenth centuries. Machiavelli and Luther did not have much in common, indeed they had opposite views on the origins of the state and of kingship, but nevertheless their views converged on the question of the kings' authority.[17] One generation later, Jean Bodin would lay the foundations of the absolute monarchy of France in his *Six livres de la république*, where he argued that sovereignty must be indivisible, that sovereign power must be concentrated in the ruler, and that nobody must challenge his authority.[18] So were ideas of divine kingship in Europe and India simply the same?

Certainly not. Ronald Inden has warned against seeing a parallel between European and Indian ideas of divine kingship.[19] The divinity of the king in India has nothing to do with divine right or absolutism, he asserts. In India, divine kingship is about the nature of cosmos and about the king's place in it.[20] R. Inden draws attention to Indian mythology, where the cosmos and everything in it issues from the Cosmic Man, it is not created *ex nihilo*. This fact is of great importance, according to Inden, because it means that the supreme Hindu God is always immanent, although transcendent in relation to society and nature. God is not outside as a bestower of kingly authority, as in Europe, we might add. This is a non-dualistic cosmos, in which the king was the microcosmic figure of the Cosmic Man symbolizing unity and order on the micro-level. But Inden seems to restrict his discussion to the world view of the Puranas and the dharma-texts. Indian theory of kingship is in a sense ambivalent. There is an opposition between the view of kingship as divine on the one hand and as a purely practical institution on the other. The legendary lawmaker Manu puts it this way:

For when this world was without a king and people ran about in all directions out of fear, The Lord emitted a king in order to guard his entire (realm), taking lasting elements from Indra, the Wind, Yama, the Sun, Fire, Varuna, the Moon, and (Kubera) the Lord of Wealth. Because a king is made from particles of these lords of the gods, therefore he surpasses all living beings in brilliant energy, and, like the Sun, he burns eyes and hearts, and no one on earth is able even to look at him.[21]

When in the *Mahabharata* worship of Krishna is added to ideas of *karmayoga* and divine kingship we have the preconditions for ideas of holy war like those found in the Old Testament. When Israel fights the peoples inhabiting the lands given to them in Palestine, God participates in the battle. When God participates in battle it has two important consequences for the belligerents' perception of the fighting. First, it makes God's party more or less invincible. Second, and more importantly from the point of view of the governance of war, it makes the battle just by definition.

In the *Mahabharata*, Krishna becomes an ally, he takes active part in the battle, he chooses sides and gives crucial advice on tactics. Krishna makes the heroes invincible and he guarantees their righteousness implicitly by his very presence and explicitly by sanctioning certain acts of deceit and fraud in the fighting. Drona, the enemy of the heroes, says: "Where dharma is, there is also Krishna, and where Krishna is, there is victory" and again "Where Krishna is, there is dharma and where dharma is there is victory."[22] Holy war is just by definition. God's participation makes the battle just, it ensures the righteousness of the belligerents.

But the fact that the war of the epic is a holy war does not make all ideas of the limitation of means irrelevant. The way in which the war is fought is a separate issue. Fundamentally, a war must be waged according to *dharma*, righteousness or the natural law of the universe. A king must not wage war by unjust means, according to the teacher Bhishma of the *Mahabharata*. What kind of ruler would rejoice in an unjust victory (*adharmavijaya*), he asks.[23] A victory won through unrighteousness weakens both the king himself and the world. The king should try to conquer by any righteous means he can, because it is his duty as king, but he must never wish to conquer through illusion or magic (*maya*) or through deceit (*dambha*).[24]

Thus, the typical view of the proper ways of waging war concerns the laws or norms associated with *dharma*. We may borrow a Western term for this ethical world view that is about following absolute rules: deontology. It is this deontological view of the ethics of war that is the core of the strand of thinking and acting that I have called *heroism*. The opposite of the deontological view is the ethical theory that is concerned with consequences of acts; this is the ethical theory that informs the strand of thinking that I have called *prudence*. At this point, we may see a concrete divergence of the two ethical traditions in their ideas about *jus in bello*, namely in their general views on trickery and deceit in warfare. The *Mahabharata*, with its deontological concern with *dharma* and its rules, will most of the time condemn deceit and trickery in war. Kamandaki, a later representative of the consequentialist statecraft to whom we shall return, takes the opposite view and asserts that by killing the enemy through deceitful warfare there is no breach of righteousness (*dharma*).[25] Heroism is about honesty, whereas prudence may necessitate deceit.

Chivalry and *jus in bello*

If we look at the more specific rules in warfare found in the *Mahabharata*, we will find that many of them seem to be part of a code of chivalry akin to that of medieval Europe. A soldier whose armour is broken, one who says "I am yours", one who folds his hands or one who has thrown down his weapons may be taken prisoner but may not be killed.[26] The aged, the children, women, one who shows he surrenders, and again one who says "I am yours" must not be killed.[27] One must not kill those who are sleeping, those who are thirsty, those who are wearied, one who is disordered or confused, one who has started out for liberation (*moksha*), one who is on the move, one who is walking, one who is drinking or eating, or one who is scattered in the mind, or one who has been struck, one who has been weakened.

The world of the *Mahabharata* is the world of individual heroes, not that of systematic warfare. Great warriors go to heaven when they die, whereas the warrior who dies in bed or runs away from danger goes to hell. The ethos of this world is summed up in the verse: "There is nothing higher in the three worlds than heroism (*shaurya*)."[28] Many of the rules for warfare seem to concern duels rather than general battles. There is the same sense of tension between the ideals of the chivalrous duel and large-scale war as that we see through the centuries in Christianity. In medieval Europe warfare meant duel. When the rules for duels were expanded to include general war, they naturally turned out to be of limited applicability to the new situation and adjustments had to be made.

The *Mahabharata* has a central position in the Hindu tradition. However, the other great Indian epic, the *Ramayana*, has probably been just as important or even more so for Hindu identity through history. Rama was the legendary king ruling India from his capital Ayodhya and his righteous rule is the paradigm of Hindu kingship. In the sphere of political power Rama's identity as a great king, warrior and statesman and, not the least, his identity as the incarnation of the high-god Vishnu is emphasized. The story about the separation of Rama from his beloved Sita ends after the siege of Lanka by Rama and his army and the battle against Ravana and his troops of demons; war is an integrated part of the epic, as in the *Mahabharata*. In fact, fighting is a prominent activity throughout the story and the *Ramayana* has nearly six thousand occurrences of terms denoting military action.[29] These are most frequent in the Book of the Battle, the *Yuddhakanda*, describing the clash between the two armies. The *Ramayana* abounds in terminology for weaponry and army formations. The most frequently mentioned type of soldier is the chariot-warrior (*maharatha*) and the most frequent type of combat is the duel between two equal opponents in chariots. It is, in fact, reasonable to talk about a kind of battle, a duel between two (*dvandvayuddha*), which is strikingly similar to the duels found in medieval European chivalry. In the *Ramayana* as in the *Mahabharata* the duel takes place in the context of a larger battle, but it is ordered in its form, the warriors are supposed to be of comparatively equal strength and nobody is allowed to interrupt or assist in any way. One reference to chariot-battle might suggest that the authors or redactors of the *Ramayana* knew more widely accepted rules for this type of warfare: in Rama's last combat with Ravana, Rama fights from the ground while his enemy is still mounted on his chariot and the gods interrupt the duel on the basis that it is unfair.[30] We recall here the similar instances in the *Mahabharata* where warriors are chastised for engaging in battles against foes with different types of weapons and armour. The rules for just warfare in the *Ramayana* belong to a world of individual heroes and when applied in the discussion of larger battles or wars, a sense of incongruity sometimes surfaces, as it does in the *Mahabharata*.

The direct references to a systematic theory of war or statecraft in the *Ramayana* are not many. However, there are hints from which we may induce the existence of a general body of statecraft related to the *arthashastra* tradition mentioned above. For instance, the monkey-god Hanuman, Rama's important ally, considers the four-fold classification of the means (*upaya*) of success in political theory. These are conciliation (*saman*), bribery or gifts (*dana*), sowing dissension (*bheda*) and the use of force (*parakrama*). These four are referred to incidentally in several places in the epic and this classification also occurs in the *Kautiliya Arthashastra* where, however, a six-fold classification is more common.[31] As to the regulation of war a number of specific rules are mentioned in the *Ramayana*. There can be no fighting during the monsoon or during the night. We find that women are inviolable, that it is a sin to kill someone who is asleep or who is drunk and that soldiers should show clemency towards those who surrender on the battlefield and, as already mentioned, the intervention of a third party in a duel is universally condemned. On the other hand, the rules for just war or the conduct of war are not discussed systematically in the way they are in the *Mahabharata*. As Brockington puts it: "Instead, we find expressed general and rather vague notions of fair play based essentially on the idea that combat should be between equals."[32] This lack of precise and systematic discussion of the rules of war fits well with the greater picture of the *Ramayana* as a less realistic and more imaginary epic on the whole than the *Mahabharata*.

Rama and Ayodhya have become central symbols in the struggle of modern Hindu nationalists of the Sangh Parivar for a hinduized India. (The Sangh Parivar, or the Sangh Family, consists of the political organizations with roots in the Rashtriya Svayamsevak Sangh (RSS), most importantly the BJP, the VHP and the RSS itself.) During the great mobilization of Hindus around the controversy of the birthplace of Rama (*ramjanmabhumi*) in late 1990 the VHP staged a great chariot procession (*rath yatra*) in which a car was decorated as the chariot of Rama and the followers dressed up as characters from the life of the god.[33] On December 6, 1992 the Babri Masjid mosque was pulled down by Hindu masses who had gathered at the call of holy men. According to nationalist history the mosque had been built by the Mughals in 1528 on the ruins of the temple to Rama and the destruction of the mosque was the first step in the process of reclaiming the sacred spot for the Hindus. The use of *Ramayana* in a nationalist discourse is a new thing, although the epic may well have been used as a source for royal and political symbols in earlier times as well. H.J. Klimkheit's sees Shivaji's campaigns as an early example of a Hindu nationalism centred on the symbolism of Hindu kingship expressed in the *Ramayana*.[34]

The lack of a *jus ad bellum*

At this point we are in a position to pose the first fundamental comparative question about the ethics of war in India and Europe. Indian writers produced plenty of literature about war but they were never concerned with *jus ad bellum*. Why did pre-modern Hindu writers take so little interest in questions of legitimate authority, just cause, right intention and the like? Alternatively, why were late medieval and early modern European writers so interested in these questions? My suggestion would be that in order to explain the fundamental difference between India and Europe we need to look at the concept of war and its place in political thought. In medieval and early modern Europe there was great interest in matters of right authority in war because European thinkers, at least from the late thirteenth century onwards, had a concept of war that made two important distinctions. First, the European concept of war distinguished violence against external enemies from violence against internal enemies. Second, the European concept of war distinguished between public and private war, between *bellum* and *duellum*. In India, there was no interest in right authority because Hindu writers on ethics and politics did not possess a concept of war that distinguished clearly between violence against external and internal enemies.

One important characteristic of the European concept of war – as it developed in the formative period of the formulation of the just war tradition in Europe in the thirteenth and fourteenth centuries – is that it is public, not private, and directed against an external group of people. On the matter of differentiating external from internal violence we might consult Thomas Aquinas. He defined war (*bellum*), brawling (*rixa*) and sedition (*seditio*) by pointing to two basic differences. First, there is the difference that both war and brawling entails actual fighting or conflict, while sedition can be either actual hostilities or preparations for them.

> The second difference is that while a war, properly speaking, is against an external enemy (*bellum proprie est contra extraneos et hostes*), one nation as it were against another (*quasi multitudinis ad multitudinem*), and brawls are between individuals, one against one or a few against a few, sedition in its proper sense is between mutually dissident sections of the same people.[35]

Sedition attacks the special good which is the unity and peace of a people. As opposed to schism, it attacks the temporal or secular unity of a people rather than the spiritual or ecclesiastical unity. When a prince is faced with a revolt or rebellion it is his duty to strike it down with force. However, this type of large-scale use of violence did not constitute real war, only an excercise of jurisdiction.[36]

We saw that in the heroic epic literature of India, war is private and duels are not conceptually distinct from the clashes of great armies. But more importantly, nowhere in classical Hindu literature do we find a distinction between the king's legitimate authority to use violence inside his realm and outside against other kings and their territories. In order to understand this crucial difference we need to understand the notion of the kingdom and the sovereignty of the Hindu king. In the European ethics of war, as it developed in the crucial period from the thirteenth century onwards, the distinction between the external and internal relations of the country was of great importance. The distinction was clear-cut and would later develop into a distinction between the functions of police and military with different rules and standards for the external and the internal aspects of the state's use of violence. At the foundation of the new distinction between external and internal affairs in Europe was the concept of sovereignty, which expressed the political autonomy of each European prince and his country in relation to other princes. In late medieval times, Europe was moving towards a consensus on the principle that only a prince without secular superior had the right to levy war.[37] The borders between the realms of the princes became sharp and only the prince without secular superior had legitimate authority in matters of public, external war, waged, at least in theory, for the sake of the common weal.

Indian political scientists did not perceive the international system as a whole with autonomous states with kings of equal standing. There were clear notions about how a king should run his country and how he should behave towards other kings but there was no notion of sovereignty in the European sense. Whether one wishes to label the typical Hindu state *feudal* or *segmentary* or something different, the fact remains that the distribution of actual military power within the kingdom was

BETWEEN PRUDENCE AND HEROISM

nothing like the early modern, bureaucratic European case.[38] The classical Hindu kingdom did not have clear borders and the military power of the king did not serve the same function as it did in early modern Europe. The peoples living in the country regions between two kingdoms belong to *both* the king and his enemy. "Country people on the other hand are common to the enemy," Kautilya says.[39] In fact, the state described by Kautilya is a state with fuzzy and permeable borders. The sovereignty and influence of the kings in the international order described by Kautilya overlap in ways that make it impossible to distinguish between external and internal affairs. This fundamentally different idea of sovereignty is significant in an exploration of the concept of war. In the words of André Wink: "In principle the stratagems to be employed by the king are the same in his own dominion and in that of his enemy. There is therefore no distinction of kind between 'external' and 'internal' politics."[40] I believe that one consequence of this was that the writers in the tradition of statecraft did not care to discuss legitimate authority in matters of war. These writers had something to say about *jus in bello* but they showed no concern for *jus ad bellum*.

In short, if we want to explain the differences between Indian writers on war and the European just war tradition we might start by observing that the distinctions between external and internal and between private and public war were not made in pre-modern India, at least not to the extent that they were in Europe. I believe that these conceptual differences go a long way to explaining why European writers were so concerned about *jus ad bellum* while Indian writers were not. In the classical Hindu world view, the legitimate authority of the king needs no defending or explanation. In the tradition of statecraft, war against another king is an extension of the proper use of violence to maintain order within the realm. The legitimate authority is self-evident in external affairs, as it is in internal affairs where it is part of the social contract where the king must maintain order and punish the evil.

Prudence: Kautilya's statecraft and the ethics of war

From the study of the great epics, Indian ideas of war seem to have made battle a goal in itself. Whereas a systematic *jus ad bellum* is lacking, there is a strong tradition in Hinduism for sanctioning the violence of the kings by referring to the general duties of kingship, the *rajadharma*. Thus, we mentioned above that the idea of divine kingship is an important element in any understanding of the ethics of war in India. But the divinity of the king was not taken for granted. Indeed, there seems to have been two very different strands of thought concerning the origin of kingship in ancient India. Basham calls them the *mystical* and the *contractual*.[41] J. C. Heesterman puts it this way: "As it is, however, kingship remains, even theoretically, suspended between sacrality and secularity, divinity and mortal humanity, legitimate authority and arbitrary power, dharma and adharma."[42]

There is an important strand of thinking, contained in both *arthashastra* and the *dharmashastra* tradition, that sees the king first of all as responsible for the maintenance of the correct order of society and in exchange for his services he collects taxes. In Indian tradition the central concept of an ordered world is the clear segmentation of the *varnas*, classes, and the *ashramas*, stages of life, and people's observation of their duty according to these two factors. The opposite of an ordered world is the state of chaos where the stronger grill the weaker as fish on a spit, where the crow eats the sacrificial cake and the dog licks the oblation, where there is no ownership and everything is upside down. The contractual idea of kingship leads to a different attitude to war and warfare than the theory of divine kingship. The battle is not a sacrifice in this tradition, *karmayoga* is irrelevant here. We saw that in the tradition of heroism war may become an end in itself. In the contractual view of kingship war is a means to achieve other things, like security and prosperity. War as a means is generally judged to be ambiguous. War is dangerous and prudence is necessary.

The greatest exponent of the idea of war and violence as a means to other ends is Kautilya. The name of Kautilya's treatise is *Kautiliya Arthashastra*. *Arthashastra* is not really a name but a generic term. It is made up of two smaller words: *artha* and *shastra*. *Artha* means worldly gains in a broad sense but to simplify a bit we may translate it by *wealth*. *Shastra* means science. A simple but reasonably exact translation of *arthashastra* would therefore be "science of worldly gains". In the last chapter of the *Arthashastra*, Kautilya gives his own definition of his science: "*Artha* is the source of the livelihood of human beings, in other words, the earth inhabited by men. The science which is the means of the attainment and protection of that earth is the *Arthashastra*."[43]

Arthashastra is the science which is the means of the attainment and protection of the earth and its riches. In order to understand this properly, we must at the outset say a few words about the goals of human life in ancient Indian thought. In India, the goals of life were often divided in three. These were religion or the cosmic order (*dharma*), worldly gain (*artha*) and enjoyment (*kama*). These three goals of human existence are often encountered in classical Indian literature. In other words, worldly gain and its science was only one of three goals of human life, although Kautilya believed that it was the most important of the three. Writers in the other two traditions would disagree with him. To complicate matters, Indian writers would often add a fourth goal, that of salvation or more exactly liberation from the cycle of rebirth (*moksha*). The literatures dealing with liberation or salvation (*moksha*) and enjoyment (*kama*) have nothing to do with our subject here, whereas the literature on *dharma* is important to understand both Kautilya and other political writers of South Asia.

Following the publication of the Sanskrit text of Kautilya's *Arthashastra*, European and American scholars started questioning the authenticity of the treatise and even the historicity of the author. The Indologist Otto Stein offered a systematic comparison of the contents of Kautilya's work with the available fragments of the Greek Megasthenes' work on India.[44] Stein wanted to find out whether the minister of Chandragupta in fact composed a work on *arthashastra* and whether it is identical with the one we have. His conclusion is that the deviations between the Greek account of India and the *Arthashastra* are great and he attributes the deviations to chronology. In general, the scholars who deny the authenticity of Kautilya's *Arthashastra* tend to place it in the third or fourth century AD, mostly from rather inconclusive internal arguments from the subject matter.[45] This is not the place to pursue arguments about the identity of the author of the *Arthashastra*, but it can be said that there are good reasons to believe that Kautilya's *Arthashastra* in fact was composed in the late fourth or early third century BC, although we cannot be certain. We might add that the treatise seems to presuppose the existence of a rather advanced tradition of statecraft.[46]

According to tradition, Kautilya was the intelligent and unscrupulous adviser of the first great Indian emperor, Chandragupta Maurya and he was the architect of the greatest of the ancient Indian empires, ruled by the Maurya dynasty. Later Indian plays depict Kautilya as the actual ruler of India at the time, Chandragupta being a weak, young king. At the end of his treatise Kautilya describes himself as the man who destroyed the Nanda dynasty.

In short, the political situation at the time of Kautilya and at the time of the composing of the *Arthashastra* was initially rather unstable but the reign of Chandragupta marked the beginnings of a long period of peace and prosperity. Pataliputra was a capital about twice the size of Rome under Marcus Aurelius and the king himself resided in a splendid wooden palace. It was a period of rapid political and economic development.[47] Cities grew as commercial centres and as political centres. The religious organizations of Buddhism and Jainism grew under the patronage of the Maurya emperors, who appreciated stability and morality.[48] Industries grew in the cities and a monetary system developed. The capital housed soldiers, ministers and religious officials employed by the king and there were moneylenders, medical practitioners, potters, weavers, dyers, reed and leaf-workers, leather-workers, architects, smiths, hunters and butchers.

In this world, Kautilya's one concern was how to make the kingdom and the king as strong and prosperous as possible. Still, on the relationship between goals and means in the thought of Kautilya there has been some debate. For instance, what is the relationship between the two traditional goals of worldly gain (*artha*) and religion and universal laws and duties (*dharma*) in Kautilya's work? The Indologist J. C. Heesterman has asserted that even Kautilya's notorious work on the *arthashastra* does not break with the literature on *dharma* – the *dharmashastra* – in order to formulate an independent *raison d'état*.[49] *Dharma* always keeps hovering over *artha* and the political science in India, according to Heesterman. I find it difficult to agree with Heesterman on this point.

Clearly, there was a complex relationship between the literature on politics and the literature on religion and cosmic order in classical India.[50] The interaction between the *dharma* tradition and the *artha* tradition, between religion and politics to put it crudely, was not one way. If the *dharmashastra* influenced Kautilya, it is also the case that Kautilya's *Arthashastra* in its turn influenced the literature on *dharma*. For instance, there are tensions within the most important book about *dharma* written by Manu because it endeavours to incorporate classical political concepts and ideas into a religious framework. The commentators on Manu borrowed extensively from Kautilya, too.[51] More importantly, I believe we must see Kautilya as more independent of the *dharma* tradition from the way he treats questions of politics. Kautilya saw the life of the king as a constant struggle to maintain order in the kingdom and gain economic and political advantages vis-à-vis his immediate neighbours. When the occasion was ripe, the king should expand his territory and fill his treasury through war. The situation *within* the kingdom was analysed in terms of economy, revenue and control through gathering of intelligence. The king should have an extensive system of spies and informers and he should kill anybody who might threaten him, especially untrustworthy ministers and servants.

The relationship *between* kingdoms was analysed as an anarchic system, where the king must see himself in the middle of a circle of states (*mandala*) and a circle of kings (*rajamandala*), where the immediate neighbours are natural enemies (*ari*) and the neighbour's neighbour is a natural friend (*mitra*) because he is the enemy of the enemy.

> The king who is situated anywhere immediately on the circumference of the conqueror's territory is termed the enemy. The king who is likewise situated close to the enemy, but separated from the conqueror only by the enemy, is termed the friend (of the conqueror). [. . .] Throwing the circumference of the Circle of States beyond his friend's territory, and making the kings of those states as the spokes of that circle, the concqueror shall make himself as the nave of that circle.[52]

This pattern of friends and enemies repeats itself in concentric circles and the king must always strive to dominate. Kautilya goes on and on giving details about the relationship between different elements of the circles according to their relative strength. In terms of foreign policy, the king is basically a conqueror in a system of alliances. As we saw, it would be a mistake to analyse this system as well-defined territorial states in a European sense. In Kautilya's world, the ends of strength, stability and prosperity justify any means. What, then, about ethics?

The great tradition of ethics that Kautilya first had to relate to as a thinker was the Vedic tradition transmitted by the powerful priestly class, the Brahmins. Their ethic may be called deontological because it emphasized the duties of the individual according to *dharma*. There was also the early form of the *arthashastra*, which may be called consequentialist in the sense that it is a pragmatic system of thought which seeks to maximize wealth. In one of the biographical accounts of the Buddha, we are told that the young prince was taught the *arthashastra* and we have other textual sources indicating that this tradition was part of the education of princes.[53] In fact, one of the most entertaining genres of classical Indian literature is the tradition of stories about animals and people, such collections as the *Tantrakhyayika*, the *Pancatantra* and the later *Kathasaritsagara*. These stories are typically short and funny and they were probably collected as a didactic tool to train young princes in the science of politics. It is in these stories that one finds the earliest traces of the *arthashastra* tradition.

In order to maintain order and to protect his people the king has *danda*, the rod of punishment. *Danda* is military power and *danda* is punishment. The execution of power is the "wielding of *danda*" (*dandaniti*). To see how important violence is to Kautilya we may look at the opening parts of his treatise, where he sets out some views about his subject. In Chapter 4 of Book 1 of the *Arthashastra*, where Kautilya lays out the goals of political science, he gives the rod a prominent place in the maintenance of an orderly world:

> Danda is the means to secure the logical inquiry, the three Vedas and economics. Its wielding is the science of politics (*dandaniti*) the purpose of which is the acquisition of what is not acquired, the preservation of what is acquired, the augmentation of what is preserved and the giving away of what is augmented to a worthy recipient. The orderly maintenance of worldly life depends on it [danda]. Therefore the king seeking the orderly maintenance of worldly life should always hold the stick lifted up to strike. For there is no such thing for the subjugation of beings, say the teachers.[54]

In Indian ideology the rod that is the symbol of the king's physical power often becomes a symbol of the king himself. I mentioned that the relationship between the literature on politics (*artha*) and the literature on religion (*dharma*) is complex and ambiguous. The writers on *dharma*, too, are very concerned with the question of legitimate violence. The most important writer on *dharma*, Manu, puts it this way:

> For (the king's) sake the Lord in ancient times emitted the Rod of Punishment, his own son, (the incarnation of) Justice, to be the protector of all living beings, made of the brilliant energy of ultimate reality. [. . .] The Rod is the King and the man, he is the inflicter and he is the chastiser, traditionally regarded as the guarantor for the duty of the four stages of life. The Rod alone chastises all subjects, the Rod protects them, the Rod stays awake while they sleep; wise men know that justice is the Rod. Properly wielded, with due consideration, it makes all the subjects happy; but inflicted without due consideration, it destroys everything. [. . .] Where the Rod moves about, black and with red eyes, destroying evil, there the subjects do not get confused, as long as the inflicter sees well.[55]

The most important difference between the passage from Kautilya and Manu about violence and the wielding of the rod may be the fact that the more religiously oriented of the two, i.e. Manu, blends all kinds of mythological ideas about the origins of kingship into his view of violence.

At first glance, it might seem that the wielding of the rod is simply one branch of the *arthashastra*, i.e. that the science of violence is a branch of the science of wordly gain. This seems reasonable when one considers how the *Arthashastra* of Kautilya discusses violence alongside other tools available to the king, like economic policy and organization of the bureaucracy. But the fact is that many writers have seen the wielding of the rod as synonymous with *arthashastra*, implying that Kautilya is really discussing subjects that are outside his proper field when he discusses peaceful things like inheritance, debts, transactions, or the offices of the controller of shipping, director of forests or superintendent of elephants. This also means that violence is the means par excellence in the tool-kit of the ruler – the Raja – according to Kautilya; the king is first and foremost a protector of order and an inflicter of punishment.

What is the relationship between the legitimate violence inflicted by the king on his subjects to maintain order and the violence inflicted against other kings and their societies? I believe that one of the main differences between Europe and India on matters of ethics and violence is the fact that Europe developed a sharper distinction between internal and external violence than India did. Perhaps it is simply about the distinction between *duellum* and *bellum* that appeared in the Middle Ages. This is not the place to speculate further on this, although I must say that I am inclined to think that one of the main variables between societies on matters of violence and ethics – China and Japan may be even more relevant than India here – is precisely the degree to which they distinguish between policing and war.

The wielding of the rod of punishment is described as potentially extremely brutal and ruthless by Kautilya. For instance, in Book 5 Kautilya has advice on how to get rid of dangerous elements without getting enmeshed in matters of law and justice: "The king in the interest of righteousness may inflict punishment in secret on those courtiers or confederacy of chiefs who are dangerous to the safety of the kingdom and who cannot be put down in open daylight."[56] Getting rid of ministers mostly involves clever traps and poisoned food. For instance, the king may invite a minister for an interview and send some of his agents to accompany the minister on his way to the palace. The agents should carry concealed weapons and when they are discovered by the palace guards, the agents should quickly admit to be involved in a plot led by the minister, who should be put to death on the spot.[57] He describes a simpler method: "A spy, under the guise of a physician, may make a seditious minister believe that he is suffering from a fatal or incurable disease and contrive to poison him while prescribing medicine and diet to him."[58]

To Kautilya, war is often discussed as an extension of internal violence and punishment. War is never an end in itself. War is always a dangerous undertaking and the king should only use military means when he knows he can achieve something substantial by it. This separates Kautilya from much of the literature on war in classical India. For instance, in the world of chivalry which is reflected in many sections of the *Mahabharata* war is a duty and fighting becomes a sacrifice or a religious game where the most important thing is not winning but fighting well according to the laws of *dharma*. In this world of bravery, running away from the battlefield is shameful. Kautilya is very much opposed to this idea of war. Chivalry has no place in his instrumental conception of military means.

When a king of poor resources is attacked by a powerful enemy, he should surrender himself together with his sons to the enemy and live like a reed (in the water). Bharadvaja says that he who surrenders himself to the strong, bows down before Indra. But Vishalaksha says that a weak king should rather fight with all his resources, for bravery destroys all troubles, this fighting is the natural duty of the warrior (Kshatriya), no matter whether he acheives victory or sustains defeat in battle. No, says Kautilya, he who bows down to all like a crab on the bank of the river lives in despair; whoever goes with his small army to fight perishes like a man attempting to cross the sea without a boat. Hence a weak king should either seek the protection of a powerful king or maintain himself in an impregnable fort.[59]

In this passage, Kautilya refers to two legendary writers with very different and opposing opinions of the very metaphysical basis of political science. Here, Bharadvaja represents the realist tradition, where the weak must bow down and forge alliances with the stronger, whereas Vishalaksha represents the *dharma* tradition, in which religious duties are more important than the outcome of the battle. To use Western terminology, we see the tension between deontology and consequentialism in Indian ideology of war. Kautilya clearly positions himself in the consequentialist camp. He rejects the idea that one should fight to the end only because fighting is a natural duty and bravery has intrinsic value. Bravery has value for Kautilya only to the extent that it makes the warriors better fit to win a battle. In order to prepare his soldiers, the king should make any argument he can. For instance, he should make his priests encourage the army by promising salvation and paradise after glorious death. Religious tradition and doctrines become instrumental.

His ministers and priest should encourage the army by saying thus: "It is declared in the Vedas that the goal which is reached by sacrificers, after performing the final ablutions, in sacrifices in which the priests have been duly paid for, is the very goal which brave men are destined to attain."[60]

In other words, he should tell his men that dying on the battlefield is a short cut to heavenly bliss. He continues later: "Soothsayers and court bards should describe heaven as the goal for the brave and hell for the timid."[61] Kautilya does not care whether what the priests, astrologers, magician and soothsayers are saying is true. His science is about winning wars here on earth. The king must promise rich rewards in the form of money to the warrior who slays the king and commanders of the enemy and Kautilya suggests a graded scale of pay for slaying different officers, destroying elephants, chariots, horses, etc.[62]

The crucial point about Kautilya's view of war becomes apparent when we compare his ideas with the typical ideas about religious and holy war in the epic literature of classical India. I have stressed the distinction between the literature on *artha* and the literature on *dharma*. Although the epic *Mahabharata* is not a systematic treatise on ideology and war, it is here that we find the most typical examples of the righteous war, the war waged according to *dharma* (*dharmayuddha*). In the *Mahabharata*, a war must be waged according righteousness or the natural law of the universe. Kautilya prefers peace because most of the time peace is more conducive to prosperity and security: "Acquisition and security (of property) are dependent on peace and industry. Effort to achieve the results of work undertaken is industry. Absence of disturbance to the enjoyment of the results achieved from work is peace."[63]

Kautilya talks prudence where the epics preach heroism. Prudence is also paramount to Kamandaki, who is one of the most important later writers in the tradition of Kautilya. The king should not be a warmonger (*ativigrahi*), says Kamandaki. Kamandaki is clearly among those who is most eager to warn the king of the dangers of war. The text presents a long list of the common causes of war and instructs the king to avoid most wars if possible.[64] A number of conciliatory measures should be adopted before thinking of war even if the king is harassed by enemies, and there is clearly an element of morality in the precepts of the manual. A king should never join an ally in a campaign if the ally is unrighteous, or *adharmic*, whereas a righteous ally should be helped even if the king risks his own life.[65]

But what is the metaphysical basis of morality if the king is seen as only one party to a contract and not as an embodiment of the divine? As Kamandaki says "All men are selfish and they always strive for the success of their self-interest."[66] Can ethics have any relevance in the politics of the king vis-à-vis other nations, then? Not really. Kamandaki's project is more descriptive than normative. Kamandaki offers a long list of the *common* causes of war and then looks at the proper responses to the different hostile situations that a king might find himself in. Kamandaki goes very far in his espousal of alternative reactions to aggression. If an enemy tries to appropriate parts or the whole of the kingdom, or kidnap members of the royal family, or take control of forts, the king should adopt conciliatory measures of gifts and should restrain his impulses towards confrontation.[67] The same strategy should be chosen if somebody damages property or transgresses laws in the kingdom, whereas the destruction of the material resources in the kingdom by an external foe may be answered by the same type of action against the opponent.[68] If the enemy causes damage to the means of transport in the kingdom or causes destruction to the academic institutions, or undermines the kingdom in other indirect ways, this should be met by patience.[69] The king must meet insults and arrogance with a show of respect and conciliation rather than aggression and if an enemy kills one of his allies, the trouble should be defused through other means than war. This prudence has little to do with a higher morality; it is a consequence of seeing war as a dangerous business. Kamandaki also has a long list of types of war that should not be entered upon. The most important point to Kamandaki is that any undertaking of the king should have good effects both here and now and in the future.[70] In other words, the political actions of the king, including wars, should contribute to the sustainability of the righteous rule of the king and to the prosperity of the realm.

The description that Kamandaki uses to characterize the accepted undertakings of the king could be understood to entail an element of moral thinking. The adjective used in his descriptions (*shuddha*) means pure, authorized, clean, faultless, right, according to rule, complete.

Heroism in the Middle Ages

"Everywhere there are warriors eminent in war," a captured swan tells prince Nala in the *Naishadhiyacarita* of the great poet king Harsha.[71] This text, which recounts the story of the love between Nala and Damayanti, was written in the twelfth century. This is one of the sources used by B. N. S. Yadava to prove a thesis that the Indian Middle Ages saw a development in ideals of chivalry which degenerated into unhealthy arrogance and led to constant warfare.[72] Yadava postulates a historical development from a high chivalry, exemplified in the great epics. This balanced chivalry dominated the early empires and it emphasized restraint, according to Yadava, as may be gathered from the caution of Kautilya and from the ideals found in early works of literature such as *Harshacarita*.[73] Yadava's argument is that chivalry peaked between the tenth and twelfth centuries with the accentuation of feudal tendencies of the post-Gupta period under circumstances similar to those found in Europe. The arrogant and individualistic morale of the warrior class of this later period led to a breakdown of military tactics, which again led to Hindu defeat at the hands of the invading Muslim armies. (A number of Indian scholars have questioned why the Hindus could not resist the Muslim armies. Yadava's thesis seems to be an attempt to answer this historical riddle.) So from a noble chivalry of the first centuries AD India developed an arrogant and destructive chivalry in the tenth to the twelfth centuries ending in destruction at the hands of invaders.

So far our study of the ethics of war in classical Hinduism has lacked a historical dimension. Yadava's thesis may provide our point of departure in a discussion of change in the ethics of war over time. Yadava's article is clearly a substantial contribution to the study of the ethics of war in India, not least because he uses a number of different sources in a creative way. It is certainly easy to find sources from the Middle Ages that seem to support the thesis that prudence was supplanted by heroism and arrogant chivalry.

It is easy to find medieval literature that praises heroism. Subandhu's romance *Vasavadatta* was probably written at the beginning of the seventh century and represents the early period of the Indian Middle Ages. The story of the beautiful Vasavadatta and the young prince is the oldest romantic novel of India. It contains the usual ideas of perfect *dharmic* kingship. King Cintamani is described as the perfect king, which naturally implies great prowess and heroic nature. Subandhu uses the *Mahabharata* as a source to decribe the king. He is likened to Bhishma; he wavered not from the path of the warrior (*kshatrapatha*).[74] His son, Kandarpaketu, "As a cloud terrifies flamingoes with showers of exceeding purity, he slew kings terrified by the edge of his flashing sword."[75]

And his sword, as if coloured with lac from the feet of the Goddess of
Victory which has been moistened with the blood of slain infantry,
elephants and horses, shone over a sea of conflict. . . . [S]ince it shone
on a sea of conflict whose shores were covered with quantities of pearls
fallen from must elephants' frontal lobes which were shattered by sharp
arrows, with flying darts, with hundreds of fleshless, white-umbrellaed
armies whose manifold charms were spread through the red waters, with
convulsing corpses, and terrible because of the fierce pride of warriors
eager to consort with the Apsarasas.[76]

In short, we have ideal heroes of the same type as found in the epics: men eager to
consort with the heavenly nymphs after death on the battlefield.

If we look at the *Subhashitaratnakosha*, which is an anthology of Sanskrit
poetry compiled by Vidyakara about AD 1100 for the declining Pala court of the
Bihar–Bengal area, we might begin to test the hypothesis of a widespread obsession
with warfare and chivalry in this period. The anthology contains some verses on
war and violence, especially in a section about the hero (*vira*). For instance, the great
poet Rajashekhara is represented in this section with six verses in which Ravana,
the villain of the *Ramayana*, boasts of how he decapitated himself to please the
god Shiva. Rajashekhara flourished under the reign of the Gurjara–Pratihara
emperor Mahendrapala at the end of the ninth and beginning of the tenth centuries.[77]
He refers to himself as the teacher and guru of the king and seems to have enjoyed
an influential position at Mahendrapala's court. Among his extant work, the
play *Balaramayana* might be the most violent one. But the war scenes of the
play are a necessary part of the play's mythological subject matter, i.e. the feats of
young Rama. Returning to Vidyakara's anthology, D. H. H. Ingalls notes in his
introduction to the translation of this section that the sentiment of heroism in the
section of the hero is pretty much the same as in the *Ramayana* itself.[78] The fact is
that Vidyakara did not include much about war or heroism in spite of giving a very
broad presentation of poets of the times and of the previous two or three centuries,
including some of the most outstanding Indian court poets of all times. "*Niti*, in
particular, is poorly represented" of the classical subjects of Indian literature, the
editors of the Sanskrit text assert.[79] Indeed, they find it necessary to provide an
explanation why "the poetry of prowess was not written" although the experience
of warfare was probably rather common.[80] The celebration of arrogant chivalry
does not seem to have been so prominent in the circles of poets after all.

Nevertheless, the medieval literature offers abundant material about warfare and
some of it may indeed be taken to corroborate Yadava's thesis. The arrogance
of King Uccala in the *Rajatarangini* is another example of the same ideology of
war.[81] In Book 8 we read the following description of King Uccala's love
of watching soldiers in combat: "He took an excessive pleasure in fights, and caused
numberless men of valour to fall in duels (*dvandvayuddha*) by raising mutual enmity
between them" (8.169). "On the monthly reception-days, at Indra-festivals and on
other occasions he presented riches to those soldiers who joined single combats"

(8.170). "There was not at that time any festival when the ground in the court of the palace was not drenched with blood, and lamentation not heard" (8.171). "Soldiers of noble race who had left their homes, as if in exultation, were carried away mutilated from the palace court by their relatives" (8.172). "When the king saw soldiers killed who had glistening black hair, fine beards and splendid apparel, he felt delight instead of pain" (8.173).[82]

This love of bloodshed is presented as a flaw in King Uccala's character. Although the author spends much energy on praising his virtues these flaws are presented at the end of the introductory description of the king. The king is also said to be jealous of the virtues, including heroism (*shaurya*) of other men (8.163). The flaws of King Uccala cause his younger brother Sussala to attempt to usurp the throne and the most interesting aspect of the fight between the two is its ambiguity. Both are seen as brave and mostly good people and both are seen to have a good reason for fighting the other (8.191–207). King Uccala repels his brother's attack but is later killed in a conspiracy in the palace because he has made too many enemies through his policy and by alienating his high civil servants or *Kayasthas*. The author breaks in after relating the slaying of the king. "The want of pity which this mighty [king] had shown towards people was to some extent atoned for by the great heroism (*viravritti*) [he displayed] at his end" (8.331). The conspirators are then attacked by people loyal to the king. One of them, called Gargacandra, takes the lead in the attack on the conspirators and the author, after gory depictions from the royal court, praises his bravery: "Of such bravery (*sahasa*) and skill (*siddhi*) in a desperate enterprise, as this illustrous [man] displayed, I have not heard anywhere, even in stories" (8.355).

On the whole, then, the *Rajatarangini* is a work which displays a very considerable interest in violence, in battles, and in the different characteristics of kings and soldiers, the vices and virtues that make them fail or succeed. In his description of warriors, Kalhana in his *Rajatarangini* praises heroism (*virya*, *shaurya*) and also heroism of the foolhardy or rash kind (*sahasa*). Nevertheless, the *Rajatarangini* is a very different work from the epics although it often uses the epics as a source for its own subjects. Parts of the *Rajatarangini* seem to be closer to real history, as opposed to much of the legendary material studied here. The author is interested in the psychology, the vices and virtues of the kings, and he has no ambition of giving a treatise in statecraft. Crucially, it is not the case that Kalhana praises foolhardiness or arrogance.

Thus, Yadava's thesis should be examined further. Is it really the case that we can see a shift in the ethics of war in India from a noble chivalry in the epics to an arrogant and individualistic heroism and a breakdown of military tactics in the Middle Ages? We may start our critique of Yadava's thesis by looking at Somadeva Suri, a teacher belonging to Jainism, the religious tradition of India that is generally held to be the most peace-loving of all.

The prudence of Somadeva

I will argue that Somadeva displays the opposite tendencies to those postulated by Yadava as dominating the medieval period. I argue that there are essentially two strands of the thinking on ethics of war and warfare in pre-Muslim India. I call these two strands the deontological and the consequentialist. The deontological tradition is famously espoused in the *Bhagavadgita*. It asserts that right acts are goals in themselves quite apart from their results, as long as they are carried out with the right intention. The consequentialist tradition is clearly formulated by Kautilya. It asserts that acts are good or bad only in respect of their results. Yadava's thesis may perhaps be reformulated to say that the consequentialist tradition declined and the deontological tradition prevailed in the Middle Ages. I believe that both these traditions were mingled in a number of writers and practitioners of state-craft both in the Middle Ages and in earlier times. Somadeva, however, offers a view of war which is clearly more consequentialist than deontological: he scorns heroism and sees war as a continuation of politics by other means. This goes against Yadava's thesis, as we shall see.

In his study of kingship in medieval South India, Burton Stein noted the significant political role of Jainism.[83] Stein points out the general lack of attention paid by scholars to the political aspects of Jainism. In South India, especially Karnataka, several kings of medieval times were Jains or had close affiliations to Jainism. A Jain monk is said to have been involved in the founding of the Ganga dynasty of the third century CE, and early Ganga kings were supporters of Jainism. The ninth-century Rashtrakuta king Amoghavarsha was the patron of Jinasena, the famous author of the *Adipurana*. Amoghavarsha is said to have retreated to a Jain monastery on several occasions during his reign. A Digambara monk is also supposed to have been instrumental in the founding of the Hoysala dynasty of the twelfth century. The early Hoysalas, who had their power base in the mountains of southern Karnataka and who would have their heyday as the Cola kingdom faded in the thirteenth century, were Jains, and their capital was an important religious centre before the king Vishnuvardhana converted to Vaishnavism and drove the Jains out.[84] The greatest success that Jainism had in northern India in terms of royal support was its relationship to Kumarapala. Hemacandra was adviser to the Hindu king, who was a devotee of Shiva, and in writing the *Yogashastra* he took care not to present Jainism so that it would alienate his powerful patron.[85]

Jinasena's account of the institution of kingship shows that Jainism, like Buddhism and Christianity, was forced to deal with the question of worldly power as the religion spread and was taken up by rulers. But it also testifies to the fact that the Jain monks who came in contact with wielders of worldly power often seized the opportunity to preach ethics and endorse the ideal of the *spiritual* warrior. This does not mean that Jain teachers taught spiritual values at the expense of statecraft.

The question is what effect Jain ethics and ideology had on the ideas and practices of kingship in India, especially South India. Stein argued that Jainism produced a particular strand of kingship, which he called *moral* kingship, as opposed to heroic and ritual kingship.[86] If we restrict our view to Somadeva, it would seem that Jainism had a view of kingship closer to the *arthashastra* tradition than to the heroic tradition, i.e. Jain monks were more inclined to look at the consequences of war and warfare rather than the inherent values of actions; their view was opposed to the *karmayoga*, opposed to arrogant chivalry. They were consequentialists rather than deontologists. Two works by Somadeva are extant, the *Yashastilaka* and the *Nitivakyamrita*. In the following, I intend to take a closer look at the ideas of ethics in war found in the latter text, which in its form is a standard treatise on statecraft. First, however, we might take a brief look at the *Yashastilaka*, the romantic story about prince Yashodhara composed towards the end of the tenth century. It is clear that this work, like the *Nitivakyamrita*, espouses the measured and pragmatic view of statecraft in general and war in particular. In his authoritative analysis of the *Yashastilaka*, K. K. Handiqui said that "*Yashastilaka* may be regarded as a sort of illustrative commentary on some topics dealt with in the formal treatises on the *nitishastra* including Somadeva's own *Nitivakyamrita*."[87] Indeed, the *Yashastilaka* and the *Nitivakyamrita* supplement each other to some extent, as Handiqui points out. The *Yashastilaka* stresses the role of the king in society both as ruler and guarantor of peace and order and as a model for other men to emulate. Among the duties of the king is the conduct of war when it is necessary for the sake of state security and integrity. To adequately deal with military affairs the king must have knowledge of weaponry and tactics and he must employ skilled commanders to carry out his orders. The commander-in-chief must be brave (*shura*) but he must also be well versed in the *arthashastra*, according to the *Yashastilaka*.[88]

In Somadeva's ideology, then, the *arthashastra* is not only an important literary tradition but it has real implications for the conduct of statecraft, contrary to the thesis of Yadava. As a political thinker Somadeva divests himself of theological bias, as Handiqui says, and his approach to the problems of statecraft is that of a pragmatic adviser with a broad knowledge of the tradition of *artha* and *niti* from Kautilya onwards. The hero of the *Yashastilaka*, Yashodhara, is said to have studied and mastered a large number of lost *nitishastras* by different authors and Handiqui analyses the presence of this tradition in the *Yashastilaka*.[89] He sums up Somadeva's ideals of kingship thus:

> Somadeva's ideal of kingship is evident from his description of the life of Yashodhara as a ruler. In presenting before us a picture of his activities, the author of *Yashastilaka* does not attempt to make him a paragon of virtue or even a hero, but is content to depict him as a prince diligent in discharging the duties that devolve upon him as the ruler of the state.[90]

If we now move to the *Nitivakyamrita*, it becomes apparent at the outset that Somadeva is very much in the tradition of Kautilya. In fact he is firmly consequentialist, as he starts his treatise with obeisance to the state, he defines *dharma* as that which leads to worldly success (*abhyudaya*), whereas *adharma*, conversely, is simply that which yields fruits contrary to the desired goals.[91] Somadeva encourages the same kind of self-restraint as Kautilya. For instance, anger (*krodha*) is one of the six enemies (1.3). The anger of the arrogant warrior has no place in Somadeva's statecraft. But this is not simply because Somadeva holds a traditional Jaina view of the karma. It has been noted by Jaina philosophers and several modern scholars that the very definition of violence in Jainism necessarily includes reference to the motivation for the action, i.e. the passions. This is perhaps most famously explained in the *Tattvarthasutra* 7.13. Bhagchandra Jain Bhaskar starts a short article on non-violence in Jainism by referring to the *Tattvarthasutra* 7.13 in order to reach a defintion of *himsa* and he compares the view of *karma* in Jainism with that of Buddhism.[92]

Robert J. Zydenbos, too, points to the definition, found in the *Tattvarthasutra*, of *himsa* as the *harming of life under the influence of passions*.[93] He argues that the preoccupation with *ahimsa* found in Jainism at all times is fundamentally about the karmic results of action and not about a concern for the well-being of other beings for its own sake.[94] The presence of passions, i.e. anger, pride, deceit and greed, determine the effect of the *karma* aquired through acts. Conversely, injuring living beings does not cause bad *karma* if it is done without the influence of passions. This is the clue to understanding the apparent paradox of, on the one hand, the insistence on *ahimsa* and, on the other hand, the historical realities of Jainism's association with political power.[95] In Zydenbos's account, it seems, the rationalization of violence in Jainism comes very close in practical consequences to the more famous *karmayoga* of the *Bhagavadgita* mentioned earlier. Indeed, in the categories employed here, the main current of Jaina thought on the subject of violence would fall under the heading of deontology, which means that Somadeva, as a consequentialist, perhaps should not be taken as a typical representative of Jaina social and political ethics. However, Somadeva is not discussed here primarily in relation to the Jaina tradition but in the context of medieval Indian political thought. As Paul Dundas pointed out, Somadeva's *Nitivakyamrita* barely shows any Jain traits at all[96] and, again, non-violence is clearly not something that confers a unique identity on Jainism in the Indian world at large.[97]

In the section on military strength, Somadeva devotes a large portion of his verses to discussing the virtues of elephants in the army as well as horses, chariots and cavalry. When he comes to the subject of manpower, Somadeva asserts that a heroic nature (*svabhavashuratva*) is one of the fundamental qualities of an army, along with sound knowledge of weapons, a core of *kshatriyas*, loyalty, etc.[98] But there is never any discussion of individual heroism. The great hero is absent from the discussion, as he is in Kautilya's work. What makes a strong army for Somadeva is the quality and numbers of men and equipment, the collective devotion of the soldiers, their treatment by the king and their training, as well as the tactics on the battlefield. Indeed, the king must be a good person, he must look after his men, he must be worth fighting for. He must pay his army well. Nevertheless, "money does not make soldiers fight so much as the honour (*prabhusammana*) of the king".[99]

Interestingly, the section on war is long. Somadeva starts out by giving the advice of caution. An arrow may miss its aim, whereas the wise man successfully achieves his goal through cunning (30.7). If we start by asking Somadeva what war really is about, we get a very measured and rational answer. "War with weapons (*shastrayuddha*)" says Somadeva, "starts when other means of conquering the enemy are exhausted", a view that is strikingly reminiscent of Clausewitz's maxim that war is the continuation of politics by other means.[100] It is also a view which is firmly consequentialist and opposed to ideas of war as ritual or royal duty according to the *dharma* of the king and the warrior. War is a means to an end and should only be resorted to when it is absolutely necessary. "That which may be obtained by peaceful means (*samasadhya*) should not be obtained by the means of war (*yuddhasadhya*)."[101]

War can never be a goal in itself to Somadeva and chivalry and heroism are quite pathetic to him. Even the very powerful (*balavat*) cannot rejoice for very long, Somadeva asserts.[102] He is often critical of bravery and haughtiness. There is more than a hint of irony when he asserts: "Everyone who does not know the use of weapons and instruments is brave (*shura*)" (30.46). He never comes close to romanticizing war or warriors. "Who is not haughty (*sadarpa*) who has not experienced the might of others?" (30.47). "The stream of heroism (*viryavega*) flows unchecked in the one who has lost hope for his life" (30.76). According to the arrogant chivalry in Yadava's thesis, retreat is far worse than death. However, Somadeva has a very different idea of what the soldier should do when hope is lost. "When total destruction is sure like moth in the flame of a lamp, one should run away from the battlefield."[103]

Somadeva has also something to say about conduct in warfare, like the treatment of opponents in battle. On this, however, his ideas are very limited. One should not kill a foe that has fallen at his feet in battle and those who fly from action should be released (30.88–9). Such ideas of conduct in warfare are more typical of the deontological tradition, where actions according to *dharma* are more important than their results. According to this tradition, which is very much present in several places in the *Mahabharata*, a soldier whose armour is broken, one who says "I am yours", one who folds his hands or one who has thrown down his weapon may be taken prisoner but may not be killed.[104] Heroism and chivalry seem to have been conditions for the development of an advanced code of ethics of war in India as they were in Europe, where during the Middle Ages the rules and regulations of the cavalier *duellum* would become the basis for a general set of rules for warfare based on the principles of proportionality and noncombatant immunity.[105]

Somadeva's thoughts on right conduct in war are not complex because he is not a great believer in ethics in statecraft. Somadeva is a believer in trust or confidence (*vishvasa*) and he denounces breach of trust in strong words (30.96–8). But this does not apply to the battlefield, for the treacherous warfare (*kutayuddha*) is praised by Somadeva (30.106–8). *Kutayuddha*, of course, is opposed to the ideals of *dharma*; it is not part of the heroism proposed by Yadava. On the contrary, it is part of the cautious tradition of *raison d'état* espoused by Kautilya. The deontological tradition condemns the idea of treacherous warfare, as mentioned above.

Yadava asserted in his theory of arrogant chivalry that *kutayuddha* disappeared in medieval times along with military tactics and diplomacy.[106] He refers to certain textual sources of the period in which *kutayuddha* is absent to demonstrate that passion rather than prudence, vanity rather than wisdom, became the norm.[107] As our reference to Somadeva shows, Yadava's thesis is incorrect. *Kutayuddha* continued to play a part in the ideology of warfare in India, as did the whole tradition of cautious but sometimes unscrupulous consequentialism and realism of the Kautilya school. Indeed, as Handiqui asserted, both the *Yashastilaka* and the *Nitivakyamrita* presuppose a large body of texts on *nitishastra*. "None of these ancient works is now extant, but there is no doubt that they were available in the 10th century."[108]

It seems safe to conclude that the Indian tradition of consequentialist and prudent statecraft did not disappear during the Middle Ages. The thesis that all thoughts of *raison d'état*, restraint in war, tactics and military cunning were overtaken by heroic chivalry celebrating death on the battlefield is untenable in the light of Somadeva's rational approach to the subject of war and the tradition that his writing presupposes.

Conclusions

In this chapter I have tried to explore whether classical Hinduism contains a tradition for just war and just warfare. I started out by looking at ideas of authority and different ideas of kingship. We saw that India produced different traditions on this point, ranging from purely divine kingship to the pragmatic contractual view of the institution. The different traditions entailed different ideas of the legitimation of political action in general and war in particular. Hinduism also produced a tradition of holy war, where God chooses sides in the battle and guarantees the righteousness of his party.

Thomas Aquinas (1225–74) proposed three basic requirements for a war to be just. First, the person who initiates the war must have the right authority to do so, second one needs a just cause, third the right intention is required of the soldiers.[109] Our discussion so far has been about the right authority to initiate war; our focus has been the king and his duties and privileges according to the *rajadharma*. We saw that the different traditions of kingship advanced diverging ideas of the right of the king to initiate wars. If we move our focus away from the person of the king and his authority, may we identify philosophical ideas about what it means to have a just cause and what it means to possess the right intention in classical Hinduism? In the *Mahabharata*, the cause of the Pandavas is perceived as just because their opponents have broken a contract when Duryodhana refused to return the kingdom to the righteous Yudhishtira as promised.[110] We may find similar cases in Indian literature, where the case for war is seen to be just because of the misbehaviour of an opponent, as in the *Ramayana*. In the *karmayoga* tradition the intention of the belligerents is the main theme of the whole approach because the intention, the mental state of the actor, determines whether an action becomes a sacrifice. A battle is a sacrifice only if the belligerent is completely detached from the fighting as means to something else, only if he is detached from the fruits of the action (*karmaphala*). But the *arthashastra* tradition, too, is interested in the intention of the king who initiates war. Kamandaki says: "A ruler should avoid taking action under the influence of lust for wealth or for material pleasures in this world or such as is likely to prejudice his spiritual benefit in the next world."[111]

The fact remains, however, that matters under *jus ad bellum* receive far less attention in Hindu thought than in the European tradition. I argued that the lack of a systematic *jus ad bellum* in the Hindu tradition must be attributed, at least in part, to the fundamentally different concept of war, i.e. one that did not distinguish between external and internal and private and public violence to the extent that one finds in Europe from the late Middle Ages. On the other hand, we saw that the classical Hindu sources on war are preoccupied with the rules of combat and it is clear that ancient India produced an extensive code of ethics for fighting, a *jus in bello*. However, as we have seen, this *jus in bello* was primarily concerned with conduct of heroes in the duels that were the paradigmatic forms of fighting in the Hindu epics. This focus on the details of the individual combatant seems to have made a larger, more generalized, conception of just warfare less relevant for Hindu thinkers. For instance, there is clearly an idea in the epic literature about proportionality, the view that the means of fighting should correspond to the military means of the opponent, although this is not exactly what is meant by proportionality in the Christian tradition. The *jus in bello* of the Hindu tradition may perhaps be described as practical and specific, not abstracted from the context of the duel, a process that was the starting point of general ethics of war in the European context.

The main contention of this chapter is that there is a tension within the Hindu tradition between heroism and prudence, between the tradition that sees war as a royal duty according to *dharma* and the tradition that sees war as a means to the ends of security and prosperity. On the one hand, I have been eager to show that it is far too narrow to identify Hindu ethics of war with the heroic ideology found in the epics. On the other hand, I wanted to show that the strand of prudent statecraft did not disappear in the Middle Ages but continued its existence alongside, and in dialogue with, the heroic tradition that emphasized *dharma*. We can make the contrast between the consequentialist and the deontological traditions clearer by contrasting some of their core ideas, values and attitudes. As we have seen, one tradition sees *dharma* as the fundamental part of human existence, whereas the other sees *artha* as the goal of all activity; one has a deontological ethical theory, whereas the other has a consequentialist theory; one sees war as an end, the other sees war as a means; one has a theory of divine kingship, whereas the other takes a contractual view of kingship; one extols bravery, the other prudence; one preaches *karmayoga*, the other *raison d'état*; one expresses devotion to God where the other objectifies religion. The deontological tradition ignores *jus ad bellum*, the consequentialist tradition ignores *jus in bello*. The heroism strand insists on proportionality, whereas the prudence strand ignores proportionality. One ideal condemns trickery, the other praises it; one is expressed mainly in the epic literature, whereas the other is contained mainly in the statecraft and scientific literature.

Notes

1 Preus, J. Samuel (1979) "Machiavelli's Functional Analysis of Religion: Context and Object" *Journal of the History of Ideas* 40(2): 171–190.
2 *The Nitisara or Elements of Polity by Kamandaki*, edited by Rajendralal Mitra, Calcutta: Bibliotheca Indica, 1982.
3 *Barhaspatya Sutram*, edited with an introduction and English translation by F. W. Thomas, Lahore, 1921.
4 Kelsay, John (1990) "Religion, Morality, and the Governance of War: The Case of Classical Islam" *Journal of Religious Ethics* 18(2): 124.
5 Aho, James A. (1981) *Religious Mythology and the Art of War. Comparative Religious Symbolism of Military Violence*, London: Aldwych.
6 Clooney, Francis X. (2003) "Pain but Not Harm: Some classical Resources toward a Hindu Just War Theory" in *Just War in Comparative Perspective*, edited by Paul Robinson, London: Ashgate: 109–126.
7 Ibid.: 115.
8 Verse 2.30ff. Edited and translated in J. A. B. van Buitenen (1981) *The Bhagavadgita in the Mahabharata*, a bilingual edition, Chicago, IL: University of Chicago Press: 76–79.
9 *The Mahabharata*, edited by V. S. Sukthankar and S. K. Belvalkar, Poona, Bhandarkar Oriental Research Institute, 1948. From now on I will simply refer to the relevant verses in the *Shantiparvan* since this is the part of the *Mahabharata* of relevance here. All references are to the same edition of the *Mahabharata*.
10 Shantiparvan, 99.1.
11 Shantiparvan, 99.13.
12 A recent example is a chapter in a book about violence in South Asia: Jatavallabhula, Danielle Feller (1999) "Ranayajna: The *Mahabharata* War as a Sacrifice" in *Violence Denied: Violence, non-Violence and the Rationalization of Violence in South Asian Cultural History*, edited by Jan E. M. Houben and Karel R. Van Kooij, Leiden: Brill. Brill's Indological Library: 97–103.
13 For a discussion of *Rajadharma*, see Derrett, D. J. (1976) "Rajadharma" *Journal of Asian Studies* 35: 597–609. Scharfe, Hartmut (1989) *The State in Indian Tradition*, Leiden: E. J. Brill.
14 *The Laws of Manu*, translated by Wendy Doniger with Brian K. Smith, London: Penguin Books: Verse 7.8.
15 Shantiparvan, 97.7.
16 Prakash, Om (1977) *Political Ideas in the Puranas*, Allahabad: Panchanada Publications. See especially chapter VI entitled "The problem of divine right and tyrannicide in the Puranas": 107ff.
17 Murray, R. H. (1960) *The Political Consequences of the Reformation. Studies in Sixteenth-Century Political Thought*, New York: Russell & Russell: 40.
18 Bodin, Jean (1992) [1583] *On Sovereignty. Four Chapters from The Six Books of the Commonwealth*, edited and translated by Julian H. Franklin, Cambridge: Cambridge University Press.
19 Inden, Ronald (1998) "Ritual, Authority and Cyclic Time in Hindu Kingship" in

Kingship and Authority in South Asia, edited by J. F. Richards, Delhi: Oxford University Press: 41–91, esp. 46–47.

20 Ibid.: 46.

21 *The Laws of Manu*, Verse 7.3–6.

22 Quoted in Simson, Georg Von (1969) "Die Einschaltung der *Bhagavadgita* im Bhishmaparvan des *Mahabharata*" *Indo-Iranian Journal* 11(3): 173.

23 Shantiparvan, 97.1.

24 Ibid.: 97.23.

25 Ibid.: 19.71.

26 Ibid.: 97.3.

27 Ibid.: 99.47.

28 Ibid.: 100.18.

29 Brockington, J. L. (1984) *Righteous Rama*, Bombay: Oxford University Press: 133.

30 Ibid.: 136.

31 Ibid.: 128–129.

32 Ibid.: 152.

33 Davis, Richard H. (1997) "The Iconography of Rama's Chariot" in *Making India Hindu*, edited by David Ludden, Oxford and Delhi: Oxford University Press: 27–54.

34 Klimkheit, Hans-Joachim (1976) "Der Politische Hinduismus der Neuzeit" in *Der Religionswandel unserer Zeit im Spiegel der Religionswissenschaft*, edited by Gunther Stephenson, Darmstadt: Wissenschaftliche Buchgesellschaft: 94–108.

35 Thomas Aquinas, *Summa Theologiae*, 2a2ae. 42, I (Question 42. sedition).

36 Russell, Frederick H. (1975) *The Just War in the Middle Ages*, Cambridge: Cambridge University Press: 146.

37 Keen, Maurice (1965) *The Laws of War in the Late Middle Ages*, London: Routledge & Kegan Paul: 72 and 78–79.

38 See introductory discussion in Kulke, Hermann (ed.) (1998) *The State in Indian Tradition: 1000–1700*, Delhi: Oxford University Press.

39 KA 8.1.27. I will refer to *Kautilya's Arthashastra* as KA from now. Here I use the translation in: *Kautilya's Arthashastra*, translated by R. Shamasastry, with an introductory note by J. F. Fleet, 1923, Mysore: The Wesleyan Mission Press.

40 Wink, André (2001) "Sovereignty and Universal Dominion in South Asia" in *Warfare and Weaponry in India 1000–1800*, edited by Jos J. L. Gommans and Dirk H. A. Kolff, Delhi: Oxford University Press: 99–133.

41 Basham, A. L. (1954) *The Wonder that was India*, London: Sidgwick & Jackson: 82.

42 Heesterman, J. C. (1985) *The Inner Conflict of Tradition*, Chicago, IL: Chicago University Press: 111.

43 KA 15.1.1–2.

44 Stein, Otto (1922) *Megasthenes und Kautilya*, Wien: Akademie der Wissenshcaften in Wien: 14.

45 Winternitz, Maurice (1985) *History of Indian Literature*, Vol. 3, Part 2: *The Scientific Literature*, Delhi: Motilal Banarsidass. Translated by Subhadra Jha: 633.

46 Ibid.: 630.

47 Thapar, Romila (1984) *From Lineage to State. Social Formations in the Mid-First Millennium B.C. in the Ganga Valley*, Bombay: Oxford University Press. Thapar, Romila (1961) *Ashoka and the Decline of the Mauryas*, Oxford: Oxford University Press.

48 Lamotte, Étienne (1976) *Histoire du Bouddhisme Indien*, Louvain la Neuve: Institute orientaliste: Chapter 3. Gombrich, R. (1996) *How Buddhism Began. The Conditioned Genesis of the Early Teachings*, London and Atlantic Highlands, NJ: Athlone Press. On the matter of motivation for joining the new religions, see Brekke, Torkel (2002) *Religious Motivation and the Origins of Buddhism*, London: RoutledgeCurzon.

49 Heesterman (1985): 111.
50 Jolly, J. (1913) "Arthashastra und Dharmashastra" *Zeitschrift der deutschen morgenlän dischen gesellschaft* lxvii: 49–69.
51 In the case of the important commentator Medhatithi, however, the borrowing was not direct from Kautilya's work but from the earlier commentator Bharuci. Bharuci often borrowed long passages from Kautilya without much adjustment. Medhatithi probably lived somewhere between 825 and 900 AD and Bharuci somewhere between 700 and 800. See Derrett, J. Duncan M. (1965) "A Newly Discovered Contact between Arthashstra and Dharmashstra: The Role of Bharuci" *Zeitschrift der deutschen morgenlän dischen gesellschaft* cxv/1: 134–152.
52 KA 6.2. Shamasastry: 312–313.
53 Lalitavistara; see Winternitz (1985) vol. 3: 608–609.
54 This four-fold ideal concerning wealth and its distribution is commonly found in Indian literature.
55 *The Laws of Manu*, Verse 7.14, 17–19 and 25.
56 KA 5.1 Shamasastry: 287.
57 KA 5.1.
58 KA 5.1 Shamasastry: 289.
59 KA 12.1.
60 KA 10.3 Shamasastry: 426.
61 KA 10.3 Shamasastry: 427.
62 Ibid.
63 KA 6.2 Shamasastry: 312.
64 *The Nitisara or Elements of Polity by Kamandaki*, chapter 10.
65 Ibid.: 10.9.
66 Ibid.: 10.39B.
67 Ibid.: 10.6.
68 Ibid.: 10.7.
69 Ibid.: 10.8.
70 Ibid.: 10.24–25.
71 *Naishadhiyacarita* 1.132. *Naishadhiyacarita*, with the commentary of Narayana, edited by Pandit Shivadatta, fourth edition, Bombay: Nirnaya Sagar Press, 1912.
72 Yadava, B. N. S. (2001) "Chivalry and Warfare" in *Warfare and Weaponry in India 1000–1800*, edited by Jos J. L. Gommans and Dirk H. A. Kolff, Delhi: Oxford University Press: 66–99. Yadava's article was originally published as part of his book *Society and Culture in Northern India in the Twelfth Century*, Allahabad, 1973.
73 Yadava (2001): 66–68.
74 *Vasavadatta* 27, 28. *Vasavadatta. A Sanskrit Romance by Subandhu*, translated by Louis H. Gray, Delhi: Motilal Banarsidass, 1962.
75 Ibid.: 53.
76 Ibid.: 54–55.
77 Warder, A. K. (1988) *Indian Kavya Literature*, vol. V, Delhi: Motilal Banarsidass: 413ff. and 441ff.
78 *An Anthology of Sanskrit Court Poetry*. Vidyakara's "Subhashitaratnakosha", translated by Daniel H. H Ingalls, Cambridge, MA: Harvard University Press, 1965: 403.
79 *The Subhashitaratnakosha*, compiled by Vidyakara, edited by D. D. Kosambi and V. V. Gokhale, with an introduction by D. D. Kosambi, Cambridge, MA: Harvard University Press, 1957: xli.
80 Ibid.: xlv.
81 Stein, M. A. (1900) *Kalhana's Rajatarangini. A Chronicle of the Kings of Kashmir*, Westminster: Archibald Constable: 133; *The Rajatarangini of Kalhana*, edited by

Durgaprasada, Bombay Sanskrit Series, Nos. XLV and LI, vol. I (1892), and vol. II (1894), Bombay: Government Central Book Depot.

82 Ibid. vol. 2: 15–16; vol. 1: 133.

83 Stein, Burton (1998) "All the King's *Mana*: Perspectives in Kingship in Medieval South India" in *Kingship and Authority in South Asia*, edited by J. F. Richards, Delhi: Oxford University Press: 133–189, esp. 142–156.

84 Stein, B. (1989) *Vijayanagara*, The New Cambridge History of India, Cambridge: Cambridge University Press: 16. Dundas, Paul (1992) *The Jains*, London: Routledge: 101–103.

85 Qvarnström, Olle (1998) "Stability and Adaptability: A Jain Strategy for Survival and Growth" *Indo-Iranian Journal* 41: 33–55.

86 Stein (1998): 142f.

87 Handiqui, Krishna Kanta (1949) *Yashastilaka and Indian Culture*, Sholapur: Jaina Samskriti Samrakshaka Sangha: 98.

88 Ibid.: 107.

89 Ibid.: 444–454.

90 Ibid.: 116.

91 *Nitivakyamritam* by Somadeva Suri, ed. and trans. by Sudhir Kumar Gupta (original text with Hindi and English translations), Jaipur: Prakrita Bharati Academy. Verse 1.2.

92 Bhaskar, Bhagchandra Jain (1987) "Conception of Non-Violence in Jainism and World Peace" in *Ideal, Ideology and Practice*, edited by N. K. Singhi, Jaipur: Printwell Publishers: 212–219.

93 Zydenbos, Robert J. (1999) "Jainism as the Religion of Non-Violence" in *Violence Denied. Violence, Non-Violence and the Rationalization of Violence in South Asian Cultural History*, edited by Jan E. M. Houben and Karel R. Van Kooij, Leiden: Brill: 194.

94 Ibid.: 185–211.

95 Ibid.

96 Dundas (1998): 176.

97 Ibid.: 185–186.

98 *Nitivakyamritam* 22.14.

99 Ibid.: 22.17.

100 Ibid.: 30.5.

101 Ibid.: 30.27.

102 Ibid.: 30.12.

103 Ibid.: 30.15.

104 Shantiparvan, 97.3.

105 Johnson, James Turner (1981) *Just War Tradition and the Restraint of War. A Moral and Historical Inquiry*, Princeton, NJ: Princeton University Press.

106 Yadava (2001): 92.

107 Ibid.

108 Handiqui (1949): 444.

109 Thomas Aquinas translated and edited by Sigmund, Paul E. (1988) *St. Thomas Aquinas on Politics and Ethics*, New York and London: W. W. Norton: 64–65.

110 For an interesting discussion of the conflict from the point of view of just warfare, see Mehendale, M. A. (1995) *Reflections on the Mahabharata War*, Shimla: Indian Institute of Advanced Study.

111 *The Nitisara or Elements of Polity by Kamandaki*, 10.26.

Bibliography

Aho, James A. (1981) *Religious Mythology and the Art of War: Comparative Religious Symbolism of Military Violence*, London: Aldwych.

Barhaspatya Sutram, edited with an introduction and English translation by F. W. Thomas, Lahore, 1921.

Basham, A. L. (1954) *The Wonder that was India*, London: Sidgwick & Jackson.

Bhaskar, Bhagchandra Jain (1987) "Conception of Non-Violence in Jainism and World Peace" in *Ideal, Ideology and Practice*, edited by N. K. Singhi, Jaipur: Printwell Publishers: 212–19.

Bodin, Jean (1992) [1583] *On Sovereignty. Four Chapters from The Six Books of the Commonwealth*, edited and translated by Julian H. Franklin, Cambridge: Cambridge University Press.

Brekke, Torkel (2002) *Religious Motivation and the Origins of Buddhism*, London: RoutledgeCurzon.

Brekke, Torkel (2004) "Wielding the Rod of Punishment – War and Violence in the Political Science of Kautilya" *Journal of Military Ethics* 3(1): 40–52.

Brekke, Torkel (2005) "The Ethics of War and the Concepts of War in India and Europe" *Numen* 52: 59–86.

Brockington, J. L. (1984) *Righteous Rama*, Bombay: Oxford University Press.

van Buitenen, J. A. B. (1981) *The Bhagavadgita in the Mahabharata*, a bilingual edition, Chicago, IL: University of Chicago Press.

Clooney, Francis X. (2003) "Pain but Not Harm: Some Classical Resources toward a Hindu Just War Theory", in *Just War in Comparative Perspective*, edited by Paul Robinson, London: Ashgate: 109–26.

Davis, Richard H. (1997) "The Iconography of Rama's Chariot" in *Making India Hindu*, edited by David Ludden, Oxford and Delhi: Oxford University Press: 27–54.

Derrett, D. J. (1976) "Rajadharma" *Journal of Asian Studies* 35: 597–609.

Derrett, J. Duncan M. (1965) "A Newly Discovered Contact between Arthashstra and Dharmashstra: The Role of Bharuci" *Zeitschrift der deutschen morgenlän dischen gesellschaft* cxv/1: 134–52.

Dundas, Paul (1992) *The Jains*, London: Routledge.

Dundas, Paul (forthcoming) "The Non-Violence of Violence: Jain Perspectives on Warfare, Asceticism and Violence".

Gombrich, R. (1996) *How Buddhism Began. The Conditioned Genesis of the Early Teachings*, London and Atlantic Highlands, NJ: Athlone Press.

Handiqui, Krishna Kanta (1949) *Yashastilaka and Indian Culture*, Sholapur: Jaina Samskriti Samrakshaka Sangha.

Heesterman, J. C. (1985) *The Inner Conflict of Tradition. Essays in Indian Ritual, Kingship and Society*, Chicago, IL: University of Chicago Press.

Inden, Ronald (1998) "Ritual, Authority and Cyclic Time in Hindu Kingship" in *Kingship and Authority in South Asia*, edited by J. F. Richards, Delhi: Oxford University Press: 41–91.

Jatavallabhula, Danielle Feller (1999) "Ranayajna: The Mahabharata War as a Sacrifice" in *Violence Denied: Violence, Non-violence and the Rationalization of Violence in South Asian Cultural History*, edited by Jan E. M. Houben and Karel R. Van Kooij, Leiden: Brill. Brill's Indological Library: 97–103.

Johnson, James Turner (1981) *Just War Tradition and the Restraint of War. A Moral and Historical Inquiry*, Princeton, NJ: Princeton University Press.

Jolly, J. (1913) "Arthashastra und Dharmashastra" *Zeitschrift der deutschen morgenlän dischen gesellschaft* lxvii: 49–69.

Keen, Maurice (1965) *The Laws of War in the Late Middle Ages*, London: Routledge & Kegan Paul.

Kelsay, John (1990) "Religion, Morality, and the Governance of War: The Case of Classical Islam" *Journal of Religious Ethics* 18(2): 124.

Klimkheit, Hans-Joachim (1976) "Der Politische Hinduismus der Neuzeit" in *Der Religionswandel unserer Zeit im Spiegel der Religionswissenschaft*, edited by Gunther Stephenson, Darmstadt: Wissenschaftliche Buchgesellschaft: 94–108.

Kulke, Hermann (ed.) (1998) *The State in Indian Tradition: 1000–1700*, Delhi: Oxford University Press.

Lamotte, Étienne (1976) *Histoire du Bouddhisme Indien*, Louvain la Neuve: Institute orientaliste.

The Laws of Manu, translated by Wendy Doniger with Brian K. Smith, London: Penguin Books, 1991.

The Mahabharata, edited by V. S. Sukthankar and S. K. Belvalkar, Poona, Bhandarkar Oriental Research Institute, 1948.

Mehendale, M. A. (1995) *Reflections on the Mahabharata War*, Shimla: Indian Institute of Advanced Study.

Murray, R. H. (1960) *The Political Consequences of the Reformation: Studies in Sixteenth-Century Political Thought*, New York: Russell & Russell.

Prakash, Om (1977) *Political Ideas in the Puranas*, Allahabad: Panchanada Publications.

Preus, J. Samuel (1979) "Machiavelli's Functional Analysis of Religion: Context and Object" *Journal of the History of Ideas* 40(2): 171–190.

Qvarnström, Olle (1998) "Stability and Adaptability: A Jain Strategy for Survival and Growth" *Indo-Iranian Journal* 41: 33–55.

Russell, Frederick H. (1975) *The Just War in the Middle Ages*, Cambridge: Cambridge University Press.

Scharfe, Hartmut (1989) *The State in Indian Tradition*, Leiden: E. J. Brill.

Sigmund, Paul E. (1988) *St. Thomas Aquinas on Politics and Ethics*, New York and London: W. W. Norton.

von Simson, Georg (1969) "Die Einschaltung der Bhagavadgita im Bhishmaparvan des Mahabharata" *Indo-Iranian Journal* 11(3): 173.

Stein, B. (1989) *Vijayanagara*, The New Cambridge History of India, Cambridge: Cambridge University Press.

Stein, Burton (1998) "All the King's *Mana*: Perspectives in Kingship in Medieval South India" in *Kingship and Authority in South Asia*, edited by J. F. Richards, Delhi: Oxford University Press.

Stein, M. A. (1900) *Kalhana's Rajatarangini. A Chronicle of the Kings of Kashmir*, Westminster: Archibald Constable.

Stein, Otto (1922) *Megasthenes und Kautilya*, Wien: Akademie der Wissenshcaften in Wien.

Thapar, Romila (1961) *Ashoka and the Decline of the Mauryas*, Oxford: Oxford University Press.

Thapar, Romila (1984) *From Lineage to State. Social Formations in the Mid-First Millennium B.C. in the Ganga Valley*, Bombay: Oxford University Press.

Warder, A. K. (1988) *Indian Kavya Literature*, Vol. V, Delhi: Motilal Banarsidass.

Wink, André (2001) "Sovereignty and Universal Dominion in South Asia" in *Warfare and Weaponry in India 1000–1800*, edited by Jos J. L. Gommans and Dirk H. A. Kolff, Delhi: Oxford University Press: 99–133.

Winternitz, Maurice (1985) *History of Indian Literature*, Vol. 3, Part 2: The scientific literature, Delhi: Motilal Banarsidass. Translated by Subhadra Jha.

Yadava, B. N. S. (2001) "Chivalry and Warfare" in *Warfare and Weaponry in India 1000–1800*, edited by Jos J. L. Gommans and Dirk H. A. Kolff, Delhi: Oxford University Press: 66–99.

Zydenbos, Robert J. (1999) "Jainism as the Religion of Non-Violence" in *Violence Denied. Violence, Non-Violence and the Rationalization of Violence in South Asian Cultural History*, edited by Jan E. M. Houben and Karel R. Van Kooij, Leiden: Brill.

4

IN DEFENSE OF DHARMA

Just war ideology in Buddhist Sri Lanka[1]

Tessa Bartholomeusz

Stanley Hauerwas has called attention to the role that cultural and religious narratives (or stories) play – whether of the Nuer or of the Christian – in shaping the moral decisions that individuals make. Like Steven Kemper, who has argued that, in the Sri Lankan context, stories do not work on people without their knowledge,[2] Hauerwas maintains that actors in ethical predicaments test stories for their efficacy.

Hauerwas's project is constructive; his aim is to "call attention to the manner in which [Jesus'] story teaches us to know and do what is right under definite conditions,"[3] a calling unrelated to this study. Nevertheless we can heed his request to pay attention to narratives as we ponder ethical systems. This study takes advantage of Hauerwas's point of view, inasmuch as it establishes the significance of narrative for ethical reflection and is concerned with the narratives that constitute a particular ethical dilemma in a particular culture – namely, defense of Buddhism in Sri Lanka. Such a study will reveal that, while there is a narrative thread in Sri Lankan Buddhist history and in contemporary rhetoric that endorses pacifism, there are Buddhist stories that argue that, for the defense of Buddhism – that is, of the Dharma – violence and war are permissible, even necessary, under certain conditions. In other words, this study will probe a type of Buddhist "just-war thinking" that calls into question scholarly obedience to the canon's narratives of pacifism. Moreover, inasmuch as the data suggest that Sri Lankan Buddhists have taken (and take) full advantage of the range of resources available to them to legitimate their ethical stance on war – namely, canonical and post-canonical stories – this study aims to demonstrate that inquiry into the full heritage of Sinhala-Buddhist ethics should not be limited to a survey of the Pali canon.[4]

Many interpreters of Sri Lankan (Sinhala) Buddhism have paid sole attention to the canonical narrative of pacifism, thus prompting us to take the imagined ultra-pacific Buddhism as the real one. This is as true of the European scholar as it is of the Sri Lankan. For instance, a Sri Lankan Buddhist monk-scholar, the Venerable Palane Siri Vajiranana, writing in 1940 during the Second World War, urged pacifism as he cited H. Fielding Hall's *The Soul of a People*:

There can never be a war of Buddhism. No ravished country has ever borne witness to the prowess of the followers of the Buddha; no murdered men have poured out their blood on their hearth-stones, killed in his name . . . He and His Faith are clean of the stain of blood. He was the preacher of the Great Peace, of love, of charity, of compassion, and so clear in His teaching that it can never be misunderstood.[5]

In this example of comparative missiology, a formulaic remnant of Buddhist–Christian relations dating to the mid-eighteenth century, Buddhism is superior to Christianity because it is non-violent. For the venerable monk, as well as for Hall, Buddhism never has allowed – nor ever will allow – for the possibility of war: the example of the Buddha's life, as well as his teachings, prove as much. There are no two ways about it.

In a more recent evaluation of Buddhism and war, Gananath Obeyesekere argues that "in the Buddhist doctrinal tradition . . . there is little evidence of intolerance, no justification for violence, no conception even of 'just wars' or 'holy wars'." In fact, Obeyesekere reinforces his claim by maintaining that "one can make an assertion that Buddhist doctrine is impossible to reconcile logically with an ideology of violence and intolerance."[6] Notwithstanding Obeyesekere's point of view, quite a few Sri Lankan Buddhists – monks and laity alike – have argued for a less clear-cut picture regarding doctrinal prescriptions for war and for peace. Some of the Sri Lankan Buddhists I interviewed[7] cited the very doctrinal tradition – with its rich mosaic of stories about the Buddha – that Obeyesekere argues is devoid of just-war ideology, to legitimate their point of view. Indeed, though the majority referred to post-canonical narratives, many nevertheless argued that the canon itself contains the seeds for a just-war ideology.

As is well known, study of European (Christian) just-war tradition has isolated a set of concerns dubbed just-war criteria. While these criteria are a product of scholarship on Christianity, as John Kelsay has made clear they are not uniquely Christian.[8] Indeed, these criteria provide a useful set of concepts for analyzing religious traditions that must balance claims of non-violence with the realities of war. For Kelsay, all religious traditions that take seriously the presumption that inflicting harm against others is morally problematic will contain just-war thinking of some sort.[9] In short, religious thinking, be it Jewish, Christian, Muslim, Hindu,[10] or Buddhist, that takes seriously the relationship of ethics, morality, and power, contains just-war thought.[11] And while here I use the tools of comparative religion, particularly Christian ethics, to illuminate Sinhala Buddhism, an overriding concern of this study, of which this chapter is a small part, is to isolate the particularly Buddhist nature of the ethical world view of Sinhala Sri Lanka.

Though, as I hope to demonstrate, just-war thinking is no stranger to Sri Lankan Buddhism, it is also obvious and indisputable that stories of pacifism abound in Sinhala Sri Lanka. The story recounted most frequently by the Buddhists I interviewed during fieldwork in the summers of 1997 and 1998 that lays a foundation for pacifism is that of the Buddha's alleged second trip to Sri Lanka, recounted in the post-canonical *Mahavamsa*. In that story, as some of my informants argued, the Buddha's actions "embody," using Hauerwas's language,[12] the ideology of pacifism: the Buddha interrupts a war between rival factions by inspiring the would-be combatants with a sermon. In short, for some of my informants, that story, as well as canonical injunctions regarding non-violence, promote pacific behavior. At the same time, as other Buddhists maintained, there are narratives, both canonical and post-canonical, which by their very nature run counter to the foundation of Buddhist pacifism and thus allow for war.

Before we refer to the stories that provide justifications for war, it is important to note that many of the (approximately fifty) monks and laity that I interviewed for this study are well known in Sri Lanka as proponents of "finishing the war," that is, of eradicating the Liberation Tigers of Tamil Eelam (LTTE) who, since 1983, have been unabashed in their claims for a "homeland" in the north of the island. In other words, the high profile of the Buddhist defenders of the government's resort to war – in and of itself – supports the premise of this chapter – namely, that Buddhists have and do justify war. And while the war that has ensued as a result of territorial claims has no readily identifiable religious component, Buddhist monks and laity alike justify – with Buddhist rhetoric – the predominately Sinhala and predominately Buddhist government's use of deadly force to quash the LTTE. As we shall see, proponents of the war – who couch their justifications in Buddhist rhetoric – argue that preservation of the integrity of Sri Lanka is tantamount to "just cause" for war. It must also be stressed, however, that those who make arguments for war – based on their interpretation of Buddhism – also maintain that Buddhism demands compassion and non-violence. How to balance the demands of non-violence with the protection of the entire island of Sri Lanka as a Buddhist territory has remained a constant feature of political and religious rhetoric in Sri Lanka since at least the 1890s, when archival resources allow for a comprehensive view.

In the 1990s, of course, with an actual war raging in the north of Sri Lanka, the discussion about war has moved from the realm of the theoretical to the reality of the deaths, since 1983, of thousands upon thousands of Tamils and Sinhalas.[13] Which has, to say the least, issued forth many responses, some of which condemn the war, others of which support it. No matter the position, it is generally supported by Buddhist stories. Indeed, in one of my interviews conducted in 1998, the Venerable Athuraliya Rathana, who is the coordinating secretary of the National Sangha Council, alleged that there are many stories in the canon that depict the Buddha as an advocate of force and violence if there is just cause.[14] Some of these stories are about the Buddha; others are told by him. The Venerable Rathana cited, among others, the *Cakkavatti Sihanada Sutta*, which depicts a king, committed to the Dharma, who is flanked by a four-fold army nonetheless. For the monk, these images suggest that even the Buddha, who taught that the paradigmatic Buddhist king is a pacifist, realized that war is a reality of life and that, for defensive measures, war can be justified.[15] For the monk, the *Cakkavatti Sihanada Sutta* provides the contemporary Sri Lankan government (which is predominately Sinhala and

Buddhist) with the Buddhist justification it needs to proceed with the war against the LTTE. A Buddhist layman, the outspoken and controversial Nalin de Silva, suggested that the reason that the king could be righteous and teach pacifism in the first place had to do with his having an army: "only after non-Buddhists saw his army could he pacify them and bring them to Buddhism." Thus, for de Silva, the army in the *sutta* is a vehicle for forcing people – through subtle manipulation – to convert to the Dharma. Moreover, in de Silva's line of thinking, the presence of the army indicates that even a righteous Buddhist king might have to fight a defensive war to protect Buddhism.[16]

In addition to canonical stories, post-canonical narratives have been used by Sri Lankan Buddhists to justify violence, even war. For example, a monk, writing in 1957 to the newspaper, the *Bauddha Peramuna* – a forum for Buddhist monks to air their grievances – employed a post-canonical Buddhist story of war to legitimate the appropriate use of violence. In fact, the monk was provoked by what he considered to be misuse of a Sri Lankan Buddhist story: he took exception to an allusion of Buddhism and war in a local paper that aligned the then prime minister, S.W.R.D. Bandaranaike, with Dutugemunu, the Buddhist hero of the fifth-century, post-canonical *Mahavamsa*. In his editorial, the monk asks Bandaranaike "to read the *Mahavamsa*," the text that chronicles the history of Buddhism in Sri Lanka, and to heed its lessons: "Dutugemunu conquered by the sword and united the land [Sri Lanka] without dividing it among our enemies [i.e. the Tamils] and established Sinhala and Buddhism as the state language and religion."[17]

In his allusion to the great Buddhist king Dutugemunu – who, according to the *Mahavamsa*, interrupted "*damila*" suzerainty over Anuradhapura, an ancient northern kingdom of the island – the monk correspondent of the *Bauddha Peramuna* justified violence against the Tamil minority who, for him, constituted the island's "enemies," just as they did (from the monk's point of view) in Dutugemunu's day. (It is important to note that, whatever the *Mahavamsa*'s meaning of the Pali word *damila*, the Sinhala word for Tamil is *demala*, while twentieth-century Sinhala interpreters of Dutugemunu's war against *damilas* translate *damila* as Tamil, *demala*.[18])

It is significant that the Sinhala-Buddhist monk reflected on Dutugemunu's story in the context of Bandaranaike's 1957 attempts to appease the Tamil minority's demands for protection of their language and territory against a vocal Sinhala (and predominately Buddhist) opposition. While Bandaranaike had the support of the *sangha*, the Buddhist monks, as he campaigned in 1956 on a "Sinhala-only" policy that, for all intents and purposes, alienated the minorities, his 1957 "about face" regarding the minorities, particularly the Tamils, enraged many monks and laity alike. Indeed, in 1959, the Venerable Mapitagama Buddharakkhita, a Buddhist monk whose name appeared in the media in conjunction with an ongoing discussion in the late 1950s on the propriety of monastic involvement in secular affairs,[19] organized Bandaranaike's assassination, while the Venerable Talduwe Somarama pulled the trigger – killing Bandaranaike – ostensibly for acquiescing to the Tamils. Though it is nearly impossible to know exactly what the monks were thinking as they plotted Bandaranaike's assassination, it is reasonable to assume that they were guided in part by readings of the *Mahavamsa*, particularly given the Buddhist rhetoric of his day that linked the island to the Sinhala-Buddhist people. For instance, it was not uncommon in the late 1950s to pick up the newspaper and read an article about a politician or other Buddhist notable referring to Sri Lanka as the island (*dwipa*) of the Dharma – *dharmadwipa* (in English transliterations, variations of *dharmadwipa* include combinations of Sinhala, Pali, and Sanskrit: *dhammadeepa*; *dharmadeepa*; *dhammadweepa*; *dhammadwipa*), a slogan whose ideology is enshrined in the *Mahavamsa*. To illustrate, Sirimavo Bandaranaike, the wife of the prime minister, in a series of speeches regarding education and its relationship to Buddhism, referred to Sri Lanka as *dharmadwipa* on various occasions,[20] while the Inspector General of Police (IGP) lamented that, given the 1958 riots in Sri Lanka, it is only by "a true understanding of the religion [Buddhism] both by precept and practice . . . that Lanka will become Dhammadwipa."[21] For both Mrs. Bandaranaike and the IGP, Sri Lanka's status as *dharmadwipa* was a status worth preserving; for others the ideology of *dharmadwipa* laid the foundation for claims that the island belonged solely to the Sinhala-Buddhist people, thus providing the justification for defensive violence.

Voices similar to our *Bauddha Peramuna* monk, whose ideas about war are shaped by the Dutugemunu story, and the involvement of monks in Bandaranaike's assassination, awaken us to something that many have refused to believe – namely, that some Buddhists, not unlike Christians, Muslims, and Hindus, have justified violence, even war, if certain criteria are met. And what are those criteria that lay the foundation for a just war in Sinhala Buddhism?

Sinhala-Buddhist just war: texts and contexts

In order to answer this, we must turn to the Buddhist narratives, to the stories, that provide models for resolving ethical quandaries. These stories are found in the Pali canon, as well as in the post-canonical *Mahavamsa*, cited by the *Bauddha Peramuna* monk. Regarding the *Mahavamsa*, since the 1980s scholarship on Sri Lanka has focused upon the *Mahavamsa* as the text that lays the foundation for the Sinhala people's claim to be *the* preservers of Buddhism. In a nutshell, that scholarship has revealed that, according to contemporary readings of the *Mahavamsa*, some Sinhalas maintain that they are the Buddha's chosen people, and that the island of Sri Lanka is the Buddhist promised land.[22] An illustration of this point of view appeared in the summer of 1998, during the ongoing controversy in the island regarding the devolution of power, which would grant Tamils in the north a certain amount of autonomy. According to a "letter to the editor" penned by a Sinhala, one S. Perera,

> Rome is sacred to the Catholics, so is Jerusalem to the Jews, and so is
> Mecca to the Muslims. The tiny island in the Indian Ocean . . . where the

Sinhalese lived for over 25 centuries . . . is the hallowed land of Sinhala Buddhists.[23]

Though the letter does not directly refer to the *Mahavamsa*, it reiterates a claim made by many who explicitly cite the text – namely, that "every sq. mm of this island is sacred to the Sinhalese."[24] For the letter writer, Sri Lanka is a sacred island because the Buddha, by word and by deed, declared it to be so: according to the *Mahavamsa*, the Buddha made three magical trips to Sri Lanka, each time colonizing another area of the island, in preparation for the formal introduction of Buddhism two centuries after his death. Thus, Perera's view – based on readings of the *Mahavamsa* – that the entire island is the sacred home of the Sinhalas *and* of Buddhism and, therefore, is not to be divided. Philosophy of Perera's ilk has been elucidated by H. L. Seneviratne, who has argued persuasively that the *Mahavamsa*'s story of the establishment of Buddhism in Sri Lanka, in which the "island of Sri Lanka and its inhabitants, as the guardians of Buddhism, are placed under divine protection,"[25] continues to resonate in the present.

In his analysis of the *Mahavamsa* story regarding the establishment of Buddhism in Sri Lanka, R. A. L. H. Gunawardana has argued that there is dissonance between the Buddha of *Mahavamsa* and the Buddha of the Pali canon, the latter of which provides the textual foundation of Sri Lankan Buddhism (and Theravada Buddhism, generally).[26] In that study, Gunawardana maintains that the *Mahavamsa* story about the Buddha's alleged first visit to the island, in which he rids Sri Lanka of forces inimical to Buddhism, provides the warrant for the use of violence for the sake of Buddhism.

According to Gunawardana's reading of the *Mahavamsa*, the Buddha's expulsion of the *yakkhas* – the non-human inhabitants of the island – contrasts with descriptions in the Pali canon of the Buddha taming similar creatures. In reinforcing the distinction, Gunawardana argues that while in the canon the Buddha uses compassion to convince non-believers of his Dharma, in the *Mahavamsa*, the Buddha uses force; in his "taming" of the *yakkhas*, the Buddha who, in the story, is referred to as the "Conqueror" (*Jina*), imposes "devious afflictions" upon the non-believers, driving them from their homeland.

Building on Gunawardana's study of the *Mahavamsa*, I would like to add that the *Mahavamsa*'s story of the Buddha's first visit to the island, "For Lanka was known to the Conqueror where his doctrine should shine in glory" (I.20), introduces, for the first time, King Dutugemunu, who is the subject of ten of the thirty-seven chapters of the *Mahavamsa*,[27] and to whom we have already referred. We meet Dutugemunu early in the *Mahavamsa*'s chapter one, immediately after the Buddha, who has eventually placated the *yakkhas*, bequeaths to Sri Lanka a bodily relic for worship. Having acceded to the requests of a deity for a relic, the Buddha gives the deity a handful of his own hair, which he allows to be encased in a reliquary to be worshiped. In recounting this episode, the author of the *Mahavamsa* then adds that, eventually, after the death of the Buddha, a collarbone of the Conqueror is brought to Sri Lanka; it is placed in the same reliquary as the Buddha's gifted hair, and the reliquary itself is fortified. The third and final fortification of the reliquary is

Dutugemunu's, "while he made war upon the damilas" (I.41) who (we learn in later chapters of the *Mahavamsa*), are illegitimate rulers of Anuradhapura. Inasmuch as relics (and their encasement) have the symbolic function of establishing Buddhism,[28] it is significant that the story of the acquisition of the island's first bodily relics of the Buddha are linked to the military campaigns of Dutugemunu. Dutugemunu's conquest of the damilas is homologized to the Buddha's conquest of the *yakkhas*, while the Buddha's bestowal upon the island of his bodily relics are completed by the warrior-king Dutugemunu who, in fortifying the reliquary, symbolically provides for the further ensconcing of Buddhism in Sri Lanka. Put differently, the *Mahavamsa*'s first-chapter comparison of the two conquerors – namely, the Buddha and King Dutugemunu – symbolized by the reliquary but obvious in their campaigns – enmeshes the two defenders of the Dharma in one lesson about the limits of, and justification for, violence and war.

To return to the scene of the *Mahavamsa* that our *Bauddha Peramuna* monk recalled in his critique of Bandaranaike, we see Dutugemunu, after his war with the damilas, looking "back upon his glorious victory, great though it was, [he] knew no joy, remembering that thereby was wrought the destruction of millions (of beings)" (xxv.101–104). Burdened by the death of millions of warriors, his troubled conscience prohibits him from celebrating his victory over the damila king, Elara. In the scene that follows, each of the criteria for "just cause," or what scholars refer to as the most important elements of just-war thought, are expounded by none other than fully enlightened beings, *arahants*, living symbols of the dhamma, symbols thus of the duty of non-violence. Indeed, we learn that just cause for war in the *Mahavamsa* includes, in the words of just-war scholars, establishing a "just order,"[29] in this case, Buddhism. Dutugemunu does not go to war for glory, but rather to protect the Dharma.[30]

Scholars who presume that Buddhism places an absolute duty of non-violence on Buddhists have argued that the *Mahavamsa* scene of the *arahants'* justification of Dutugemunu's protection of the Dharma itself warrants justification.[31] Many of my informants' reading of the episode, however, is that the scene contains its own justification. According to some of the Buddhists I interviewed in the summers of 1997 and 1998, Dutugemunu's saga provides contemporary Buddhists with the criteria to argue for just war (*dharma yuddhaya*); the saga reminds them that they can be faced with conflicting obligations – namely, the obligation of non-violence and the duty to protect the Dharma, which might call for violence. Put differently, according to my informants' reading, the *Mahavamsa*'s rendering of ethical duties is based on prima facie responsibilities rather than on absolute duties. In other words, the duty of non-violence can be overridden – though the justification to do so is extremely weighty – if certain criteria are met. In the *Mahavamsa*, just-war thinking provides a scenario in which Dutugemunu's violent actions are justified and in which non-violence – rendered palpable by Dutugemunu's guilt – remains the guiding force.

The reading that Dutugemunu's duty of non-violence has been overridden by his duty to establish Buddhism further throughout the island is plausible in light of the exchange between the *arahants* and the troubled king. With their power to read the king's mind, they discern his profound discomfort for having taken life (that is, the lives of King Elara with sixty thousand men), and eight of them travel to his side to console him. He asks them how he will ever find comfort, considering what he had done, that he had killed such a lot of people. The *arahants* respond with their own just-war thinking:

> Only one and a half human beings have been slain here by thee, O lord of men. The one had come unto the (three) refuges, the other had taken unto himself the five precepts. Unbelievers and men of evil life were the rest, not more to be esteemed than beasts. But as for thee, thou wilt bring glory to the doctrine of the Buddha in manifold ways; therefore cast away care from the heart, O ruler of men.
>
> (xxv.108–112)

In other words, the enlightened beings counsel Dutugemunu with their criteria for assessing his war with the damila king, which includes Dutugemunu's sacrifice of his obligation as a Buddhist not to take life. For the *arahants*, spreading the religion constitutes just cause for war; it constitutes sacrificing one moral obligation for another.

In the narrative of Dutugemunu's angst and the *arahants*' logic, the monk-author of the text lays the foundation for an internal dialog regarding ethical responsibilities. Indeed, some of my monk and lay informants volunteered that the story demonstrates that Dutugemunu would have preferred not to have used violence, but nonetheless had a responsibility to engage in a war in order to defend the Dharma. Cast in the language of ethics, the rhetoric hinges on the notion that some ethical obligations, no matter how weighty, must be compromised if there is just cause. In other words, in the Dutugemunu narrative the ethical obligation to practice Buddhist non-violence is compromised for a very good reason, namely the spread or protection of the Dharma. Which allows for the *arahants*' logic that only one and one-half persons were actually killed, or the idea of proportionality in just-war discourse. And proportionality, or the criterion that in the end more good than evil has been performed,[32] had been met from the point of view of the enlightened beings.

In a 1998 example of the idea of proportionality and of just cause, a Buddhist, who refers to himself or herself in the press as "a student," argues that the war in Sri Lanka against Tamil terrorism can be justified from a Buddhist point of view: "Many people opposing the war . . . say . . . that it is very unBuddhistic and say . . . that the Buddhists [who advocate the war] are going against the teachings of Lord Buddha and support killing."[33] The editorial's Buddhist argument for just war then proceeds like this: if your house is attacked by wasps, and you try to protect your house and, if in the protection, wasps are killed, "It's not actual killing that takes place."[34] In this line of thinking, the Buddhist obligation of non-violence should be compromised in order to protect, recalling the logic of the *arahants* in the *Mahavamsa*. Moreover, the deaths that ensue – in this case, they are rationalized away – are proportional to the need for violence, even war.

The just-war thinking reflected in the editorial is not limited to apolitical discourse. Indeed, in the summer of 1998, General Ratwatte, the architect of the present government's war against the LTTE, was homologized to Dutugemunu on various occasions.[35] The comparison was first made by the Buddhist monk, the Venerable Sobitha Thera, a proponent of "finishing the war," on Ratwatte's birthday.[36] Now labeled by some as the modern-day Dutugemunu, Ratwatte – who like Dutugemunu has waged a war against the "Tamils" – has become the embodiment of contemporary Buddhist just-war ideology in Sri Lanka. Moreover, as the Venerable Sobitha's remarks indicate, the rhetoric regarding General Ratwatte is an instance of the power of stories, in this case of the *Mahavamsa*, to shape the ethical life, thus reminding us of Hauerwas's theory of narrative and ethics.

Conclusion

In the present, as my study indicates, Sri Lankan Buddhists avail themselves of a variety of Buddhist stories – canonical and post-canonical – to support their point of view regarding war. And because there are no pronouncements in the stories attributed to the Buddha or in those stories told about him that declare un-equivocally and directly that war is wrong, the military metaphors of the stories allow for a variety of interpretations. Some Buddhists, as we have seen, argue that the stories directly or indirectly permit war under certain circumstances, while others argue that war is never acceptable. Whether they justify war or not, these Buddhists engage the stories – sometimes the very same ones – to argue their points of view. Put differently, and using Charles Hallisey's presentation of Buddhist ethics, one might say, then, that Buddhist stories are "discursive sites where Buddhists [have] debated the scope and validity of the different ethical theories."[37] Like Hauerwas, Hallisey sees in Buddhist moral stories a reflection of the ethical quandaries that religious people debate and their resolution, as well as models of and for behavior.

Moreover, Hallisey argues that Theravadin stories reveal that when Buddhists make moral decisions, they sometimes assume a kind of "ethical particularism," which may make them appear more inconsistent in their moral choices than the pluralism of the tradition might otherwise suggest. In short, Hallisey maintains that some Theravada Buddhist ethics insist on a sensitivity to context. For Hallisey, ethical particularism is tantamount to prima facie duties, a subject taken up (without reference to Buddhism) by W. D. Ross.[38] Hallisey suggests that "Ross's account of prima facie duties does not suggest that some moral principles are more important than others; it also eschews any attempt to discover any consistency in the things which we take to matter morally."[39] (I find useful Ross's language of prima facie responsibilities, and Hallisey's expression of them, even though Ross fails to capture the texture of moral theory that Hauerwas's nuanced discussion of narratives offers.) Inasmuch as the just-war thinking reviewed here suggests that when Sri Lankan Buddhists discuss the war in their country, they are sensitive to the context, it can reasonably be concluded that their thinking, like the Buddhist stories they embody, reflects a type of ethical particularism rather than an ethical system of absolutes.

The subject of just-war thinking in (Sinhala) Buddhism demands a larger inquiry than space allows here. Though this chapter is part of a larger project that explores the relationship between canonical and post-canonical Buddhist narratives and their use in Sri Lankan political and religious rhetoric since the late nineteenth century, my hope is that, by presenting some of my ideas at this early stage, I will help to nurture a scholarly conversation that takes seriously a dimension of Buddhism that we very often fail to notice.

Notes

1 A version of this chapter was read at the 27th Annual Conference on South Asia, Madison, Wisconsin, October 16, 1998. I would like to thank Charles Hallisey, Aline Kalbian, John Kelsay, and Jonathan Walters for their contribution to this study.
2 Kemper, Steven (1991) *The Presence of the Past: Chronicles, Politics, and Culture in Sinhala Life*, Ithaca, NY: Cornell University Press: 19.
3 Hauerwas, Stanley and L. Gregory Jones (1989) *Why Narrative? Readings in Narrative Theology*, Grand Rapids, MI: William B. Eerdmans Publishing: 159.
4 For a similar argument, see Hallisey, Charles (1995) "Ethical Particularism in Theravada Buddhism," *Journal of Buddhist Ethics*, vol. 3: 6.
5 Cited in Venerable Palane Siri Vajiranana Maha Nayaka (1940) "Light to All the World," *The Buddhist*, vol. xi, no. ii (June): 25.
6 Obeyesekere, Gananath (1995) "Buddhism, Nationhood, and Cultural Identity," in *Fundamentalisms Comprehended*, edited by Martin E. Marty and R. Scott Appleby, Chicago, IL: University of Chicago Press: 233.
7 In the summer of 1997, my research was funded by a generous grant from the American Institute of Sri Lankan Studies, while in 1998, the study was funded by a Florida State University Committee on Faculty Research Support grant.
8 John Kelsay has argued that "just war criteria, while historically connected with Christian moral thinking, are nevertheless not strictly 'Christian'." See Kelsay, John (1989) "The Just War Tradition and the Ethics of Nuclear Deterrence," *International Journal on the Unity of the Sciences*, vol. 2, no. 2 (Summer): 229–252.
9 In a further exposition of just-war criteria and non-Christian tradition, Kelsay explores the moral perspective of Muslims as they prepared for, and justified, the Iran–Iraq conflict and the Gulf War. See Kelsay, John (1993) *Islam and War: The Gulf War and Beyond*, Louisville, KY: Westminster Press.
10 See Obeyesekere's study of the *Bhagavad Gita* in (1993) "Duttagamini and the Buddhist Conscience," in *Religion and Political Conflict in South Asia*, edited by Douglas Allen, Delhi: Oxford University Press: 141–142.
11 Here, I have expanded upon Kelsay's ideas in "The Just War Tradition,": 231.
12 Hauerwas, Stanley (1986) *The Peaceable Kingdom*, Notre Dame, IN: University of Notre Dame Press: 120.
13 From the Sri Lanka Net: COLOMBO, Dec. 9 (Reuters): "Battle casualties in Sri Lanka's ethnic war have risen sharply since the ruling People's Alliance coalition came to power in 1994 on a platform of peace, according to official statistics published on Wednesday. The Daily News, quoting defence ministry figures, said 19,457 people, including 1,338 civilians, had been killed in major battles since November 1994, shortly after the government of President Chandrika Kumaratunga came to power. The state-owned newspaper said 8,208 troops and 9,911 Liberation Tigers of Tamil Eelam

rebels had died. The statistics mark a sharp rise in battle casualties. In the 11 years before November 1994, a total of 15,655 soldiers, rebels and civilians were killed in major battles while 8,635 troops were wounded and 1,087 soldiers and 218 civilians were listed as missing, the newspaper said. It said 17,492 soldiers were wounded in major battles in the last four years alone, while 1,321 troops and 187 civilians had been classified as missing in that time. The government two years ago estimated the total number of people killed in the war at 50,000. The People's Alliance came to power after elections in August 1994 pledging to talk to the rebels to bring peace to Sri Lanka. But talks broke down and in 1996 the government launched Operation Jayasikuru (Sure of Victory) to wrest control of a bitterly contested strategic highway to the north of the country. The government said last Friday that Jayasikuru had ended, but that it had launched a fresh offensive against the rebels."

14 Space does not permit a fully detailed account of these passages. Among them, the Venerable Rathana cited the *Kutadanta Sutta*, the *Alavika Sutta*, and the *Baka Jataka*.

15 Interview with the Venerable Athuraliya Rathana, August 22, 1998, Colombo. My assistant, Yashodara Sarachchandra, conducted the interview.

16 Interview with Nalin de Silva in Maharagama on July 30, 1998.

17 *Bauddha Peramuna* (untitled editorial), 21 September 1957, 2.

18 According to the Oxford English Dictionary, "Tamil" is the "native name (known in the 8th century) of the people and language; in Pali and Prakrit Damila, Davila, Dravida, Sinhalese Demala, Sanskrit Dramila, Dramida, Dravida."

19 See, for instance, the letter to the editor, "Wither LSSP," *Daily News*, 14 October 1958.

20 For instance, "'Religious Education is Lacking' – PM's Wife," *Daily News*, 18 October 1958; and "PM's Wife on the Role of Dhamma Schools," *Daily News*, 15 November 1958.

21 "'Follow Example of Gunananda Thero,' says IGP," *Daily News*, 23 September 1958.

22 For a summary of this scholarship, see Bartholomeusz, Tessa J. and Chandra R. de Silva (1998) "Buddhist Fundamentalism and Identity in Sri Lanka," in *Buddhist Fundamentalism and Minority Identities in Sri Lanka*, edited by Tessa J. Bartholomeusz and Chandra R. de Silva, Albany, NY: State University of New York Press: 1–35.

23 S. Perera, "Sinhala Grievance – the Metadata" *The Daily News*, 25 August 1998.

24 Ibid.

25 Seneviratne, H. L. (1997) "Identity and the Conflation of Past and Present," in *Identity, Consciousness and the Past*, edited by H. L. Seneviratne, Oxford: Oxford University Press: 8. (First published in *Social Analysis*, no. 5, September, 1989.)

26 Gunawardana, R. A. L. H. (1976) "The Kinsmen of the Buddha: Myth as Political Charter in the Ancient and Early Medieval Kingdoms of Sri Lanka," Colombo: Social Scientists' Association, n.d.: 53–62. (Reproduced from *Sri Lanka Journal of Humanities*, vol. 2, no. 1, 1976.)

27 Seneviratne (1997): 8.

28 For more on the role of relics in Sri Lankan Buddhism, see Trainor, Kevin (1997) *Relics, Ritual, and Representation in Buddhism: Rematerializing in the Sri Lankan Tradition*, Cambridge: Cambridge University Press.

29 Childress, James (1982) *Moral Responsibility in Conflicts*, Baton Rouge, LA: Louisiana State University Press: 75.

30 In his meditation of Dutugemunu's conscience, Obeyesekere notes that "Duttagamini claims that his war was not for the joy of sovereignty but to establish the doctrine of the Buddha." See Obeyesekere (1993): 142.

31 Among them, see Greenwald, Alice (1978) "The Relic on the Spear: Historiography and the Saga of Duttagamini," in *Religion and Legitimization of Power in Sri Lanka*, edited by Bardwell Smith, Chambersburg, PA: Anima Publishers: 13–35.

32 Childress (1982): 77.
33 "That's Not Killing!," *The Island*, 13 May 1998.
34 Ibid.
35 For example, "Princely Warrior Not for Polls," *Sunday Leader*, 2 August 1998.
36 "Splits in the Alliance and Protest Campaigns over Polls," *Sunday Leader*, 19 July 1998.
37 Hallisey (1995): 3.
38 It is important to acknowledge that Ross is at odds with Hauerwas, particularly regarding the manner in which we come to know what the rules of ethical behavior are.
39 Hallisey (1995): 4.

Bibliography

Bartholomeusz, Tessa J. and Chandra R. de Silva (1998) "Buddhist Fundamentalism and Identity in Sri Lanka," in *Buddhist Fundamentalism and Minority Identities in Sri Lanka*, edited by Tessa J. Bartholomeusz and Chandra R. de Silva, Albany, NY: State University of New York Press: 1–35.

Childress, James (1982) *Moral Responsibility in Conflicts*, Baton Rouge, LA: Louisiana State University Press.

Greenwald, Alice (1978) "The Relic on the Spear: Historiography and the Saga of Duttagamini," in *Religion and Legitimization of Power in Sri Lanka*, edited by Bardwell Smith, Chambersburg, PA: Anima Publishers.

Gunawardana, R. A. L. H. (1976) "The Kinsmen of the Buddha: Myth as Political Charter in the Ancient and Early Medieval Kingdoms of Sri Lanka," Colombo: Social Scientists' Association, n.d.: 53–62. (Reproduced from *Sri Lanka Journal of Humanities*, vol. 2, no. 1, 1976.)

Hallisey, Charles (1995) "Ethical Particularism in Theravada Buddhism," *Journal of Buddhist Ethics*, vol. 3.

Hauerwas, Stanley (1986) *The Peaceable Kingdom*, Notre Dame, IN: University of Notre Dame Press.

Hauerwas, Stanley and L. Gregory Jones (1989) *Why Narrative? Readings in Narrative Theology*, Grand Rapids, MI: William B. Eerdmans Publishing.

Kelsay, John (1989) "The Just War Tradition and the Ethics of Nuclear Deterrence," *International Journal on the Unity of the Sciences*, vol. 2, no. 2 (Summer): 229–252.

Kelsay, John (1993) *Islam and War: The Gulf War and Beyond*, Louisville, KY: Westminster Press.

Kemper, Steven (1991) *The Presence of the Past: Chronicles, Politics, and Culture in Sinhala Life*, Ithaca, NY: Cornell University Press.

Obeyesekere, Gananath (1993) "Duttagamini and the Buddhist Conscience," in *Religion and Political Conflict in South Asia*, edited by Douglas Allen, Delhi: Oxford University Press: 141–142.

Obeyesekere, Gananath (1995) "Buddhism, Nationhood, and Cultural Identity," in *Fundamentalisms Comprehended*, edited by Martin E. Marty and R. Scott Appleby, Chicago, IL: University of Chicago Press.

Seneviratne, H. L. (1997) "Identity and the Conflation of Past and Present," in *Identity, Consciousness and the Past*, edited by H. L. Seneviratne, Oxford: Oxford University Press.

Trainor, Kevin (1997) *Relics, Ritual, and Representation in Buddhism: Rematerializing in the Sri Lankan Tradition*, Cambridge: Cambridge University Press.

Part III

EAST ASIA

5

MIGHT MAKES RIGHT

Just war and just warfare in early medieval Japan

Karl Friday

"War," observed Michael Walzer, "is always judged twice," first in regard to the reasons for fighting, and then in regard to the methods. Medieval writers, he notes, formulated this distinction as "a matter of prepositions," distinguishing *jus ad bellum* from *jus in bello*.[1] To this one might add that the wars of peoples like the Japanese are always judged thrice by Western audiences, as they are further measured against the military conventions that evolved in Europe.

Japan's famous warrior order arose during the early part of the Heian period (794–1185), as part of a generalized trend toward the privatization of government functions. Its genesis was a shift in imperial court military policy that began in the middle decades of the eighth century: bit by bit, the government ceased trying to draft and drill the population at large and concentrated instead on co-opting the privately acquired skills of martially talented elites, through a series of new military posts and titles that legitimized the use of the personal martial resources of this group on behalf of the state. In essence, the court moved from a conscripted, publicly trained military force to one composed of privately trained, privately equipped professional mercenaries. As it happened, government interest in the martial talents of provincial elites and lower-ranked court nobles dovetailed with growing private demands for these same resources spawned by competition for wealth and influence among the premier houses of the court. This fusion of state and private needs opened new opportunities for advancement to young men with military talent. The greater such opportunities became, the more enthusiastically and the more seriously such young men committed themselves to the profession of arms. The result was the gradual emergence of the *bushi*, an order of professional fighting men in the countryside and the capital.

In 1180, Minamoto Yoritomo, a dispossessed heir to a leading *bushi* house, adeptly parlayed his own pedigree, the localized ambitions of provincial warriors, and a series of upheavals within the imperial court into the creation of a new institution – called the shogunate, or *bakufu*, by historians – in the eastern village of Kamakura. The first shogunate was a government within a government, at once a part of and distinct from the imperial court in Kyoto. Its principal functions were to oversee eastern Japan and the country's military affairs, based on authority delegated it by the court. But the establishment of this new institution also set rolling a snowball that would expand until it bowled over and completely destroyed Japan's classical polity. In the thirteenth century, shogunal vassals across the country discovered that they could manipulate the insulation from direct court supervision offered them by the Kamakura regime, to lay stronger and more personal claims to the lands they ostensibly administered on behalf of the powers-that-were in the capital. During the next two centuries, a new warrior-dominated system of authority gradually supplanted the older, courtier-dominated one, and real power over the countryside began to spin off from the center to the hands of local figures.

By the second quarter of the fourteenth century, this evolution had progressed to the point where the most successful of the shogunate's provincial vassals had begun to question the value of continued submission to Kamakura. Thus when a deposed emperor, posthumously known as Godaigo, issued a call to arms against the shogunate, among those who answered him were Ashikaga Takauji and Nitta Yoshisada, both descendents of Minamoto Yoritomo and sometime commanders of Kamakura armies. In 1333 Yoshisada captured Kamakura and destroyed the shogunate. Two years later Takauji broke with Godaigo and drove him from the capital. In 1336, after annihilating Yoshisada's army in the Battle of Minatogawa, he established a new shogunate, under himself, headquartered in the Muromachi district of Kyoto. Under the new regime warriors not only dominated the countryside, but overshadowed the imperial court as well.

The circumstances attendant to the birth and childhood of the samurai, then, differed markedly from those of the knights of northern Europe. This chapter will explore the ways that the socio-political climate in which the early *bushi* functioned shaped early medieval (tenth to fourteenth century) Japanese customs and beliefs regarding just war and the ethics of battle, and the reasons these conventions diverged so widely from European notions of *jus ad bellum* and *jus in bello*.

Justifying war

The Western tradition of just war theorizing has its earliest roots in pre-Christian cultures, but just war doctrine proper was developed by Catholic theologians, who incorporated earlier ideas into their philosophies and whose positions were in turn later combined and secularized by legal and military thinkers. Augustine, Gratian, Thomas Aquinas, and other Church canonists and theologians began from the fundamental question: is it ever justifiable for Christians to participate in war? The just war theory they evolved permits Christians to take part in certain forms of violence under particular conditions, but also demands limitations on the form and extent of such violence.[2]

Japan generated no explicit literature or dialog of its own on what circumstances rendered it morally acceptable for the state to direct its military power at its own subjects or at outsiders, and instead seems to have drawn the philosophical base it needed for such decisions from Chinese – predominantly Confucian – principles.[3] Chinese ideas about war were carried into Japan along with other bits of sinology over the course of the sixth and seventh centuries, and provided the framework for the military institutions of the *ritsuryo* codes, which in turn served as the guiding principles of the state's military system from the eighth through the end of the fourteenth centuries.[4] Following the Chinese model, the Japanese court viewed warfare with foreign powers and peoples as an extension of domestic law enforcement and justified it accordingly. For the most part this was easy, inasmuch as nearly all of Japan's encounters with foreign enemies during the classical and medieval periods were defensive.[5]

The court's efforts to establish control over the northeastern part of Honshu, ongoing from the late seventh to the early ninth centuries, represented the only significant offensive military action of the era undertaken against an enemy outside the control of the imperial state.[6] Court communications cast these campaigns as "pacification" efforts (*seii*), and the *emishi* people against whom they were directed, as criminals and rebels:

> Because [military action] brings hardship to the people, We have long embraced the broad virtue [and have eschewed war]. [But] a report from Our generals makes it clear that the barbarians have not amended their wild hearts. They invade Our frontiers and ignore the instructions of the Sovereign. What must be done cannot be avoided. . . . Immediately dispatch the army to strike down and destroy in a timely fashion.[7]

> These bandits are like wild-hearted wolf cubs. They do not reflect on the favors We have bestowed upon them but trust in the steepness of [the terrain around their bases] and time and again wreak havoc upon Our frontiers. Our soldiers are a formidable weapon, but they cannot stop [these depredations]. Be it thus: mobilize 3000 troops and with these cut off the rebel progeny; with these put out the smoldering embers.[8]

From the perspective of the law – of the state as a corporate entity – the fighting between *bushi* that constituted most of the warfare of the early medieval period was judged by the same criteria. Recourse to arms was just when and only when it was sanctioned by the state *in advance*. The principle that final authority and formal control rested with the central government was a key feature of Japan's military and police system from the late seventh century until well into the fourteenth. The state jealously guarded its exclusive right to sanction the use of force throughout the Heian and Kamakura periods and attempted to do so, albeit with lessening success, under the Muromachi regime as well.

Throughout the Heian period all major military officers were appointed by the imperial court; all but the most minor criminal problems were first reported upward, and the appropriate action was decided upon and ordered by the Council of State.

Any form of military action undertaken without a Warrant of Pursuit and Capture (*tsuibu kanpu*) was subject to punishment.[9]

After the 1180s, many of the court's military/police functions shifted to the shogunate, but the essential premise of central control over the right to violence remained intact. The Kamakura regime's first and most important piece of legislation, the *Goseibai shikimoku*, was unequivocal on this issue: "No person, even one whose family have been hereditary vassals of the shogun for generations, shall be able to mobilize troops for military service without a current writ."[10]

The Muromachi regime had similar policies. A 1346 supplement to the shogunate's legal code, the *Kemmu shikimoku*, made this clear:

> Even those who have cogent, long-standing complaints must first petition the Shogun and follow his judgment. To willfully initiate hostilities with attendant loss of life constitutes a crime that cannot easily be tolerated. In the case of offensive warfare, even when the original petition is justified, usurpation of [the Shogun's authority in this area] constitutes a crime that will not be tolerated. Still more so when there is no justification. Henceforth, this will be strictly forbidden. Violators shall, in accordance with the original law [of the *Goseibai shikimoku*], have their property confiscated and be subject to exile. Accomplices shall also have their property confiscated. If they have no property, they shall be exiled, in accord with the details just outlined. Cases of defensive warfare by persons other than the lawful holder of the lands shall constitute the same crime as offensive warfare. If a person acts out of justifiable reason, judgment shall be made according to the particulars of the case.[11]

Thus until the mid-fourteenth century at least, Japanese law made an unambiguous distinction between lawful military action, in which one (or more) of the parties involved possessed a legal warrant, and unlawful, private fights. It is tempting then, to simply equate just war with the former, and dismiss the latter as criminal behavior.

But there are important complications to what might otherwise be a very simple picture here. For, legalities notwithstanding, it is clear that warriors did engage in fighting for reasons other than being called to service on behalf of the state, that they were doing this from the very beginning of their history, and that they felt morally justified in doing so.

Private warfare among the Bushi

One of the most important forms of private warfare during the late classical and early medieval periods was *bushi* involvement in the political intrigues of the upper court aristocracy. Throughout the Heian period, intensifying competition for wealth and influence created a demand among the great houses of the court for bodyguards and other private military resources.[12] Dramatic or large-scale examples of recourse to arms in pursuit of political aims were rare, but attempts at assassination and intimidation were by no means uncommon.[13]

The attitude of warriors toward participation in this sort of affair is neatly showcased in an anecdote involving Minamoto Yorinobu, said to have taken place around 990:

> Yorinobu was a retainer of [Fujiwara Michikane]. Now and then he would say, "If I were to be ordered by my lord to kill [his rival, Michitaka], I would take up my sword and run to his home; who could defend him against me?" When [Yorinobu's father] Yorimitsu heard this, he was greatly surprised, and restrained Yorinobu, saying, "In the first place, the likelihood of successfully killing him would be exceedingly small. In the second place, even if you were to succeed, this evil deed would prevent your lord from becoming Chancellor. In the third place, even if he were to become Chancellor, you would have to protect him unerringly for the rest of his life, which would be all-but impossible."[14]

Clearly neither Yorinobu nor his father were bothered by the fact that the action he was contemplating was illegal, and therefore ostensibly unjust. Their concerns about the advisability of the action center exclusively on its practicality. The fact that the hypothetical assassination would be ordered by Yorinobu's patron, and that it would stand a reasonable chance of success (or, as their discussion determined, that it would not) was justification enough for them.

From the perspective of the warriors involved, military actions undertaken on behalf of aristocratic employers were not, of course, very far removed from actions conducted in possession of warrants. In either case the warrior was acting on orders from above. From the mid-ninth century the state itself was becoming privatized: among the upper nobility, a growing identity developed between hereditary status and government office-holding, and many key government functions came to be performed through essentially private channels. Correspondingly, public and private rights and responsibilities became increasingly hard to separate.[15] Under such circumstances, warriors probably made little practical distinction between orders from state officials and (private) orders from courtier patrons.

But not all private warfare was initiated by or for the aristocracy. Early *bushi* had a highly developed sense of personal honor, and were quick to the saddle in order to protect or advance it. Breaches of etiquette and failure to show proper respect often led to violent consequences. In 989, for example, two *bushi* in the capital got into a quarrel over drinks and "went to war," in the process shooting down several officers sent to quiet them. In 1241 Miura Yasumura and some of his relatives were having a drinking and dancing party in a "lascivious house" near Shimoge Bridge in Kamakura, while warriors of the Yoki, Oyama, and Naganuma households were having a similar party near the other end of the bridge. At some point during the festivities, Yoki Tomomura took it into his head to practice some long-distance archery, and began chasing and shooting at a dog outside the house. Unfortunately, one of his arrows went wild, and ended its flight in a screen in the house where the Miura were gathered. Tomomura sent a servant to ask for the arrow back, but the Miura refused, instead scolding Tomomura for his rudeness. An argument quickly ensued and before long both sides had assembled mounted troops and began a full-scale battle.[16]

Malicious gossip carried between warriors by third parties also appears to have frequently prompted *bushi* to gather troops and take to the field.[17] The seriousness of gossip and personal insults is reflected in the language of shogunal laws:

> Battle and killing often arise from a base of insults and bad-mouthing of others. In momentous cases the perpetrator shall be punished by exile; in lighter cases, he shall be punished by confinement. If, in the course of judicial proceedings, one party should bad-mouth the other, the dispute shall be settled in favor of his enemy. Further, if his argument is otherwise without merit, he shall have another of his holdings confiscated. If he has no holdings, he shall be punished by exile.[18]

Filial piety and familial honor were a third cause of private warfare.[19] Large-scale vendettas were surprisingly rare, but attempts to avenge slights or crimes against family members were common enough and troublesome enough to merit specific mention in twelfth-century shogunal law:

> Next, in the case of a son or grandson who kills the enemy of his father or grandfather, said father or grandfather shall also be punished for the crime, even if he protests that he had no knowledge of it, because the father or grandfather's enmity was the motive that gave rise to the act. Next, if a son should kill in order to seize a man's post or steal his valuables, the father shall not be judged guilty, provided he maintains he had no knowledge of the act and has documentary proof of this.[20]

Overt attempts at self-aggrandizement by armed force provided yet another source of unsanctioned military encounters. Such skirmishes were a minor, albeit ongoing, phenomenon from the tenth century, and became increasingly common-place during the Kamakura and Muromachi periods.[21]

And warriors were sometimes drawn into the quarrels of their vassals and retainers. Taira Masakado's rebellion (935–940), which first became a matter of concern to the central government when Masakado led troops into Hitachi province, to plead the case of one of his men with the acting governor of Hitachi, is probably the most famous example of this phenomenon.[22]

Bushi values and courtier values

In principle, the state's exclusive right to sanction violence ought to have robbed private war of any righteousness but clearly it did not. Instead, the notion of just war seems to have broadened over the course of the tenth to thirteenth centuries, making increasing room for the existance of legitimate battle, even in the absence of formal legality. Significantly, but not surprisingly, this expansion of the parameters of what constituted just cause for employing organized violence paralleled the rise of the *bushi*. In particular, the state's willingness to tolerate at least small-scale military activities conducted for enhancing or preserving personal profit grew at a pace just a few steps behind the court's dependence on private warriors for law enforcement. The government's increasingly liberal attitude toward private conflicts between *bushi* can be seen in the punishments meted out to violators of the peace, which varied considerably with time and political circumstance.

During the Heian period, warriors engaged in private fighting at their peril: in 1049, for example, Minamoto Yorifusa, a former governor of Kaga, clashed with troops belonging to Minamoto Yorichika, the governor of Yamato, near a temple in Nara, causing the deaths of several monks by stray arrow shots. The court responded by arresting both warriors, and exiling them. Similarly, in 988, Taira Korehira and Taira Muneyori found themselves banished as the result of a private feud. A century later Fujiwara Motohira was called swiftly to task for his armed attempt to defend long-held perquisites over his lands in Mutsu province, and escaped punishment only by pleading ignorance and offering the troop commander during the incident, his nephew and retainer Inunoshoji Sueharu, as a scapegoat; Sueharu was executed, along with five of his men.[23]

The court was only slightly more tolerant when unauthorized military actions served the public interest. The most celebrated case in point began in 1083, when Minamoto Yoshiie, serving as governor of Mutsu, found himself drawn into a conflict between two powerful warriors resident in the province, Kiyowara Sanehira and Kiyowara Iehira. As Yoshiie prepared to move against Iehira, he informed the court that the Kiyowara were in rebellion against the state, and asked for authorization to proceed. But the court, suspecting that Yoshiie's motives were more personal than public, refused to endorse the campaign. Undaunted, Yoshiie went ahead anyway, launching what became known as the "Latter Three Years' War" of 1083–87. Once he had secured his victory, Yoshiie petitioned the Council of State for rewards for himself and his men. The court, however, stood firm in its refusal to sanction the action, forcing a frustrated Yoshiie to reward his troops from his own pocket. Yoshiie had violated the court's rules of war, and thus no reward could be forthcoming. Perhaps, however, because his campaign was helpful to the state, or perhaps because of his tremendous popularity in both the provinces and at court, he was able to avoid serious punishment. A scant four years before the campaign in the north, Yoshiie himself had been sent by the court to "pursue and capture" Minamoto Shigemune for engaging in a private fight with Minamoto Kunifusa in Mino.[24]

The Kamakura shogunate, forced to maintain a delicate balancing act between satisfying its mandate from the court to maintain law and order, and not alienating its vassals, on whose support it depended for continued existence, was much more tolerant than the imperial court of small-scale private warfare in the provinces. In

Kamakura times armed incursion into neighboring lands and use of force to extort estate residents and proprietors alike became commonplace. While shogunal edicts described attempts at self-aggrandizement through force of arms as "outrages" (*ranbo*), "evil acts" (*akugyo*), or "depradations" (*rozeki*), severe punishments were almost never imposed. Most often, those judged guilty of activities of this sort were simply ordered to cease and desist. Occasionally recalcitrant warriors were threatened with fines, imprisonment, or the confiscation of their lands and titles, but such threats were seldom carried out. Warrants for arrests were issued and punitive campaigns conducted only when a warrior's military activities were judged to threaten the security of court or the shogunate itself.[25]

During the fourteenth century, the existence of rival imperial courts made it impossible to distinguish public from private war, inasmuch as both courts claimed to be issuing public calls to arms. *Bushi* could therefore justify almost any recourse to violence as public, which lent an unprecedented legitimacy to feuding, with the predictable result that violence became endemic. The inability of central authority to provide meaningful protection for property rights, or to secure public safety, made self-help an essential component of dispute resolution between warriors. Sixty years of this sort of ambiguity reified the custom of warrior self-help, and the shogunate found itself unable to recover control of the situation, even after the era of two courts ended, in 1392.[26]

It is clear, then, that warriors engaged in private warfare with growing frequency and impugnity over the course of the early medieval period. But it is also clear that this represented not a broadening of central government acceptance of private warfare, but a shrinking ability to stop it. In this respect early medieval Japan differed markedly from early medieval Europe, where feuds and duels were essentially legal instruments serving clearly defined purposes and with clearly defined rules and boundaries.[27]

The proliferation of private warfare that occurred over the course of the early medieval period was symptomatic of a fundamental change in Japanese definitions of just war, one that centered on the replacement of courtier values with those of the *bushi* themselves. While the former focused narrowly on central government sanction, the latter broadly embraced the right of warriors to fight on the personal authority of courtier or *bushi* patrons, as well as in pursuit or defense of private profit or matters of honor. The new ethic was nascent during the Heian period, but *bushi* remained politically constrained enough that they were obliged to bow to courtier rules and definitions governing their *droit de guerre*. The Gempei Wars (1180–85) unleashed widespread local violence conducted under the banner of public war, and the Kamakura shogunate that emerged from this fighting found itself unable to fully constrain small-scale private conflicts, because it depended for its existence as much on the backing of its own warrior vassals as on the credibility of its promises to the court to maintain law and order. The fourteenth century witnessed six decades of more-or-less constant civil war, fueled by two competing centers of political legitimation, which made it both possible to wrap almost any private fight in the banner of the larger public war, and impossible for either government to restrain its warriors, lest they simply change allegiance to the other side. The result was the end of any meaningful distinctions between public and private warfare and of the ability of governments in Japan to assert the primacy of centrally dictated law over warrior self-help. Henceforth, *bushi* notions of just war would prevail.

Ethics in war

The Peace of God and Truce of God movements of the tenth and eleventh centuries, and the Second Lateran Council of 1139, were the most systematic attempts by the Church to restrain war by regulation. But the real origins of the principles that governed *jus in bello* in Europe lay outside the Church. During the same period, military, social, technological and economic changes in Europe brought with them a sharp division between the armed noble and the rest of society. The emerging knightly class inherited and thus broadened application of long-established codes of conduct for nobles on the battlefield. The body of custom that emerged seems to have been concerned primarily with regulating the profits, and mitigating the rigors, of conflict. Except in the case of violations of specific disciplinary regulations issued by specific commanders, violations of this body of custom lacked the force of law and were thus not enforceable in any judicial sense. But they became generally accepted – if not universal – through frequent repetition, and because of their innate practical value. The application and observation of such customs of war depended first on their pragmatic advantages, and second on the dictates of honor and reputation.[28]

Scholars have long postulated the existence of gentlemanly norms and conventions underlying the conduct of fighting between the early samurai. Indeed, the two terms that crop up most consistently in descriptions of early samurai warfare are "ritual" and "formalism." Early medieval battles are usually portrayed as set pieces, following an elaborate choreography determined by customary rules, in which the conduct of the fighting often seems to have been more important than the result. Eiko Ikegami's characterization of early medieval warfare as "a complex social ritual of death, honor and calculation," and "actual combats on the medieval battlefield" as "colorful rites of violence, death and honor," is a case in point.[29]

But this vision of early medieval warfare is more epic than epoch, arising not from the battlefield exploits of the *bushi* themselves, but from the imaginations of later littérateurs and *jongleurs* who recounted them. Such creative nostalgia found its most eloquent and best-known expression on the pages of the great medieval war tales: the *Hogen monogatari*, the *Heiji monogatari*, the *Heike monogatari*, and the *Gikeiki*. Modern literary scholars have demonstrated, however, that much of the compelling detail contained in these narratives was in fact largely the product of formulaic techniques of oral composition, not remembered history.[30]

Analyses and descriptions of the gentlemanly rules alleged to have governed early samurai warfare all begin from the common premise that such rules did in fact exist. Historians who have identified and endeavored to explain ritual and formality

167

on early medieval battlefields have done so because they *expected* to find it there. The blinders imposed by preconceptions appear to have restricted these scholars' views of their sources, and precluded serious consideration of alternative interpretations. But closer, more careful analysis of the sources, even the most familiar ones, indicates that Heian and Kamakura period warriors were a good deal less gentlemanly in their battlefield antics than was previously believed. The revised view that has been emerging over the past two decades fits the military culture of this era much more comfortably between the "anything goes" fighting depicted in the ancient legends of the *Kojiki* and *Nihon shoki*, and the equally unapologetic warfare of later medieval times. It is now clear that there was no mysterious degeneration of warrior values and standards of behavior between the late twelfth and late fourteenth centuries; *bushi* approached their craft with substantially the same attitudes in both eras.[31]

Warrior reputation and honor

In early medieval Japan, as in Europe, honor and reputation lay at the heart of a warrior's self-perception, and provide the context within which adherence to the conventions of war must be evaluated. Reputation, honor, and pride, which centered on a man's prowess in combat and his feats of arms, were almost tangible entities that took precedence over all other obligations. Slights to reputation or honor were often catalysts to belligerence and bloodshed. Warriors might refuse orders from their superiors, risk the loss of valuable retainers, and even murder men to whom they owed their lives, all for the sake of their reputations. As a thirteenth-century commentary enumerating the "seven virtues of a warrior" concludes, "To go forth to the field of battle and miss death by an inch; to leave behind one's name for myriad generations; all in all, this is the way."[32]

Honor – or conversely, shame – could reach beyond the warrior himself, and even beyond his lifespan. *Bushi* could prosper through the inherited glory of their ancestors or suffer the stigma of their disgrace. Thus even a warrior's life could be of less consequence to him than his name and image, and we find in accounts of battles numerous sketches of warriors choosing to sacrifice themselves in order to enhance their reputations or those of their families.[33]

We must, however, be careful about making anachronistic or ethnocentric assumptions about the nature of honor or about the sort of battlefield conduct it might be expected to engender. For while concepts of honor and shame were of the profoundest importance to the self-perception of the early *bushi*, honor turned on one's military reputation, which turned first and foremost on one's record of victories. Early medieval Japanese concepts of honor and of honorable conduct in battle appear to have been flexible enough to permit successful warriors to rationalize almost any sort behavior.[34] Thus, unlike their European counterparts, *bushi* were seldom, if ever, faced with choosing between military advantage and adherence to chivalric norms. Pragmatism, self-interest, and tactical, strategic, or political advantage proved to be much more powerful determinants of early medieval Japanese military conventions than abstractions like honor. Warriors in the various sources appear as cool, rational men possessing powerful forces of will and equally powerful egos, and valuing results and success above all else.

Deception, guile and surprise

One of the most important features of the European corpus of customs pertaining to behavior in battle were the rules governing the onset of hostilities. Feudal lords saw a fundamental need to cleanly mark the transition from a state of peace to one of war. It was a serious matter to claim that someone had begun an attack "without keeping his honor" or "without issuing a challenge."[35]

Japan developed no such convention. Although *bushi* did sometimes issue challenges and even set times and places for battle, such promises were honored far more often in the breach than in the event. In fact, the preferred stratagem of early *bushi* was to catch opponents offguard: ambushes, night attacks, and other surprise tactics appear to have been employed in the majority of both public and private military encounters, and the preference for this sort of fighting is reflected even in the later medieval war tales.[36] Heian period audiences considered surprise attacks so normal that an early eleventh-century text begins a description of the archetypal *bushi*, "the greatest warrior in the land," by informing us that "he was highly skilled in the conduct of battles, *night attacks*, archery duels on horseback, and *ambushes*" (emphasis added).[37]

The aplomb with which the early samurai applied deceit and even treachery is striking. The acceptance of both warrior and non-warrior audiences of this sort of behavior is even more so. One of the most revealing accounts of the degree to which Japanese warriors embraced surprise and perfidy in battle concerns a feud between two late tenth-century warriors, Taira Koremochi and Fujiwara Moroto:[38] a dispute over a piece of land festered, fueled by gossip, until at length a challenge was issued and date and place agreed upon. As the day of battle approached, Moroto found himself outnumbered nearly three to one and, apparently deciding discretion to be the better part of valor, fled instead to a neighboring province. The text that records the tale, informs us that "Those who spoke between the two warriors also pronounced favorably on this."

Koremochi, upon receiving this news, determined things were safe and demobilized his men, who had been pestering him to allow them to return to their homes. But shortly thereafter, Koremochi and his household were startled from their sleep by Moroto, approaching with a sizeable force. Moroto's men surrounded Koremochi's compound, set fire to the buildings, and shot down anyone who emerged. When the fire had burned itself out, they searched the ashes, "discovering men of high and low rank, children and the like – all told more than eighty persons – burned to death."

In route home, Moroto stopped near the home of his brother-in-law, to give his troops a rest. The brother-in-law, identified only as okimi ("the great prince"), sent food and *sake*, upon which Moroto's men gorged themselves, until they passed out.

Unbeknownst to them, however, Koremochi was not dead. He had escaped by seizing a robe from one of his serving women, and slipping past the attackers under the cover of the smoke.[39]

"Dropping into the depths of a stream to the west, he carefully approached a place far from the bank where reeds and such grew thickly, and clung to the roots of a willow," where he hid until the fighting was over and Moroto's troops had withdrawn. Some of his own troops who had not been in the house later found him, and re-supplied him with clothing, weapons, and a horse, while he explained what had happened, adding that he had chosen not to flee into the mountains at the beginning of the attack because he feared that "this would leave behind the reputation of one who had run away." His men counseled him to wait and reassemble his forces before going after Moroto, whose troops outnumbered them five or six to one. But Koremoto shook off this advice, arguing:

> Had I been burned to death inside my house last night, would my life exist now? I escaped in this manner at great cost, yet I do not live. To show myself to you for even one day is extremely shameful. Therefore I will not be stingy with this dew-like life. You may assemble an army and fight later. As for myself, I will go [on to attack] alone. . . . No doubt I will send off [only] a single arrow and then die, but to choose otherwise would be a limitless shame for my descendents. . . . Those of you who begrudge your lives need not come with me; I will go alone.

Koremochi and his men then fell upon Moroto's troops, taking them completely by surprise. Drunk and sated, Moroto's side was able to offer only a half-hearted defense, and was soon utterly destroyed. After taking Moroto's head, Koremochi moved on to his home, which he put to the torch.

Building on tactics of betrayal and deception to secure victory was not, of course, by any means unique to Japan. European knights too, applauded cunning, guile, and surprise, even in tournaments, and acknowledged them as fundamental and ubiquitous elements of war.[40] Even so, the Japanese attitude stands out. For in Europe, betrayal and deception were acceptable only within limits, restricted by conventions of war that sought to regulate fighting to the mutual benefit of both sides in any struggle. They were legitimate only because of legalistic loopholes that arose from the formalized rules governing oaths, truces, declarations, and challenges.

Japanese custom lacked all such qualifications. Promises and truces were violated with impunity, as Minamoto Yoritomo demonstrated in his campaign against Satake Hideyoshi, in 1184. Finding that Hideyoshi had ensconced himself behind fortifications, Yoritomo, using Taira Hirotsune, a relative of the Satake, as an intermediary, persuaded Hideyoshi's father, Yoshimasa, to meet him alone, at the center of a bridge leading to Yoshimasa's home. When Yoshimasa reached the meeting point, however, Hirotsune abruptly cut him down, causing many of Yoshimasa's followers to surrender and others to turn and flee.[41]

In plotting strategy, early medieval Japanese warriors seem, for the most part, to have concerned themselves only with the most efficient means to bring about the desired result, with the ends justifying almost any means. The notion that certain sorts of tactics might be "fair" while others were "unfair" was not only inapposite to such deliberations, it was utterly extraneous to *bushi* culture.

Prisoners of war

Another of the key components of medieval European military custom was the conventions surrounding the treatment of surrendered enemies. These centered on the practice of ransoming captured knights back to their families, in exchange for payments in cash or arms, a routine that had precedents in ancient Greek hoplite battle and reappeared in early Frankish warfare, becoming well established by the mid-eleventh century. Knights were not supposed to kill other knights unless it was absolutely necessary. The code of chivalry demanded that a beaten enemy be given quarter and that prisoners be treated as gentlemen to be ransomed for sums not beyond their means to pay. Captivity came to be a form of contract, originally established orally on the field but recorded in writing once the battle was over.[42]

Japanese warriors developed no comparable customs of quarter, custody, and ransom. Instead, the fate of a captured *bushi* depended entirely on the particulars of his case. Some were executed, others released, and still others were recruited into the service of their captors.[43] The divergence of Japanese from European conventions pertaining to prisoners was the result of differing political, social, and technological circumstances.

In point of fact, capture was rare in Japanese warfare. Most prisoners mentioned in the sources were taken into custody as the result of surrender, rather than seizure. One reason for this was probably the nature of the weapons employed by the early *bushi*, inasmuch as it is difficult to use a bow in a manner designed to capture rather than kill – although some attempts to do just this, such as by aiming at horses rather than riders – appear to have been made.[44]

More fundamentally, European feudal custom sanctioned the right to redress personal grievances through force-of-arms, rendering much of the fighting between Christian lords akin to a lawsuit pursued through other means. Warfare was a direct means of securing some form of profit and usually centered on limited, clearly defined objectives. This situation was logically conducive to self-imposed restraints. For when the belligerents could be satisfied by the accomplishment of more limited objectives, there was little reason to gratuitously destroy an opponent, and largesse could readily be seen as a function of enlightened self-interest. Moreover, if the winner achieved his immediate objective by means that brought him the censure of the society around him, he would have realized no long-term profit. The convention of ransom thus satisfied both the desire of knights for financial gain and their desire for self-preservation.

The political structure of early medieval Japan, however, made no allowance for the pursuit of private ends through violence. Rather, the court – and later the shogunate – jealously reserved for itself the exclusive right to sanction the use of armed force. While central authorities were forced, with increasing frequency, to look the other way during private squabbles between warriors, they never dignified such activities with the veneer of legal respectability. Early *bushi* warfare was, therefore, always legitimized under the rubric of criminal, rather than civil, law. One side in any conflict was, by definition, acting in the name of the state, while those on the other were cast as rebels or outlaws. In practice, these labels could shift back and forth over the course of a long drawn war – as they did during the Gempei War, and the *Nambokucho* wars – but in the end the winners could justify their victory only in terms of law enforcement and defense of the polity. This characterization of the purpose of warfare not only made winning the only real imperative (and thereby justified any actions taken toward that end), it defined captured or surrendered enemy warriors as criminals and set the parameters for dealing with them accordingly.

European chivalry, moreover, was a code of conduct for knights – noble warriors – that served to intensify the separation of the knight from the rest of society and, at the same time, to define his obligations to other knights and to other orders. Significantly, the customs that that governed ransom applied only to knights and squires, because they were made practical only by mutual recognition of status and the expectation of reciprocity of treatment.

Early *bushi* had a far less developed sense of group identity and separateness than did their Western counterparts. By the eleventh century, in northern Europe, knights formed the ruling class and nearly all secular rulers were knights. Kings, counts, and other feudal lords all self-consciously identified themselves as *miles*, members of the same *ordo militaris* or *ordo equestris* as their warrior retainers. The awareness of a common bond of knighthood, and concomitant feelings of professional empathy were enhanced by ecclesiastical efforts to define the role of knighthood in Christian society, and by the institution of the tournament, which, among other things, gave knights practice in, and incentive to develop, skills at unseating and capturing opponents relatively unharmed.[45]

The Japan of this same period was still ruled by civil authority; its socio-economic hierarchy still culminated in a civil, not a military, nobility; and the idea of a warrior order was still more nascent than real. Warrior leaders, scions of the lower and middle tiers of the court nobility, still looked to the center and to the civil ladder for success, and still saw the profession of arms largely as a means to an end – a foot in the door toward civil rank and office. And *bushi* at all levels in the socio-political hierarchy still identified more strongly with their non-military social peers, than with warriors above or below them in the hierarchy.[46]

A sense of warriors as a separate estate did not begin to emerge until after the first shogunate was in place. The new institution, which was in essence a kind of warriors' union, created the category of shogunal retainer (*gokenin*), as a self-conscious class of individuals with special privileges and responsibilities. It also narrowed the range of social classes from which *bushi* came. Yoritomo consciously helped foster this new sense of warrior identity by holding hunts and archery competitions.[47]

Thus the different purpose of war, the different weapons employed, and the different view of who they were, and of their responsibilities to one another and to the rest of society, all mitigated against the *bushi* developing customs resembling those of quarter and ransom. Their place and function in the socio-political structure prevented warriors from seeing battle as a sport-like activity properly pursued only by a particular order of sportsmen and also from perceiving prisoners as human booty that could be exchanged for a profit. During the early medieval period, prisoners did not belong to their captors, they belonged instead to the higher authority who sanctioned the military action in the first place.

From the foregoing – and from ideas about medieval samurai values popularized by Second World War era propaganda – one might expect capture to have been regarded as a matter of great shame.[48] And indeed, this conclusion is supported by several passages in late medieval literary works.

One of the most interesting tells of the pursuit by a warrior named Sho Shiro Takaie of one Taira Tsunemasa, in the aftermath of the battle of Ichinotani (1184). Takaie calls to Tsunemasa to turn back to fight him, but Tsunemasa simply looks back, replies, "I'm not running away, I disdain you," and hurries his horse onward. An enraged Takaie declares his intention to "shame him by capturing him alive." He calls to two retainers, and all three take up the chase. But just as they catch up with him, Tsunemasa leaps from his horse and cuts open his belly.[49]

Other sources, however, give a completely different impression – and address the issue more directly. One particularly interesting case in point occurred in 1189, during Minamoto Yoritomo's northern campaign against Fujiwara Yasuhira. Usami Heiji Sanemasa, a member of Yoritomo's army, captured Yuri Korehira, one of Yasuhira's senior retainers, and brought him to Yoritomo's camp. But another warrior, Amano Norikage, disputed Sanemasa's account, claiming instead that he had made the capture. Yoritomo thereby directed Kajiwara Kagetoki to ask the prisoner who caught him. But when Kagetoki attempted to do so, Korehira responded, "Your tone goes too far. . . . To exhaust one's luck and a become prisoner is an ordinary thing for a warrior. You have no call for insolence."

Kagetoki, now furious, reported this to Yoritomo, who agreed that Kagetoki had behaved badly, and directed another retainer, Hatakeyama Shigetada, to take over the questioning. Shigetada took an entirely different tack, kneeling before Korehira, bowing, and arguing that, "To those who deal in bow and horse, becoming the prisoner of an enemy is ordained everywhere, in China as well as our homeland. It is not necessarily to be called shameful. . . . You, sir, now bear the status of prisoner, but ought you create a deep and lasting enmity? I have heard that you are praised in the six districts of Mutsu province as a great warrior leader; need we dispute between us that it was because of your meritorious service as a valiant that you were captured? You must speak now of . . . the man who captured you." A much placated Korehira readily answered Shigetada's questions. Following a brief conversation, Yoritomo entrusted Korehira to Shigetada's care, specifying that he be treated with respect and consideration. Six days later, Yoritomo ordered Korehira pardoned and freed, although he also directed that he not be given back his weapons or armor.[50]

Up through the early 1200s, the fate of prisoners varied, but largely reflected tenets of criminal law. The central figures of enemy armies – those deemed responsible for the conflict – were sometimes severely punished, but the majority of the warriors on the losing side were usually pardoned.[51] It does appear, however, that treatment of captured or surrendered enemy troops hardened over the course of the thirteen and fourteenth centuries. During the fourteenth century, as war became more pervasive, more frequent, and more open-ended, commanders displayed an increased willingness to embrace deserters and turncoats. Warriors, particularly powerful ones, who capitulated or otherwise changed sides before any actual fighting could expect generous treatment and confirmation by their new lord of all or part of their lands. On the other hand, commanders became much less willing than they might once have been to deal with enemy troops captured in battle, perhaps fearing that pardoned troops would simply return to the fight later. Prisoners were viewed as liabilities. Most were summarily executed. The rest were imprisoned, interrogated, and (in most cases) executed later.[52]

Rights of non-combatants

A key premise underlying modern views on military ethics is the notion that war is, or should be, combat between combatants; that those who cannot or do not fight – women, children, old men, priests, neutral tribes or states, and wounded or captured soldiers – are entitled to some degree of immunity from attack. Indeed, some scholars have argued that rules protecting non-combatants are natural, and nearly universal across time and cultures.[53] But while there may be some universality to the sentiment that war ought to be between warriors and only between warriors, in practice the definitions that separate non-combatants from proper belligerents have been closely bound to time and circumstances.

Non-combatants can be defined in terms of their social function – those who by virtue of their occupation cannot or do not make war – or by their circumstances – those who cannot or are not bearing arms at any given time. European notions of who can and cannot be a morally acceptable target or casualty of military action embraced both definitions, being rooted in the medieval Church's efforts to establish immunity for its property and its personnel, and in knightly condescension, born of pride of class, which dictated that knights should defend rather than harm the weak and innocent. But the socio-political structure of early medieval Japan mitigated against the emergence of strong imperatives for non-combatant immunity based on either sort of definition, with the predictable result that warrior treatment of those not directly involved in a particular fight was shaped largely by circumstances of the moment.

In contrast to the monolithic dominion of the Church in Europe, ecclesiastical authority in Japan was fragmented between a half-dozen or so autonomous institutions representing different schools and sects, and maintaining a consciously controlled religious balance among themselves that one historian terms a "doctrinal multitude." The great temples and shrines, moreover, not only competed with one another for patrons and followers, they also contended for secular power with the elite noble houses of the court and (from the late twelfth century) with the shogunate. By the eleventh century, the larger religious institutions had organized themselves along lines parallel to those of the great court houses. Each had its own private administrative headquarters (*mandokoro*), portfolio of rights and perquisites (*shiki*) over private estates (*shoen*), and head abbot, usually of noble or imperial birth, who represented the institution and served as a channel of communication to the other powers-that-were, or *kenmon* (as Kuroda Toshio dubbed them). Many also maintained sizeable private military forces to police their lands, defend the grounds and personnel of the main temple, and enhance their political clout within the capital. Thus the medieval Japanese religious establishment lacked a unified voice through which to dictate military ethics to warriors; and was insufficiently separate from the secular realm to make compelling claims that its lands and its clergy deserved immunity and shelter from warrior activities.[54]

At the same time, early medieval warriors could scarcely have looked upon all non-warriors as inferiors in need of mercy and protection. Defined more by craft than by pedigree, and drawn from lower and middle ranks of the court nobility and the upper tiers of rural society, they were servants and officers of the powers-that-were, not a ruling order unto themselves. And their responsibilities were delimited accordingly.

A description recounted in a thirteenth-century Japanese anthology – and paraphrased in part from the ancient Chinese classic, *Spring and Autumn Annals* – observes that, "the functions of warriors are: to caution against violence, to suppress weapons, to preserve the great, to determine merit, to soothe the people, to pacify the masses, and to enrich assets." It is noteworthy that while this passage enjoins warriors to serve their rulers by controlling the rest of the population, it says nothing about *defending* or *protecting* the people.[55]

Except under unusual circumstances, warriors were seldom prone to worry about non-combatants. Women, children, and others in the proximity of early medieval battles were indiscriminately slaughtered along with the warriors. Raiding, which entailed burning the fields, plundering the houses, and killing the inhabitants of an enemy's lands, was a common tactic. So were sieges of enemy strongholds, which often involved surrounding the compound, setting fire to its buildings, and shooting down any and all occupants who attempted to escape the flames. In at least one case, the houses of a nearby village were demolished for use as kindling for the fire! Women who somehow survived raids, sieges, and other battles – even women of status, such as the wives and daughters of enemy officers – might be handed over to victorious troops to be robbed of their clothing or raped. Those who wished to avoid this fate sometimes committed suicide.[56]

In the rare instances in which *bushi* did take care to distinguish non-combatants, there were specific reasons for doing so. The account of Taira Koremochi's attack on Fujiwara Moroto's home discussed earlier, for example, notes that,

When the flame had been put to all the buildings, Koremochi said, "Lay not a hand on the women, high or low. As for those you might call men,

175

shoot them down as you see them." Standing outside the flames, they shot them all dead.

It is abundantly clear, however, that Koremochi's motive was not mercy or chivalry, but the very practical desire to avoid creating trouble with Moroto's brother-in-law, Okimi:

> After the flames had burned out, Koremochi and his troops returned in the twilight. Approaching the gates of Okimi's house, Koremochi sent in the message, "I cannot come in person. But we have shown no shame to the wife of Lord Koremochi. As she is your younger sister, I have respectfully refrained from any such actions and respectfully present her to you now."

Koremochi's order safeguarding all the women in the household was thus necessary to avoid the possibility that Okimi's sister might have been accidentally or mistakenly harmed. This appears to have been a wise precaution. A few decades earlier, two of Taira Masakado's commanders captured the wives of two of his principal opponents. When Masakado heard about this, he issued orders that they "not be shamed" but he was too late; some low ranking troops (*fuhei*) had already assaulted them, stripping one of the wives naked. In apology, Masakado wrote her a poem and presented her with a set of clothing.[57]

On or off the battlefield, early medieval *bushi* appear to have held little concern for the lives of others, or for distinctions between warriors and non-combatants. Neither the warriors themselves, nor those who chronicled their exploits seem to have attached much impropriety to killing, except under extraordinary circumstances.

But as shocking and brutal as this sort of behavior appears, disregard of medieval *bushi* for the lives and property of non-combatants arose from detachment, professionalism, and pragmatism rather than savagery or cruelty. Their willingness to kill was at least in part related to their willingness to die. In an anecdote that relates Minamoto Yorinobu's rescue of a child taken hostage by a thief, Yorinobu expresses this sentiment dramatically, when he admonishes the child's distraught father – who was also the son of Yorinobu's wetnurse – for losing his composure over the matter:

> Is this a thing to cry about? You must think you have taken on a devil or a deity or some such thing! To cry like a child is a foolish thing. Only one small child – let him be stabbed to death. With this sort of heart does a warrior stand! To think of yourself, to think of wife and children, is to abandon all that is proper to a warrior and his honor. To speak of fearing nothing is to speak of thinking naught of oneself, of thinking naught of wife and child.[58]

Even more fundamentally, however, *bushi* indifference to the fate of third parties stemmed from a single-minded focus on the ends of their actions, with little attention to the moral character of the means. This in turn was at least in part a consequence of *bushi* tactics and ethics having evolved in an age in which military force was mostly employed either in pursuit of criminals, or in pursuit of criminal activity. Non-combatants were viewed as either accomplices to the criminal, or simply as "collateral damage" (to borrow a term from the modern US military).

While just war theorizing has often been portrayed as timeless, especially in the abstract theological treatment of the Thomist circle, it has in fact usually been closely tied to specific times and places. Chivalry was ultimately a uniquely European construct, deeply influenced by the values and the politics of the Church, as well as those of the knightly order that governed secular society.

There is a tempting, superficial resemblance between the military circumstances of early medieval Europe and early medieval Japan – the privatization and pro-fessionalization of war-making, the elite status of men-at-arms, and the tactical focus on mounted warriors – but in the final analysis, the differences in the conditions under which early knights and early samurai lived and fought proved more telling than the similarities. The continued existence of a centralized polity in Japan, the low pedigrees and political weakness of even warrior leaders, the weaker identification of the *bushi* as a class, the existence of a civil nobility above them, the absence of tournaments, the diversified religious establishment, and the military technology of Japanese warriors all combined such that war and the ethics of war bore scant resemblance to the European traditions of *jus ad bellum* and *jus in bello*.

Warfare between early medieval *bushi* was sometimes analogous in purpose to European *bellum hostile*: open, public conflicts between Christian knights who honored – in the intent, if not always in the event – gentlemanly rules of battle, particularly the customs of quarter, ransom, and formal declaration of hostilities. But its conduct much more closely resembled the conditions of *guerre mortelle*, or *bellum Romanum*, fought without privilege of ransom or distinction between combatant and non-combatant.[59]

The two military cultures were, moreover, evolving in opposite directions. In Europe, the parameters of both *jus ad bellum* and *jus in bello* became more restricted and codified as time passed. In Japan, the idea of just war broadened over the course of the medieval period, to incorporate more and more rights to self-help and private (non-centrally sanctioned) conflicts.

Notes

1 Walzer, Michael (1977) *Just and Unjust Wars: A Moral Argument with Historical Illustrations*, New York: Basic Books: 21.
2 Johnson, James Turner (1981) *Just War Tradition and the Restraint of War*, Princeton, NJ: Princeton University Press: xxi–xxxv; Bainton, Roland H. (1960) *Christian Attitudes Toward War and Peace: A Historical Survey and Critical Re-Evaluation*, New York: Abingdon Press: 91–121; Russell, Frederick H. (1975) *The Just War in the Middle Ages*, London and New York: Cambridge University Press: 293–96.

3 Chen-Ya, Tien (1992) *Chinese Military Theory*, Oakville, Ontario: Mosaic Press: 21–22.

4 The *ritsuryo* were the legal codes that defined the structure and operation of the imperial state. There were four such codes, each superseding its predecessors: the Omi Codes of 668, the Kiyomihara Codes of 689, the Taiho Codes of 702, and the Yoro Codes of 718. Only the Yoro Codes remain extant, although it is possible to reconstruct much about the earlier codes from early ninth-century commentaries on the Yoro Codes. See Friday, Karl (1992) *Hired Swords: The Rise of Private Warrior Power in Early Japan*, Stanford, CA: Stanford University Press: 8–69, for a detailed discussion of the ritsuryo military system.

5 Japanese defensive military encounters with foreigners during the classical and medieval periods included scattered and inconsequential troubles with the Korean kingdom of Silla during the ninth and early tenth centuries, an attack by Jurchen forces in 1019, and the Mongol invasions of 1274 and 1281. See Toyohiko, Fukuda (1993) "Senshi to sono shodan," in *Ikusa*, ed. by Fukuda Toyohiko, Tokyo: Yoshikawa kobunkan: 89–92; Tei, Morita (1979) *Ocho seiji*, Tokyo: Kyoikusha: 142–44; Conlan, Thomas (2001) *In Little Need of Divine Intervention: Scrolls of the Mongol Invasions of Japan*, Ithaca, NY: East Asia Program, Cornell University; Kyotsu, Hori (1967) "The Mongol Invasions and the Kamakura Bakufu" (PhD dissertation, Columbia University); Kyotsu, Hori (1974) "Economic and Political Effects of the Mongol Wars," in *Medieval Japan: Essays in Institutional History*, ed. by John W. Hall and Jeffrey P. Mass, New Haven, CT: Yale University Press: 184–200; Koki, Ota (1997) *Moko shorai: sono gunji shiteki kenkyo*, Tokyo: Kinshosha; or Ichiro, Kaizu (1998) *Moko shorai: taigai senso no shakaishi*, Tokyo: Yoshikawa kobunkan.

6 Studies on the *emishi* pacification campaigns in English include: Friday, Karl (1997) "Pushing Beyond the Pale: The Yamato Conquest of the *Emishi* and Northern Japan," *Journal of Japanese Studies* 23, no. 1: 1–24; and Farris, William Wayne (1992) *Heavenly Warriors: The Evolution of Japan's Military, 500–1300*, Cambridge, MA: Harvard University Press: 81–104.

7 *Shoku Nihongi*, in *Shintei zoho kokushi taikei*, Tokyo: Yoshikawa kobunkan: 774 7/23.

8 *Shoku Nihongi*, 780 02/11.

9 Friday (1992): 122–66.

10 *Goseibai shikimoku*, in *Shinko gunsho ruijo*, ed. by Hanawa Hokinoichi, vol. 17, *buke bu 1* (Tokyo: Meicho fukyokai, 1930), 357. An English translation of the entire code appears in Hall, John Cary (1906) "Japanese Feudal Law: The Institutes of Judicature: Being a Translation of 'Go Seibai Shikimoku'; the Magisterial Code of the Hojo Power-Holders (AD 1932)," *Transactions of the Asiatic Society of Japan* 34: 1–44.

11 *Kemmu shikimoku tsuika-ho*, in *Shinko gunsho ruijo*, ed. Hanawa Hokinoichi, vol. 17, *buke bu 1* (Tokyo: Meisho fukyokai, 1930), 366–406. An alternative translation appears in Grossberg, Kenneth A. (1981) *The Laws of the Muromachi Bakufu*, Tokyo: Monumenta Nipponica Monograph: 40.

12 For details see Friday (1992): 32–69, 78–92.

13 See, for example, *Ruijo sandaikyaku*, in *Shintei zoho kokushi taikei* (Tokyo: Yoshikawa kobunkan, 1983), 896 4/2, 905 8/25, 905 11/03; *Honcho seiki*, in *Kokushi taikei* (Tokyo: Yoshikawa kobunkan, 1964), 941 9/19; *Nihon kiryaku*, in *Shintei zoho kokushi taikei* (Tokyo: Yoshikawa kobunkan, 1985), 969 2/7; *Shoyoki*, in *Dainihon kokiroku* (Tokyo: Iwanami shoten, 1959), 985 3/22, 996 1/16; *Heian ibun*, edited by Takeuchi Rizo (Tokyo: Tokyodo, 1965), 15 vols., doc. 372; *Gonki*, in *Zoho shiryo taisei* (Kyoto: Rinsen shoten, 1965), 1000 11/3; *Mido kampakki*, in *Dainihon kokiroku* (Tokyo: Iwanami shoten, 1952), 1016 5/25, 1017 3/11; *Choyoki*, in *Zoho shiryo taisei* (Kyoto: Rinsen shoten, 1965), 1113 4/30, 1114 5/27.

14 *Kojidan*, ed. Kobayashi Yasuharu, *Koten bunko*, vol. 60–62 (Tokyo: Gendai shichosha, 1981), tale #317.

15 Hall, John W. (1966) *Government and Local Power in Japan 500–1700: A Study Based on Bizen Province*, Princeton: Princeton University Press: 116–28.

16 *Nihon kiryaku*, 989 11/23; *Azuma kagami, in Shintei zoho kokushi taikei* (Tokyo: Yoshikawa kobunkan, 1968), 1241 11/29.

17 See, for example, *Konjaku monogatari-sho*, in *Nihon koten bungaku zensho* (Tokyo: Shogakkan, 1971), 23.13, 25.3, and 25.5.

18 *Goseibai shikimoku*, 358–59.

19 See, for example, *Suisaki*, in *Zoho shiryo taisei*, vol. 12 (Kyoto: Rinsen shoten, 1965), 1079 8/30; *Shomonki*, edited by Hayashi Rokuro (Tokyo: Imaizumi seibunsha, 1975), 65; *Mutsuwaki*, in *Gunsho ruijo* (Tokyo: Shoku gunsho ruijo kanseikai, 1941), 23; *Heian ibun*, doc. 2467; *Konjaku monogatari-sho*, 25.4, 25.9; *Shoyoki*, 989 4/4; *Azuma kagami*, 1219 1/27.

20 *Goseibai shikimoku*, 358.

21 Friday (1992): 78–88, 155–56; Yasunori, Oyama (1976) "Kodai makki no togoku to saigoku," in *Iwanami koza Nihonshi kodai 4*, Tokyo: Iwanami shoten: 231–69; Yukio, Endo (1983) "Shuba no to no kodo to seikaku," in *Nihon kodai shi ron'en*, ed. by Endo Yukio, Sensei shoju kinen kai (Tokyo: Kokusho kangyokai), 3–17; Okuno Nakahiko (1985) "Heian ji no gunto ni tsuite," in *Minasho undo to sabetsu-josei*, ed. Minshoshi kenkyokai (Tokyo: Oyama kaku), 5–27; Mass, Jeffrey P. (1974) *Warrior Government in Medieval Japan: A Study of the Kamakura Bakufu, Shugo and Jito*, New Haven, CT: Yale University Press; Mass (1979) *Development of Kamakura Rule 1180–1250: A History With Documents*, Stanford: Stanford University Press dissertation; Mass (1989) *Lordship and Inheritance in Early Medieval Japan: A Study of the Kamakura Soryo System*, Stanford, CA: Stanford University Press; Harrington, Loraine F. (1982) "Social Control and the Significance of the Akuto," in *Court and Bakufu in Japan: Essays in Kamakura History*, ed. Mass, New Haven, CT: Yale University Press: 221–50; Arai Takashige (1990) *Chosei akuto no kenkyo* (Tokyo: Yoshikawa kobunkan); Kaizu Ichiro (1993) "Chosei kokka kennryoku to akuto," *Rekishigaku kenkyo* 646 (6): 9–18; Amino Yoshihiko (1995) *Akuto to kaizoku: Nihon chosei no shakai to seiji* (Tokyo: Hosei daigaku shuppankyoku); Conlan, Thomas (1998) "State of War: The Violent Order of Fourteenth Century Japan" (PhD dissertation, Stanford University): 203–43; Davis, David L. (1974) "Ikki in Late Medieval Japan," in Hall and Mass, *Medieval Japan*: 221–47.

22 Summary histories in English of the Masakado affair appear in Friday (1992): 144–47; and Farris (1992): 131–42.

23 *Fuso ryakki*, in *Kokushi taikei* (Tokyo: Yoshikawa kobunkan, 1965), 1049 12/28, 1050/1/25; *Konjaku monogatari-sho*, 23.13; *Kojidan*, #330.

24 Friday (1992): 109, 175–76; Farris (1992): 233–41; *Fuso ryakki*, 1079 8/17.

25 See, for example, *Kamakura ibun*, edited by Takeuchi Rizo (Tokyo: Tokyodo, 1971), docs. 169, 2231, 2946, 2973, 6254, 6721, or 7354; *Azuma kagami*, 1200 11/1–11/4, 1201 2/3, 1201 4/2–4/6, 1205 6/22, 1205 8/7, 1207 9/24, 1218 1/12, 1241 11/29, 1247 5/21–6/22. The workings of the Kamakura judicial system are discussed in detail in Mass (1979). In the late thirteenth century, Kamakura did make an attempt to rejuvenate its enforcement of centrally dictated law with respect to the right to fight, but by then it was too late, widely perceived as tyrannical and proved the catalyst to rapidly growing vassal hatred of the shogunate. For details, see Conlan (1998): 208–20.

26 Conlan (1998): 220–42.

27 Brunner, Otto (1992) *Land and Lordship: Structures of Governance in Medieval Austria*, translated by Howard Kaminsky and James Van Horn Melton, revised edition, Philadelphia, PA: University of Pennsylvania Press; Johnson (1981): 41–49; Stacey, Robert C. (1994) "The Age of Chivalry," in *The Laws of War: Constraints on Warfare*

179

in the Western World, ed. Michael Howard, George J. Andreopoulos, and Mark R. Shulman, New Haven, CT: Yale University Press: 28–29.

28 Strickland, Matthew (1996) *War and Chivalry: The Conduct and Perception of War in England and Normandy, 1066–1217*, New York and London: Cambridge University Press: 31–54; Stacey (1994): 28–32; Johnson (1981): 123–31.

29 Ikegami, Eiko (1995) *The Taming of the Samurai: Honorific Individualism and the Making of Modern Japan*, Cambridge, MA: Harvard University Press: 97, 98; fuller discussions of early medieval warfare appear on pp. 97–103. Other examples of recent scholarship that has portrayed early medieval warfare as ritualized include: Ishii Shiro, "Kassen to tsuibu," in *Nihon kokuseishi kenkyo II: Nihonjin no kokka seikatsu* (Tokyo: Tokyo daigaku shuppankai, 1986), 14–24; Nishimata Fuso, "Kassen no roru to manaa," in *Gempei no soran*, ed. Yasuda Motohisa (Tokyo: Daiichi hogen, 1988), 146–47; Okada Seiichi, "Kassen to girei," in *Ikusa*, ed. Fukuda Toyohiko (Tokyo: Yoshikawa kobunkan, 1993), 154–81; Seki Yukihiko, "'Bu' no kogen: kocho to yumiya," in *Ikusa*, ed. Fukuda Toyohiko (Tokyo: Yoshikawa kobunkan, 1993), 1–38; Varley, H. Paul (1994) *Warriors of Japan as Portrayed in the War Tales*, Honolulu, HI: University of Hawaii Press; Takahashi Masaaki, "Nihon chosei no sento: yasen no kijosha o choshin ni," in *Tatakai no shisutemu to taigai senryaku (jinrui ni totte tatakai to ha #2)*, ed. Matsugi Takehiko and Udakawa Takehisa (Tokyo: Toyo shorin, 1999), 234–43; Farris (1992): 8–9, 132–33, 231–33, 237–38, 269–70, 298–300; Farris, W. Wayne (1999) "Japan to 1300," in *War and Society in the Ancient and Medieval Worlds: Asia, the Mediterranean, Europe, and Mesoamerica*, ed. Kurt Raaflaub and Nathan Rosenstein, Cambridge, MA: Center for Hellenic Studies, Harvard University: 60–62, 66–67. The image of ritual and formalism in early medieval warfare has been virtually reified in popular and textbook accounts. See, for example, Hane, Mikiso (1991) *Premodern Japan: A Historical Survey*, Boulder, CO: Westview Press: 73–74; Turnbull, Stephen R. (1982) *The Book of the Samurai: The Warrior Class of Japan*, New York: Gallery Books: 19, 22–36; Turnbull, Stephen R. (1990) *The Lone Samurai and the Martial Arts*, London: Arms & Armour Press: 14–28; Newman, John (1989) *Bushido: The Way of the Warrior*, Wigston, Leicester: Magna Books: 13–14, 16–17.

30 Butler, Kenneth D. (1966) "The Textual Evolution of the *Heike Monogatari*," *Harvard Journal of Asiatic Studies* 26: 5–51; Butler, Kenneth D. (1969) "The *Heike Monogatari* and the Japanese Warrior Ethic," *Harvard Journal of Asian Studies* 29: 93–108.

31 A growing body of scholarship implicitly or explicitly rejects the idea of early samurai warfare as ritualized or formalistic. This includes studies by Kondo Yoshikazu, Kawai Yasushi, Fujimoto Masayuki, Yamamoto Koji, Gomi Fumihiko, Thomas Conlan, and myself. In English, see Friday, Karl (1983) *Mononofu: The Warrior of Heian Japan*, Master's thesis, University of Kansas; Friday, Karl (1993) "Valorous Butchers: The Art of War During the Golden Age of the Samurai," *Japan Forum* 5, no. 1 (April): 1–19; Conlan (1998) and (2001); Conlan, Thomas (1999) "The Nature of Warfare in Fourteenth-Century Japan: The Record of Nomoto Tomoyuki," *Journal of Japanese Studies* 25, no. 2: 299–330.

32 *Konjaku monogatari-sho*, 25.6, 29.5; *Kokon chomonjo*, in *Shintei zoho kokushi taikei* (Tokyo: Yoshikawa kobunkan, 1985), 9.13.347, 9.12.333; Strickland (1996): 98–131.

33 See, for example, *Mutsuwaki*, 23, 25–6; *Azuma kagami*, 1180 8/26, 1184 4/21, 1205 6/22, 1221 6/6, 1241 11/29.

34 Matthew Strickland observes that, "despite drawing on established concepts, honor [is] ultimately a personal issue [.] governed by the conscience and self-esteem of the individual" Strickland (1996): 125–31.

35 Strickland (1996): 42–43; Brunner (1992): 65. Brunner notes that, "The *Summa legum* of Raymond of Wiener Neustadt contended that to kill someone 'without a challenge, without open enmity' (*sine diffidacione et sine manifesta inimicitia*) was just murder."

36 Out of 60 episodes recounted in various sources for the tenth to twelfth centuries in sufficient detail to permit judgments concerning the order of battle, 43 involved ambushes or surprise attacks of one form or another. Friday (1993): 8.

37 *Shin Sarugakki*, in *Nihon shiso taikei*, vol. 8 Kodai seiji shakai shiso (Tokyo: Iwanami shoten, 1986), 138.

38 This incident is recounted in *Konjaku monogatari-sho*, 25.5.

39 *Azuma kagami*, 1184 4/21 recounts a similar incident involving a warrior escaping danger disguised as a woman, and even getting a friend to impersonate him and draw off pursuers.

40 Strickland (1996): 128–31.

41 *Azuma kagami*, 1180 11/4.

42 Strickland (1996): 133–38; Ober, Joseph (1994) "Classical Greek Times," in Howard *et al.*: 13–17; Johnson (1981): 126; Stacey (1994): 36–38.

43 *Mutsuwaki*, 25, 26, 31–34; *Choya gunsai*, in *Kokushi taikei* (Tokyo: Yoshikawa kobunkan, 1964), 1058 3/29; *Azuma kagami*, 1187 8/15, 1190 8/16. See also Kawai Yasushi, *Gempei kassen no kyozo o hagu*, 194–97.

44 Strickland (1996): 176–82 raises similar considerations with regard to infantrymen in medieval Europe.

45 Brown, R. Allen (1973) *Origins of English Feudalism*, London: George Allen & Unwin: 23–27; Strickland (1996): 149–53; Johnson (1981): 131–50; Stacey (1994): 36–38.

46 See Friday (1992); and Farris (1992) especially pp. 367–80.

47 Takahashi Masaaki, *Bushi no seiritsu*, 130–34, 144–48, 210–26; Nakazawa Katsuaki, *Chosei no buryoku to jokaku* (Tokyo: Yoshikawa kobunkan, 1999), 99–107; Noguchi Minoru, *Buke no toryo no joken: chosei bushi o minaosu* (Tokyo: Choo koronsha, 1994), 56–64.

48 See Friday, Karl (1994) "Bushido or Bull? A Medieval Historian's Perspective on the Imperial Army and the Japanese Warrior Tradition," *History Teacher* 27, no. 3 (May): 339–49, for a discussion of modern and medieval Japanese ideas on military ethics.

49 *Gempei josuiki*, ed. Nagahara Hajime (Tokyo: Shinjinbutsu oraisha, 1989) vol. 5:98–9.

50 *Azuma kagami*, 1189 9/7, 9/13. *Azuma kagami*, 1184 3/28 offers another example of a warrior (Taira Shigehira) arguing that there is no disgrace to capture.

51 Kawai Yasushi, "Jisho joei no nairan to chiiki shakai," *Rekishi gaku kenkyo*, 11, no. 730 (1999): 11–12.

52 Conlan (1999): 320–21.

53 Walzer, Michael (1974) "Political Action: The Problem of Dirty Hands," in *War and Moral Responsibility*, ed. Marshall Cohen, Thomas Nagel, and Thomas Scanlon, Princeton, NJ: Princeton University Press: 42–43; Nagel, Thomas (1974) "War and Massacre," in ibid., 3–24; Brandt, R. B. "Utilitarianism and the Rules of War," in ibid., 25–45; Hare, R. M. "Utilitarianism and the Rules of War," in ibid., 46–61.

54 For a fuller description of the role of temples in the socio-political and economic structure of early medieval Japan, see Adolphson, Mikael (1997) "Enryakuji: An Old Power in a New Era," in *The Origins of Japan's Medieval World: Courtiers, Clerics, Warriors, and Peasants in the Fourteenth Century*, ed. Jeffrey P. Mass, Stanford, CA: Stanford University Press: 237–60; Collcutt, Martin (1981) *Five Mountains: The Rinzai Zen Monastic Institution in Medieval Japan*, Cambridge, MA: Harvard University Press; Piggott, Joan R. (1982) "Hierarchy and Economics in Early Medieval Todaiji," in *Court and Bakufu in Japan: Essays in Kamakura History*, ed. Jeffrey P. Mass, New Haven, CT: Yale University Press: 45–91.

55 *Kokon chomonjo*, 9:12:333.

56 See, for example, *Shomonki*, 117–19, 99, 125–27; *Mutsuwaki*, 27, 31–34; *Choya gunsai Sessho ke osesho*, 986 10/20, pp. 179–80; *Konjaku monogatari-sho*, 23.13,

25.1, 25.5; *Heian ibun*, docs. 797, 007, 2090, 2583; *Fuso ryakki* 902 9/26, 919 5/23; *Nihon kiryaku*, 947 2/14; *Choshoki*, 1094 3/8.
57 *Shomonki*, 117–19; *Konjaku monogatari-sho*, 25.1.
58 *Konjaku monogatari-sho*, 25.11.
59 *Bellum hostile* and *bellum Romanum* are described in Stacey (1994): 27–36.

Bibliography

Adolphson, Mikael (1997) "Enryakuji: An Old Power in a New Era," in *The Origins of Japan's Medieval World: Courtiers, Clerics, Warriors, and Peasants in the Fourteenth Century*, ed. Jeffrey P. Mass, Stanford, CA: Stanford University Press: 237–60.

Bainton, Roland H. (1960) *Christian Attitudes Toward War and Peace: A Historical Survey and Critical Re-Evaluation*, New York: Abingdon Press.

Brandt, R. B. (1974) "Utilitarianism and the Rules of War," in *War and Moral Responsibility*, ed. Marshall Cohen, Thomas Nagel, and Thomas Scanlon, Princeton, NJ: Princeton University Press: 25–45.

Brown, R. Allen (1973) *Origins of English Feudalism*, London: George Allen & Unwin.

Brunner, Otto (1992) *Land and Lordship: Structures of Governance in Medieval Austria*, translated by Howard Kaminsky and James Van Horn Melton, revised edition, Philadelphia, PA: University of Pennsylvania Press.

Butler, Kenneth D. (1966) "The Textual Evolution of the *Heike Monogatari*," *Harvard Journal of Asiatic Studies* 26: 5–51.

Butler, Kenneth D. (1969) "The *Heike Monogatari* and the Japanese Warrior Ethic," *Harvard Journal of Asiatic Studies* 29: 93–108.

Chen-Ya, Tien (1992) *Chinese Military Theory*, Oakville, Ontario: Mosaic Press.

Collcutt, Martin (1981) *Five Mountains: The Rinzai Zen Monastic Institution in Medieval Japan*, Cambridge, MA: Harvard University Press.

Conlan, Thomas (1998) "State of War: The Violent Order of Fourteenth Century Japan," PhD dissertation, Stanford University: 203–43;

Conlan, Thomas (1999) "The Nature of Warfare in Fourteenth-Century Japan: The Record of Nomoto Tomoyuki," *Journal of Japanese Studies* 25, no. 2: 299–330.

Conlan, Thomas (2001) *In Little Need of Divine Intervention: Scrolls of the Mongol Invasions of Japan*, Ithaca, NY: East Asia Program, Cornell University.

Davis, David L. (1974) "Ikki in Late Medieval Japan," in *Medieval Japan*, ed. John W. Hall and Jeffrey P. Mass, New Haven, CT: Yale University Press: 221–47.

Farris, W. Wayne (1992) *Heavenly Warriors: The Evolution of Japan's Military, 500–1300*, Cambridge, MA: Harvard University Press.

Farris, W. Wayne (1999) "Japan to 1300," in *War and Society in the Ancient and Medieval Worlds: Asia, the Mediterranean, Europe, and Mesoamerica*, ed. Kurt Raaflaub and Nathan Rosenstein, Cambridge, MA: Center for Hellenic Studies, Harvard University: 60–62.

Friday, Karl (1983) "Mononofu: The Warrior of Heian Japan," Master's thesis, University of Kansas.

Friday, Karl (1992) *Hired Swords: The Rise of Private Warrior Power in Early Japan*, Stanford, CA: Stanford University Press.

Friday, Karl (1993) "Valorous Butchers: The Art of War During the Golden Age of the Samurai," *Japan Forum* 5, no. 1 (April): 1–19.

Friday, Karl (1994) "Bushido or Bull? A Medieval Historian's Perspective on the Imperial Army and the Japanese Warrior Tradition," *History Teacher* 27, no. 3 (May): 339–49.

Friday, Karl (1997) "Pushing Beyond the Pale: The Yamato Conquest of the *Emishi* and Northern Japan," *Journal of Japanese Studies* 23, no. 1: 1–24.

Grossberg, Kenneth A. (1981) *The Laws of the Muromachi Bakufu*, Tokyo: Monumenta Nipponica Monograph: 40.

Hall, John Cary (1906) "Japanese Feudal Law: The Institutes of Judicature: Being a Translation of 'Go Seibai Shikimoku'; the Magisterial Code of the Hojo Power-Holders (A.D. 1932)," *Transactions of the Asiatic Society of Japan* 34: 1–44.

Hall, John W. (1966) *Government and Local Power in Japan 500–1700: A Study Based on Bizen Province*, Princeton, NJ: Princeton University Press: 116–28.

Hane, Mikiso (1991) *Premodern Japan: A Historical Survey*, Boulder, CO: Westview Press: 73–74.

Hare, R. M. (1974) "Utilitarianism and the Rules of War," in *War and Moral Responsibility*, ed. Marshall Cohen, Thomas Nagel, and Thomas Scanlon, Princeton, NJ: Princeton University Press: 46–61.

Harrington, Loraine F. (1982) "Social Control and the Significance of the Akuto," in *Court and Bakufu in Japan: Essays in Kamakura History*, ed. Jeffrey P. Mass, New Haven, CT: Yale University Press: 221–50.

Ikegami, Eiko (1995) *The Taming of the Samurai: Honorific Individualism and the Making of Modern Japan*, Cambridge, MA: Harvard University Press.

Johnson, James Turner (1981) *Just War Tradition and the Restraint of War*, Princeton, NJ: Princeton University Press.

Kyotsu, Hori (1967) "The Mongol Invasions and the Kamakura Bakufu," PhD dissertation, Columbia University.

Kyotsu, Hori (1974) "Economic and Political Effects of the Mongol Wars," in *Medieval Japan: Essays in Institutional History*, ed. by John W. Hall and Jeffrey P. Mass, New Haven, CT: Yale University Press: 184–200.

Mass, Jeffrey P. (1974) *Warrior Government in Medieval Japan: A Study of the Kamakura Bakufu, Shugo and Jito*, New Haven, CT: Yale University Press.

Mass, Jeffrey P. (1979) *Development of Kamakura Rule 1180–1250: A History With Documents*, Stanford, CA: Stanford University Press dissertation.

Mass, Jeffrey P. (1989) *Lordship and Inheritance in Early Medieval Japan: A Study of the Kamakura Soryo System*, Stanford, CA: Stanford University Press.

Nagel, Thomas (1974) "War and Massacre," in *War and Moral Responsibility*, ed. Marshall Cohen, Thomas Nagel, and Thomas Scanlon, Princeton, NJ: Princeton University Press: 3–24.

Newman, John (1989) *Bushido: The Way of the Warrior*, Wigston, Leicester: Magna Books: 13–14, 16–17.

Ober, Joseph (1994) "Classical Greek Times," in *The Laws of War*, ed. Michael Howard, George J. Andreopoulos, and Mark R. Shulman, New Haven, CT: Yale University Press: 13–17.

Piggott, Joan R. (1982) "Hierarchy and Economics in Early Medieval Todaiji," in *Court and Bakufu in Japan: Essays in Kamakura History*, ed. Jeffrey P. Mass, New Haven, CT: Yale University Press: 45–91.

Russell, Frederick H. (1975) *The Just War in the Middle Ages*, London and New York: Cambridge University Press: 293–96.

Stacey, Robert C. (1994) "The Age of Chivalry," in *The Laws of War: Constraints on Warfare in the Western World*, ed. Michael Howard, George J. Andreopoulos, and Mark R. Shulman, New Haven, CT: Yale University Press.

Strickland, Matthew (1996) *War and Chivalry: The Conduct and Perception of War in England and Normandy, 1066–1217*, New York and London: Cambridge University Press.

Turnbull, Stephen R. (1982) *The Book of the Samurai: The Warrior Class of Japan*, New York: Gallery Books: 19, 22–36.

Turnbull, Stephen R. (1990) *The Lone Samurai and the Martial Arts*, London: Arms & Armour Press: 14–28.

Varley, H. Paul (1994) *Warriors of Japan as Portrayed in the War Tales*, Honolulu, HI: University of Hawaii Press.

Walzer, Michael (1974) "Political Action: The Problem of Dirty Hands," in *War and Moral Responsibility*, ed. Marshall Cohen, Thomas Nagel, and Thomas Scanlon, Princeton, NJ: Princeton University Press: 42–43.

Walzer, Michael (1977) *Just and Unjust Wars: A Moral Argument with Historical Illustrations*, New York: Basic Books.

6

THE JUST WAR IN EARLY CHINA

Mark E. Lewis

Like many peoples, the Chinese have elaborated a body of doctrine dealing with the causes that justify recourse to organized, large-scale violence and the constraints within which it should be practiced. While they unsurprisingly had no concept exactly corresponding to the Western notion of "just" or "justifiable" war, the phrase *yi bing*, literally "righteous," "just," or "dutiful" war, came to serve as a rubric for many comparable ideas. These ideas developed gradually in the centuries leading up to creation of the first unified empire in 221 BC, and during the first imperial dynasties. Although later centuries witnessed new ideas about warfare introduced by followers of Buddhism and by nomadic conquerors, the theories formulated in this early period remained the classic Chinese justification of warfare into the twentieth century. Both their similarities to and differences from the Western tradition make them useful for comparative study.

To summarize the early Chinese teachings on *yi bing*, they argued that war was justifiable primarily as the highest form of punishment through which the ruler could suppress large-scale deviance or criminality and thereby bring peace to the people and order to the world. A second key point in the early *yi bing* doctrine was that warfare was natural and inevitable, that it had existed since the origins of time and that no ruler could do without it. Thus the primary targets of the *yi bing* doctrine, as the early texts make clear, were not those who argued for absolute warfare free from all rules or constraints – a position which did not exist – but those near pacifists who argued that the compelling moral power of a true king would make war unnecessary, or that only defensive wars were permissible. Third, the idea of *yi bing* appeared during the Warring States (481–221 BC) and Qin (221–207 BC) periods, when a single, autocratic ruler was emerging as the center and defining element of the Chinese state. Consequently, ideas of just war were linked to the theory that proper warfare was possible only under the command of a semi-divine ruler who brought killing in the world of men into harmony with the violence of nature. All these points share similarities with the Western tradition whose founder, Augustine, justified warfare against the radical pacifism of certain Christian traditions through his appeal to the need to protect the innocent and punish the guilty, and placed the principles of legitimate authority acting with proper intentions at the center of his justification of war.[1] All these doctrines, both of *yi bing* and of

Augustine, dealt almost entirely with the right to make war (*jus ad bellum*), and they linked the idea of a just or righteous war to a doctrine of sovereignty that held a monopoly of legitimate force. Thus the doctrine in China of the justifiable war was above all a defense of the power of the absolute ruler in his roles as source of law, highest judge, and the ultimate dispenser of life and death.

A final principle of the *yi bing* doctrine that emerged only in the course of the Han dynasty (206 BC–AD 220) was the idea that since proper warfare was intended to bring peace to the people, the people themselves should play no part in it. This doctrine also has a Western counterpart in the principle that formed the core of the rules of war (*jus in bello*), that of *discrimination* between combatants and non-combatant and some attempt to spare the latter.[2] However, here an important distinction must be noted, for whereas the Western version of this doctrine emerged within the context of chivalric society, where warfare was to be restricted to a warrior nobility, China had no such nobility since the Spring-and-Autumn period (770–481 BC) and the practice of warfare was instead restricted to barbarians, criminals, and troublemakers. This fact increasingly linked participation in war to alienation from proper society, and made any restrictions in the targets of violence more a matter of tactical calculations than some sense of moral restraint or noble obligation.[3] This distinction in the social character of warfare and its regulation marks one of the key differences between the histories of China and Europe.

In this chapter I will trace the textual and institutional emergence of these Chinese doctrines of *yi bing*, with occasional remarks on comparisons with the West. I will begin with a brief consideration of sources, the historical background from which the doctrine emerged, and finally analyze the development of each of the major principles sketched above.

Systematic thinking in China about the uses and nature of warfare began in a series of treatises written in the Warring States period on the subject of military action. This was an age in which a once dominant warrior aristocracy that had fought in chariot armies was being supplanted by mass infantry armies commanded by specialist officers in the service of territorial lords. Consequently the texts, of which the most famous is the celebrated *Sunzi*, developed arguments on the means by which the skillful use of armies could preserve a state, expand its territory, and increase its power.[4] While these texts generally accepted warfare as inevitable and devoted little effort to justifying it, they articulated many of the ideas that were later combined in the theories of just war. These theories themselves were developed within the philosophical texts written in the same period, which sought to incorporate ideas about warfare into broader theories about the political and social orders. Theories of the just war achieved full form in major philosophical compendia sponsored by leading political actors under the Qin and the early Han, and then figured as elements in the propaganda and political debates of these dynasties. In this form they appear in stone inscriptions sponsored by rulers, in memorials, and in records of political debates.

Prior to the middle of the Warring States period there is evidence of attempts to justify specific campaigns and their results, but there are no expositions justifying warfare as an institution or defining the conditions for its correct practice. During the Shang (c.1600–c.1050 BC), Western Zhou (c.1050–771 BC), and Spring-and-Autumn periods warfare seems to have been accepted as a fact of life by all political actors, much as it was in classical antiquity.[5] Although we have few reliable sources from the early periods, passing remarks in the early chapters of the *Shang shu* justify the Zhou conquest of the Shang, and the Zhou temple hymns celebrate the conquerors. Warfare as a general phenomenon, however, was not called into question. Somewhat later the pre-battle oaths recorded in the *Zuo zhuan*, speeches attributed to the period from 770–476 BC, and their fictional equivalents in the later chapters of the *Shang shu* provide elaborate justifications for specific battles and rules for their conduct. However, these emerged from a society in which warfare was still a regular, virtually annual occurrence that defined the ruling elite.[6] In the absence of any calling into question of warfare as routine practice, there was as yet no need for any systematic defense or justification.

Certain arguments preserved in the *Zuo zhuan*, however, do suggest the immediate ancestry in the middle of the Warring States period of the later *yi bing* doctrine. First, speakers articulate rules and rituals for the conduct of armies on campaign, the existence of which posits a distinction between proper and improper warfare as understood by the hereditary nobility of the period.[7] More important for later developments, a handful of speeches articulate a theory in which yi, "justice" or "righteousness," is assigned to certain motives for war which are held to be superior to others. Specifically, those motives are described as *yi* which involve punishing criminal behavior or defending smaller states from an aggressor, in contrast to those which involve the annexation of territory or some material gain. In the relevant stories a victor is accused of initiating a war for justice (*yi*), only to use the victory as a means of expanding his state's territory.[8] In response to this criticism the man accused will usually renounce the territory or the unreasonable demands that he had imposed. These arguments, which may well themselves be products of the Warring States period, indicate a model in which war was made just or righteous through the proper intent of those who conducted it, particularly where that intent focused on the punishment of deviance. However, some of these campaigns were waged by nobles against the objections of their lord, and hence were not strictly licit, and there is still nothing to suggest that only those motives which are yi could justify a war. Thus these stories simply indicate how certain arguments took shape among the Zhou nobility that would later be incorporated into a broader discourse justifying warfare as the monopoly power of the emergent territorial lords.

While certain nobles, or scholars working within the mental universe of the nobility, first began to speak of the highest motives for wars as "justice," it was the Warring States philosophical traditions that for the first time made warfare itself a topic of speculation and argument. In the fourth century BC military texts such as the *Sunzi* still posited the centrality of war as an axiom, but other philosophical traditions began to call it into question. Thus the *Mencius* in the late fourth century asserted that those who advocated war and military expertise were criminals, while the moral power of the true ruler would make all people choose to serve him and thus obviate the need for war.[9] At roughly the same time a set of three chapters in the Mohist canon argued that all offensive wars were criminal and that combat was justified only for defensive purposes. In these arguments we see how, as the warrior aristocracy declined and the scale of warfare increased, certain observers challenged the ancient assumptions that war was inevitable and noble, and instead viewed it as a destructive force that should ideally be curbed or eliminated. It was in response to these open challenges to the propriety of warfare that Chinese writers supporting the emergent territorial states first articulated a systematic theory of *yi bing* in which war was held to be necessary and proper, so long as it was used by a legitimate ruler to curb violence.

It is unclear who were the earliest figures to make such an argument. The *Sima fa*, a military treatise of uncertain Warring States date, begins with the argument that ancient rulers had based themselves on benevolence and justice or righteousness (*yi*), but when these failed to preserve order they had recourse to war.

> For this reason if one must kill men to give peace to the people, then killing is permissible. If one must attack a state out of love for their people, then attacking is permissible. If one must stop war with war, although it is war it is permissible.

The balance of the first chapter describes how the earlier kings put their states in order through rites and music, and how they wielded punishments to suppress or correct specified categories of malefactors.[10] Another military text from approximately the same period, the *Wuzi*, also argued that rulers should seek to achieve order through rites and virtue, and use military force only to punish the refractory. This text repeatedly cites *yi* as a basis of rule and refers to the highest form of military action as *yi bing*. It defines this as that which "suppresses the violently perverse and rescues the people from chaos."[11] Thus in the late Warring States period several military treatises began to insist on the virtuous power of the ruler as the basis of all proper military action, and to justify such action as a means by which the ruler could preserve social order. A military treatise from the same period also made the argument, which became central to the justification of war, that combat existed even in nature in the form of animal armaments – horns, claws, and stings – and that human violence was similarly a direct outgrowth of man's nature.[12]

Arguments that the ruler's virtues were the basis of all military action and that the preservation of order was the sole justification for war appeared in the chapter "Debate on Warfare" in the *Xunzi*, a "Confucian" philosophical work compiled in the third century BC.[13] The chapter, which begins as a debate between Xun Kuang and a fictional military expert but soon turns into a series of lectures, first delivers an extended attack on the *Sunzi*'s emphasis on maneuver and deception. Such amoral military expertise, Xun Kuang asserts, would be no match for the power of a people completely united by the humanity, virtue, and righteousness of their ruler. In response to inquiries on the principles of warfare, Xun Kuang reiterates the position that the worthiness of the ruler and the ritual principles that he imposes are the decisive factors. Although certain rules for the ordering of an army and conduct in the field are later introduced, these are always treated as secondary. As for the purposes of warfare, the text argues that it serves only to punish those who cause disorder among the people. "In the rule of a true king there are punitive expeditions but no warfare." As in the *Sima fa* (and in the theories of St. Augustine) this use of warfare to "prohibit violent and aggressive behavior and to prevent harm to others" is justified as an expression of the ruler's love for his people and his desire to stop those who would do injury to them.

These texts, which develop from or seek to refute the earlier military traditions articulated in the *Sunzi*, are notable for placing the emphasis on the ruler as the only proper source and guarantor of licit warfare. They thus indicate the steady decline of the old martial elite and the rearticulation of warfare as a mode of state power which was proper only if guided by a single supreme ruler.[14] This new model of warfare as one of the ruler's tools for justice and social order was given its clearest articulation in the *Lü shi chun qiu*. This is particularly important because this work was produced in Qin state between 250 and 240 BC under the sponsorship of Lü Buwei, chief minister of the man who later became First Emperor, and it clearly expressed a vision of Qin state as an emergent world empire. It is in a series of writings produced in Qin or identified with this state that the full-blown form of warfare as *yi bing* first took shape, and which defined the doctrine for subsequent dynasties.

The chapters in the *Lü shi chun qiu* devoted to warfare appear in the initial, calendrical section of the work.[15] They are gathered in Books Seven and Eight, the chapters pertaining to the first and second months of autumn. The significance of their assignment to autumn will be discussed below. They begin with a discussion placed under the rubric of *yi bing* of the nature and history of warfare.

> The ancient sage-kings had righteous weapons/warfare (*yi bing*), but none of them abolished weapons. Weapons/warfare originated in high antiquity, appearing at the same time as the human race. As a general principle weapons are what intimidates and what intimidates is force. People's being intimidated by force is their essential nature. It is received from Heaven. It is not that which people can contrive. No soldier can eliminate it or artisan change it.

The passage then amplifies this assertion of the antiquity of weapons with a list of ancient rulers who employed them, and asserts that control in human affairs invariably devolved to the victor in battle. From this proposition it elaborates a model of the evolution of political authority from tribes to states to an empire based on the fact of constant fighting.

> Even before the time of Chi You [a mythic inventor of metal weapons] people certainly fought with branches from which they had peeled the bark, and the victor became the chief who controlled them.[16] When chiefs

proved insufficient to control them, they established princes. When princes were still insufficient to control them, they established a Son of Heaven. The Son of Heaven derived from the princes, the princes derived from the chiefs, and the chiefs derived from fighting. The origins of fighting and conflict are ancient; they cannot be banned. Thus the ancient sage-kings had righteous weapons/warfare, but none of them abolished weapons.

Having established that weapons had existed as long as humankind, and made this fact fundamental to the possibility of having a world ruler, the authors then articulated the principle that weapons were justified as the highest form of punishment.

If a family has no painful whips, then their children will immediately commit offenses. If a state lacks punishments, then officials and the common people will immediately violate the laws and abuse one another. If the world lacks punishing expeditions, then the feudal lords will immediately commit violence against one another.

From this the authors assert the necessity of warfare to maintain order in the world, and repeat the refrain that the sage rulers of antiquity, mythic models for contemporary monarchs, never abolished weapons. The balance of the chapter rings changes on the idea that warfare is indispensable, universal, and an attribute of the true ruler, returning again and again to the line with which it began.

The next two chapters are devoted to the rejection of the Mohist doctrine that only defensive wars were permissible. Having established that warfare was necessary as a means of punishing the enemies of public order, the authors argued that such punitive wars would have to employ offensive campaigns, and that wars to defend a given city or state would entail defending the criminals within that state. The criterion to distinguish proper wars from improper ones was not their use of attack or defense, but the moral character or conduct of their targets. Thus the authors defended a full range of options for the ruler, who in the name of justice would be entitled to initiate attacks on any foe deemed to be a threat to his order.

The final chapter of Book Seven describes the conduct of "righteous troops" engaged in a punitive expedition. It stipulates that such troops will avoid all acts of pillage and inflict no harm on the civilian population. The army should target solely the enemy ruler and his followers, in an attempt to secure the support of the populace, or at least avoid its active intervention. The campaign should be accompanied by an extended propaganda campaign in which heralds publicly list the crimes of the government, and proclaim that the army has come simply to punish the malefactors and protect the people. Those who submit are promised tangible rewards, which are increased in accord with the number of followers that they can bring with them.

The chapters in Book Eight begin with a definition of *yi* as the guideline for all actions and the origins of all social hierarchy, and at one point they list *yi* as the highest military virtue. However, the contents are largely devoted to the more explicitly military questions of training men to act in unison, selecting the best troops and weapons, inspiring the troops with courage, securing their loyalty, and maneuvering in the field. Most of these ideas and arguments are drawn from the military treatises. The key points for the Chinese doctrine of the just war were those sketched in the preceding book: warfare is natural and necessary, it is the tool of the true ruler, it is a form of punishment used to secure order, and its conduct aims to minimize damage to the civil populace and to divide the enemy leaders from their people. These points, for the first time all drawn together and placed under the rubric of *yi bing*, form the core of later Chinese theories about the justification of warfare.

The theory of *yi bing* as a hallmark of the true ruler and a necessary element of statecraft was not restricted to philosophical texts, for it was also employed in government propaganda. As part of a series of triumphal processions through his newly conquered territory on the eastern seaboard, the First Emperor placed on selected mountain tops a series of stelae inscribed with lengthy panegyrics written in four-character verse celebrating the glories of his achievements and the commencement of a new era in human history. Copies of these texts were made and circulated through the realm. One passage from the inscription placed at Kuaiji reads:

> The sage of Qin gazed down on the states,
> For the first time fixing the punishments and titles.
> He clearly laid out the old regulations,
> And first settled laws and standard.
> He distributed administrative tasks
> In order to fix a constant standard.
> The kings of the six states were self-willed and rebellious.
> Covetous, refractory, arrogant, and savage,
> They led their hosts to strengthen themselves.
> Violent, cruel, and capricious,
> Arrogant in the certainty of their strength,
> They repeatedly mobilized their armored troops.
> Secretly linking up through spies and emissaries,
> They formed horizontal and vertical alliances,
> Acting as fractious provincials.
> Within they developed treacherous schemes,
> Outside they invaded our borders,
> And thus brought about calamities and disaster.
> Just (*yi*) and awesome, our ruler punished them,
> Extinguishing the violent and disobedient.
> The bandit rebels were destroyed.[17]

The inscription continues with an account of how the emperor's blessings covered the whole world and how his just punishments corrected all conduct.

This text is a classic expression of the *yi bing* doctrine. It focuses on the virtuous power of the ruler, elaborates the iniquity of his foes, insists on the justice or right-eousness of his military action, identifies his conquests as a form of punishment, and points out how the use of force creates a universal peace that benefits all creatures. This is the only inscription that explicitly describes the emperor's military actions as *yi*, and it also gives the most elaborate account of the criminality of the other rulers. However, as Martin Kern has pointed out, all the inscriptions are composed from a set of recurring topoi and stock themes. Among these is the depiction of the Warring States period as a time of rampant criminality, and the Qin unification as a punishing power that imposed order on the world. In the five inscriptions that deal with the theme, the Qin campaigns of conquest are always described as punitive expeditions, and the Qin empire is justified through its imposition of justice and order in a world of criminal chaos.[18] Consequently the theme of *yi bing* outlined in the *Lü shi chun qiu*, and the propaganda methods that were an element of this theme, played a major role in Qin celebrations of their new world empire.

While the inscriptions are our only demonstration from Qin sources of the political use of the *yi bing* doctrine, both the rubric and principles are written into Han accounts of the Qin. Writing around 100 BC, more than a century after the fall of Qin, Sima Qian records as follows the memorial from a group of ministers proposing the adoption of a new title for the ruler in order to proclaim the unprecedented nature of Qin's achievement.

> In ancient times the Five Emperors had a territory of 1,000 *li* square. Outside the feudal lords submitted and the barbarians submitted, but sometimes the feudal lords attended the court and sometimes they did not. The Son of Heaven could not control them. Now Your Majesty has raised up your righteous troops (*yi bing*) to punish the cruel bandits and to establish order in the world. All within the seas has become your administrative districts, and all laws come from a single authority. This is without precedent from the most ancient times to the present day.[19]

While it is uncertain whether and in what manner Sima Qian could have had access to Qin policy discussions, this passage at least demonstrates that within the first century of Han rule the rubric and the basic ideas of *yi bing* had become conventional in Chinese political discourse.

The same point is demonstrated in the same historian's accounts of the rebellion against Qin and the establishment of the Han. In these narratives several people assert that Qin relied on force or deceit without justice (*yi*), or that the troops of the Han founder Liu Bang were themselves *yi bing*. At one point a speaker calls upon Liu Bang to lead his *yi bing* to "punish the criminal Qin." Sima Qian himself not only describes Liu Bang's campaigns as "expeditions in support of justice," but retroactively applies the same terminology to earlier dynastic shifts such as the Zhou conquest of the Shang, as well as the wars between Wu and Yue in the fifth century BC.[20] These arguments not only indicate general acceptance of the doctrine of *yi bing* as a justification for military action and a hallmark of the ruler, but also demonstrate how it was an argument that cut in two directions. Just as Qin had described its former rivals as criminals and its own actions as the imposition of justice and order, so those who rebelled against Qin insisted on the moral deviance of the Qin regime and portrayed their own actions as punitive campaigns in the cause of righteousness. In all later Chinese histories the rebel armies that founded a new dynasty were invariably described as *yi bing*. As will be discussed below, the ruler's military actions were ultimately justified through the support of Heaven, which was demonstrated only by victory. Thus the *yi bing* doctrine, like so many claims to virtue in politics, came to serve equally an established regime and the rebels who opposed it.

Shortly before Sima Qian wrote his history, a synthesizing philosophical compendium entitled the *Huainanzi* included a chapter "The Essentials of Military Action" that directly adopted the principles of *yi bing* as articulated in the *Lü shi chun qiu*. The opening section of this chapter consists largely of paraphrase, elaboration, and direct quotation from the Qin work. After asserting that in ancient times people used armies in order to "reduce to order disturbances in the world and eliminate that which harmed the people," it continues that warfare is natural, was created by Heaven, and has existed since earliest times. It pushes this argument further than the *Lü shi chun qiu* by pointing out that even animals are endowed with weapons such as horns, claws, and teeth. After noting that combat is inevitable among people due to the competition for scarce goods – an argument previously articulated in such late Warring States philosophical texts as the *Xunzi* and the *Han Feizi* – it narrates the introduction of weapons and asserts, like the *Lü shi chun qiu*, that political authority emerged in response to this primitive state of constant warfare. After running through a list of early rulers and their use of weapons, the text again asserts that weapons cannot be abandoned, even using the same verb as the *Lü shi chun qiu*. The sage-kings' use of armies is compared to the necessity of weeding a field, or killing animals that harm the flocks or the fish that people reared. At this point in the argument the authors specifically asserted that proper military action is in support of "justice/righteousness (*yi*)" and that it served to punish the unjust and thereby preserve the people. These actions are named "Heaven's punishments." This introductory section of the chapter then concludes with an invocation of the highest form of *yi bing*, in which actual combat is no longer necessary.[21]

Thus, like Sima Qian, this early Han compilation essentially accepted the Qin doctrine of *yi bing* as a given, and it differed only in introducing elaborate, Daoist-tinged accounts of the conduct of war by a ruler or commander who patterns himself on the forces of nature. Even this theme of natural pattern was already anticipated in the *Lü shi chun qiu*, for the first twelve chapters of this text present a calendar of the ruler's rituals and policies based on the principle of the imitation of Heaven. Bestowing mercy, encouraging agriculture, and furthering life in the spring and summer, the ruler in the autumn and winter follows Heaven's example by turning harsh and killing. These are the seasons of punishments, military training, imprisonment, and a general sealing up of the world. This calendrical rationalization of combat – which appeared in the *Lü shi chun qiu*, the "Monthly Ordinances" of the *Li ji*, the calendrical chapter of the *Huainanzi*, and an early Han silk manuscript discovered at Mawangdui – provided an ultimate foundation in nature for the ruler's use of violence to impose his order.[22] Given the importance that both the *Lü shi chun qiu* and the *Huainanzi* assigned to the origins of warfare in natural patterns and the "bestowals" of Heaven, this calendrical model was clearly fundamental to all justifications of warfare in the period.

Further evidence of the role and uses of the *yi bing* model in the Han appears in the *Discourses on Salt and Iron* by Huan Kuan. This work is presented as a transcription or reconstruction of a debate held at the Han court in 81 BC between leading officials defending the state's use of monopolies on salt and iron along with regulated trade, and a group of Confucian or classicist (*ru*) scholars from the region of modern Shandong who attacked these policies. While the precise links of the text to the actual debates cannot be known, and a high degree of authorial liberty and even fictionalization is certain, this account represents positions being articulated in the second century of Han rule. Interestingly, key points of the *yi bing* argument, specifically the dispute over the necessity of warfare and the possibility of its abolition, figure within the debates.

The argument appears in several chapters, but in each case it follows the same pattern. The officials argue that the raids of the Xiongnu tribesmen who "rebelled against our authority" had wreaked havoc at China's frontiers. In order to end this scourge, Emperor Wu had launched a series of military expeditions, and to pay for these expeditions without placing too great a burden on the peasantry he had resorted to the reintroduction of monopolies. These military campaigns, described by the officials as "punishment for unruliness and lawlessness," were thus justified precisely as the actions of *yi bing* (although the term itself was not used) that demonstrated the greatness of the Han emperor and his concern for his people. Interestingly, the officials cite Qin as a positive precedent that demonstrates the value of correctly used military force. In response the scholars reply that the true ruler should simply cultivate his virtue, and the enemy would submit without the need for a battle. They even employ the *Mencius*'s argument that the ruler who practices benevolence will have no enemies (or no "match") in the world.[23]

This debate, to the extent that it is not completely fictional, suggests some of the political realities underlying the appeal to *yi bing*. It demonstrates once again that the doctrine was above all about the power of the ruler and his right to impose his laws by force, an imposition justified in terms of the social benefits that would flow from the preservation of order. The willingness to cite Qin as a positive example in such arguments also highlights the links of the *yi bing* doctrine to Qin state, and to all those who advocated an activist government with a powerful ruler. The advocates of the possibility of rule without force are described as *ru* and textually linked to the Mencian tradition. This hostility of the *ru* to the theory of just or righteous wars is also indicated in a *Shi ji* anecdote that tells of a *ru* official during the Qin–Han interregnum who scorns strategic advice because "righteous troops do not use deceitful stratagems or unusual plans". As a result he was crushed in battle.[24] Thus the suspicion of Warring States Confucians towards military action seems to have carried forward into certain intellectual currents in the Han, while the theory of *yi bing* was advocated largely by those interested in maximizing the powers of the ruler and his officials.

A final demonstration of the significance of the *yi bing* theory in Han thought is the "Monograph on Punishments" in the *Han shu*, a history of the Han state compiled with imperial sanction in the first century AD. This chapter, as the title indicates, deals with the roles of law and punishments, but it also includes substantial discussions of military action.[25] We have already seen how the *Lü shi chun qiu* listed a hierarchical series of types of punishments, from those within the household to those within the state, and finally military action. The *Han shu* monograph adopted the same model. After demonstrating people's need to form groups and the consequent necessity of rulers, the text argued that such rulers must employ punishments that "emulate the killing and destruction of Heaven's thunder and lightning." When it listed the categories of punishments it began with the "great punishments" carried out with weapons and armor, i.e. warfare. Like the earlier accounts of *yi bing*, it asserted that warfare dated back to the beginnings of human history and listed examples of the use of combat by the ancient sages. These ancient precedents were followed by an elaborate account of military institutions from the Zhou dynasty down to the Western Han. Thus all the main points of the *yi bing* theory, and several of the arguments used in earlier texts to justify it, are incorporated directly into this officially sponsored Han account of judicial practice.

While all of the above Han arguments are largely repetitions of the theory of *yi bing* as articulated in the Qin, there was at least one major shift in Han military practice that introduced a new theme into the arguments justifying war. With the formal abolition of universal military service in AD 32, combat was increasingly restricted to non-Chinese peoples, convicts, and local troublemakers.[26] As a result, several writers argued that properly conducted warfare was also marked by the non-participation of the peasantry, and linked to this the expulsion of deviant elements to the frontier.

However, even this one Han innovation was anticipated in writings linked with Qin. A philosophical work entitled the *Shang Jun shu* (*Book of Lord Shang*) identified itself both in name and in content with the reform program carried out by Wei Yang in Qin in the middle of the fourth century BC. While this text does not refer to *yi*, except in one passage advocating the "joining of justice (*yi*) with violence," it argues repeatedly that the purpose of warfare is to punish deviance, impose order, unite the world, and thereby attain peace. It even employs the formula found in the *Sima fa* that one should use war to end war.[27] While these are all conventional *yi bing* ideas, the *Shang Jun shu* introduces a unique argument on the manner in which warfare can lead to social order. It argues that given the inevitable competition among men, the populace's growing strength would necessarily lead to internal conflict. This threat was to be countered in two ways. First, the people as individuals and households had to be weakened, which formed the subject of two chapters. Second, the power and aggression of one's own people had to be channeled into the army and then dispatched into enemy territory in the form of military campaigns. In a striking image, the strength and aggression of one's own people was described as a poison that had to be expelled into enemy territory or it would destroy one's own.[28]

However, these arguments in the *Shang Jun shu* are still based on a world in which the entire free peasantry was trained and mobilized for military service. To the extent that it recognized any possibility of separating combatants from noncombatants, it was the indigenous inhabitants of Qin who were to serve in the army and thus depart from the state, while recently settled immigrants stayed behind to work the fields.[29] The Han case was quite different. As warfare became a frontier phenomenon in the wake of unification, mass infantry armies based on a rota of peasant service proved useless. They were gradually replaced by professionals and convicts who manned garrisons, and non-Chinese nomads who provided cavalry strike forces. The overthrow of the usurper Wang Man, who had established his own dynasty from AD 9–23, demonstrated how regular peasant training and mobilization provided both the tools and occasions for launching rebellions. Consequently all training of peasants was abandoned and local military offices abolished. The Eastern Han armies came to be composed largely of convicts exiled to the frontiers, local toughs and troublemakers press-ganged into professional service, and nonChinese tribesmen providing cavalry. It was armies composed of such forces that finally defeated the nomadic Xiongnu armies in the AD 80s, and several texts such as a stone inscription on the decisive victory over the Xiongnu and a memorial submitted in AD 88 noted that these triumphs were achieved without disturbing the common people. At the same time we find evidence, such as a successful general's declining to take an office at court because he had spent his life in armies at the frontier surrounded by criminals, that the military forces were themselves increasingly regarded as deviant elements who were suspect, foreign, and even polluting. Thus their expulsion to the frontier furthered internal order, just as in the theory of the *Shang Jun shu*.

By the middle of the Eastern Han the idea had thus developed of a clear separation between those who fought and the civil population, and the highest form of war, the truly "just war," was one that impinged as little as possible on the latter. This pattern carried forward in the subsequent centuries of political disunion, when armies in the north of China were composed of non-Chinese nomads or Chinese who had assimilated to nomadic life, while armies in the south were formed from refugee populations kept on separate population registers. Early Tang dynasty (AD 618–906) armies – hereditary troops at the capital, Turkic allies, and the separately registered divisional army (*fu bing*) – were also based on the separation of fighters from the mass of the civil populace. However, unlike the West where the fighting men formed a nobility that extracted income from the peasantry, in China it was the state and powerful clans who taxed the peasants, while the fighting men were tied to the state through cash payments, alliances, or some form of personal, patron–client tie with the ruler. While military men might sometimes dominate a court, particularly in the early reigns of a dynasty, the long-term consequence in China of the separation of soldiery from the populace was the general devaluation of the fighting man.

Conclusion

The key point to note about the Chinese theory of the "just war" or *yi bing* was that it was primarily a justification of the role of the ruler within a centralized state, and thus a defense of the power of the emperor. By justifying war as a mode of punishment carried out by the legitimate authority to create social order, it made all proper combat ultimately a manifestation of the power of the chief lawgiver and highest judge. This idea was anticipated in the Warring States philosophical text, the *Xunzi*, which denied the importance of military expertise and insisted on the absorption of combat into state administration under the auspices of the ruler. It culminated in Qin with the systematic articulation of the *yi bing* model in the *Lü shi chun qiu* and its proclamation in the First Emperor's stone inscriptions. Carried forward into the Han in the *Huainanzi* and *Shi ji*, it again served in debates over the salt and iron monopolies as an argument for an activist, powerful imperial state. The grounding of licit violence in the calendrical model of state violence also tied it to the function of the ruler as cosmic fulcrum and earthly embodiment of Heaven.

Another feature of the Chinese doctrine, closely related to the first, is that the focus was largely on *jus ad bellum* rather than *jus in bello*. Having justified the use of violence as a method of securing order, little attention was paid to restraints on the forms or degree of violence. While one text cited above argued that the army should attack only the guilty and leave the rest of the people alone, such distinctions had little reality in actual practice. Although many later imperial armies tried to alienate rebel forces from their leaders by promising pardons for those who surrendered, few actual constraints were imposed on the methods employed to suppress challenges to imperial power. This pattern was much like that in the Western theological tradition of the just war, which also dealt largely with *jus ad bellum* and devoted little attention to the limits on the conduct of belligerents. Indeed claims for the justice of one's cause, culminating in proclaiming a holy war commanded by God, were invoked to criminalize or even demonize the enemy, and consequently to justify the most savage actions against them. Actual restraints on the conduct of war (*jus in bello*) derived largely from chivalric codes and other forms of rules imposed by fighting men on themselves.[30] Given the absence of any warrior nobility in imperial China, there was no comparable source for such limits, and whatever restraints were actually imposed was largely a matter of calculation or convenience. The most brutal methods could be applied when necessary, and the model of warfare as a form of punishment justified virtually any conduct.

As noted above, it justified even rebellion. So long as the ultimate role of combat was to impose order under a single, supreme ruler, then in the event of a civil war the *yi bing* doctrine would justify the violence of anyone who could restore peace. This idea is already indicated in the *Lü shi chun qiu*'s account of righteous war, which traced a history where chieftainship, princedom, and ultimately world rule all derived from victory in battle. The justification of war through order ultimately sanctioned the rule of any conqueror. Of course this legitimation of whoever had the power to finally impose his will also has a Western equivalent, as given in the classic formulation by Sir John Harrington:

> Treason doth never prosper, what's the reason?
> For if it prosper, none dare call it treason.
> Instead we call it justice.

Notes

1 Johnson, James Turner (1981) *The Just War Tradition and the Restraint of War: A Moral and Historical Inquiry*, Princeton, NJ: Princeton University Press: xxiv–xxxi, 4–6, 44–59, 150–65, 170–79; Russell, Frederick H. (1975) *The Just War in the Middle Ages*, Cambridge: Cambridge University Press, ch. 1.

2 Best, Geoffrey (1980) *Humanity in Warfare*, New York: Columbia University; Johnson (1981): 127–28, 131–50, 196–228.

3 On China's warrior aristocracy and its disappearance, see Lewis, Mark Edward (1990) *Sanctioned Violence in Early China*, Albany, NY: State University of New York, esp. ch. 1–2. On the Han relegation of warfare to those outside proper society, see Lewis, Mark Edward (2000) "The Han Abolition of Universal Military Service," in *Warfare in Chinese History*, ed. Hans van de Ven, Leiden: Brill: 48–75.

4 On the social background and basic ideas of the texts, see Lewis (1990) ch. 3. For translations of the major surviving treatises, see *The Seven Military Classics of Ancient China*, tr. Ralph Sawyer (Boulder, CO: Westview, 1993); *Sun Pin: Military Methods*, tr. Ralph Sawyer (Boulder, CO: Westview, 1995).

5 Russell (1975): 3–11; Johnson, James Turner (1991) "Historical Roots and Sources of the Just War Tradition in Western Culture," in *Just War and Jihad*, ed. John Kelsay and James Turner Johnson, New York: Greenwood Press: 7–12; Zampaglione, Gerardo (1973) *The Idea of Peace in Antiquity*, tr. Richard Dunn, Notre Dame, IN: University of Notre Dame; Watson, Alan (1993) *International Law in Archaic Rome: War and Religion*, Baltimore, MD: Johns Hopkins University Press; Vernant, Jean-Pierre (1968) "Introduction," *Problèmes de la guerre en Grèce ancienne*, Paris: École des Hautes Études en Sciences Sociales: 10–19.

6 On the pre-battle oaths see Lewis (1990): 18, 24–25. On the routine nature of warfare and its function as a hallmark of the elite, see ibid. ch. 1, esp. pp. 17–28, 36–43.

7 Lewis (1990): 22–26, 38–39.

8 *Chun qiu Zuo zhuan zhu* (Beijing: Zhonghua, 1981), Lord Xuan year 11, pp. 714–15; Lord Xuan year 17, pp. 771–74; Lord Cheng year 2, pp. 797–99; *Shi ji* (Beijing: Zhonghua, 1959) ch. 32, pp. 1497–98; ch. 36, p. 1580; ch. 39, pp. 1677–78; ch. 40, p. 1702; *Chun qiu Guliang zhuan zhu shu, in Shisan jing zhu shu*, vol. 7 (Taipei: Yiwen, 1976) Lord Xuan year 4, ch. 12, pp. 5b–6a.

9 For the major Mencian discussions of war see Lewis (1990): 129–30, 209.

10 *Seven Military Classics*: 126–28.

11 *Seven Military Classics*: 207–09.

12 *Sun Pin*: 116.

13 This chapter, entitled "Debate on the Principles of Warfare," is translated in *Xunzi: A*

Translation and Study of the Complete Works, vol. 2, tr. John Knoblock (Stanford, CA: Stanford University, 1990): 218–34.

14 On this shift within the Chinese military tradition, and the new focus on the figure of the ruler as center of proper warfare, see Lewis (1990) ch. 2, 4–5, 6, pp. 231–39.

15 These are translated in *The Annals of Lü Buwei: A Complete Translation and Study*, tr. John Knoblock and Jeffrey Riegel (Stanford, CA: Stanford University, 2000): 175–87, 193–204.

16 On myths dealing with Chi You, the Yellow Emperor, and the invention of weapons, see Lewis (1990): 157–212.

17 *Shi ji*, ch. 6, p. 261. A translation appears in *Records of the Grand Historian: Qin Dynasty*, tr. Burton Watson (New York: Columbia University, 1993): 60.

18 Kern, Martin (2000) *The Stele Inscription of Ch'in Shih-huang: Text and Ritual in Early Chinese Imperial Representation* (American Oriental Series Vol. 85), New Haven, CT: American Oriental Society: 132–34.

19 *Shi ji*, ch. 6, p. 236; Watson, *Qin*: 42–43.

20 *Shi ji*, ch. 8, p. 376; 67, p. 2199; 74, p. 2345; 92, p. 2612; 97, p. 2692; 118, p. 3086; 130, p. 3303.

21 *Huainanzi*, in *Xin bian zhu zi ji cheng*, vol. 7, Taipei: Shijie, 1974: 251–53.

22 On the role of natural pattern as a rationalization or justification of warfare and punishments, see Lewis (1990): 137–150, 213–39.

23 *Discourses on Salt and Iron*, tr. E. M. Gale (reprint edn, Taipei: Ch'eng Wen, 1973), pp. 3–6, 12–13, 35–39, 41–49, 51–52, 74–80, 88–91, 92–93, 99–103, 195, 199–200.

24 *Shi ji*, ch. 92, pp. 2615–16.

25 A complete translation of the monograph is available in Hulsewe, A. F. P. (1955) *Remnants of Han Law*, vol. 1, Leiden: Brill: 321–422. Pages 351–422 are the notes.

26 On the reasons for and consequences of this Han innovation, see Lewis (2000): 33–76.

27 *The Book of Lord Shang*, tr. J. J. L. Duyvendak (reprint edn, Chicago, IL: University of Chicago, 1963), pp. 185, 189–90, 194, 196–97, 200, 207–08, 210, 219, 221–22, 227, 232, 257, 268, 275–76, 283, 285 – this is the passage on using war to abolish war, 286, 292, 325.

28 *The Book of Lord Shang*: 198–99, 211–12, 216, 235–36, 253–54, 290.

29 *The Book of Lord Shang*: 270.

30 The classic account of the holy war as a distinct type is Bainton Roland (1960) *Christian Attitudes towards War and Peace: A Historical Survey and Critical Re-evaluation*, Nashville, TN: Abingdon Press. As James Turner Johnson has pointed out, Bainton's attempt to clearly distinguish holy war from just war does not fit with actual historical cases, where the one easily turns into the other. See Johnson, James Turner (1975) *Ideology, Reason, and the Limitation of War*, Princeton, NJ: Princeton University Press: 25, 81–149; Johnson (1981): xxv–xxxi; 54–59, 158–61, 230–37; While Johnson has questioned Bainton's assertion that holy wars tend to be more vicious than others, his own data often demonstrate the contrary. This blurring of just war into holy war and the consequent extremity of violence is also demonstrated in Little, David (1991) "'Holy War' Appeals and Western Christianity: A Reconsideration of Bainton's Approach," in *Just War and Jihad. Historical and Theoretical Perspectives on War and Peace in Western and Islamic Traditions*, ed. John Kelsay and James Turner Johnson, New York: Greenwood: 121–39. On the primary origin of *jus in bello* in the values of the fighters, see Johnson, J. T. (1977) *Ideology, Reason and the Limitation of War: Religious and Secular Concepts 1200–1749*, Princeton, NJ: Princeton University Press: 25, 64–80; Johnson (1981) ch. 5; Howard, Michael "*Temperamenta Belli*: Can War be Controlled?" in *Restraints on War: Studies in the Limitation of Armed Conflict*, ed. Michael Howard, Oxford: Oxford University Press: 1–15; Best (1980): 3–16.

Bibliography

Bainton Roland (1960) *Christian Attitudes towards War and Peace: A Historical Survey and Critical Re-evaluation*, Nashville, TN: Abingdon Press.

Best, Geoffrey (1980) *Humanity in Warfare*, New York: Columbia University.

Howard, Michael "*Temperamenta Belli*: Can War be Controlled?" in *Restraints on War: Studies in the Limitation of Armed Conflict*, ed. Michael Howard, Oxford: Oxford University Press: 1–15.

Hulsewe, A. F. P. (1955) *Remnants of Han Law*, vol. 1, Leiden: Brill: 321–422.

Johnson, James Turner (1975) *Ideology, Reason, and the Limitation of War*, Princeton, NJ: Princeton University Press.

Johnson, James Turner (1981) *The Just War Tradition and the Restraint of War: A Moral and Historical Inquiry*, Princeton, NJ: Princeton University Press.

Johnson, James Turner (1991) "Historical Roots and Sources of the Just War Tradition in Western Culture," in *Just War and Jihad*, ed. John Kelsay and James Turner Johnson, New York: Greenwood Press: 7–12.

Kern, Martin (2000) *The Stele Inscription of Ch'in Shih-huang: Text and Ritual in Early Chinese Imperial Representation* (American Oriental Series Vol. 85), New Haven, CT: American Oriental Society.

Lewis, Mark Edward (1990) *Sanctioned Violence in Early China*, Albany, NY: State University of New York.

Lewis, Mark Edward (2000) "The Han Abolition of Universal Military Service," in *Warfare in Chinese History*, ed. Hans van de Ven, Leiden: Brill: 48–75.

Little, David (1991) "'Holy War' Appeals and Western Christianity: A Reconsideration of Bainton's Approach," in *Just War and Jihad. Historical and Theoretical Perspectives on War and Peace in Western and Islamic Traditions*, ed. John Kelsay and James Turner Johnson, New York: Greenwood: 121–39.

Russell, Frederick H. (1975) *The Just War in the Middle Ages*, Cambridge: Cambridge University Press, ch. 1.

Sawyer, Ralph (trans.) (1995) *Sun Pin: Military Methods*, Boulder, CO: Westview.

Sawyer, Ralph (trans.) (1993) *The Seven Military Classics of Ancient China*, Boulder, CO: Westview.

Vernant, Jean-Pierre (1968) "Introduction," *Problèmes de la guerre en Grèce ancienne*, Paris: École des Hautes Études en Sciences Sociales: 10–19.

Watson, Alan (1993) *International Law in Archaic Rome: War and Religion*, Baltimore, MD: Johns Hopkins University Press.

Zampaglione, Gerardo (1973) *The Idea of Peace in Antiquity*, tr. Richard Dunn, Notre Dame, IN: University of Notre Dame.

AFTERWORD
Ethics across borders

Henrik Syse

It is a cliché, but nonetheless true: the world is becoming smaller, and inter-dependence and cooperation across borders – indeed, across the entire globe – are facts of life to a degree hitherto unheard of in world history. Ideally, such a world should be peaceful: a meeting place for ideas and trade, a global community of understanding and goodwill. Such is not the case. While the number of armed conflicts seems to be declining as we enter the twenty-first century, few would say that we inhabit a world of peaceful coexistence, or that we are anywhere near doing so.[1]

The twentieth century saw the worst wars in the history of humankind, in terms of destruction as well as geographical extension. But that same century also produced hitherto unseen international structures for dealing with war and conflict, most prominently the United Nations. The charter of the United Nations and many of its other documents, such as the Universal Declaration of Human Rights, reflect the truly international state of world politics. They express a number of ethical and political ideals, but without referring to one particular philosophical or religious position to justify them. Rather, they follow the pattern of what American political philosopher John Rawls has called "overlapping consensus"[2] – they express claims that (for most people) do stand in need of philosophical or theological underpinnings, but they leave it open to the reader which tradition to refer to. They thus concentrate on conclusions that adherents of *different* religions and world views should all be able to embrace, based on their own terminology and inventory of ideas. In other words: in spite of a plurality of philosophical premises, we expect humankind to be able to agree on certain conclusions, for the sake of peace and human dignity.

Seeing the success, in theory if not always in practice, of the UN Charter, the Declaration of Human Rights, and a number of other documents in international law, ethicists should be inspired to strive for the same sort of overlapping consensus in other fields. Certain moral questions are of such importance, and deal with issues so seriously in need of cross-cultural agreement and understanding, that the call for consensus and cooperation is highly pertinent. Medical ethics and research ethics are two such fields much debated in the philosophical community, but the ethics of war can arguably be said to be the most pressing concern.

Admittedly, documents in international law (such as the UN Charter and the Geneva Conventions and Protocols) have achieved part of the task of formulating a cross-cultural consensus on rules of war. Yet, the ethics of war comprises more than legal rules. After all, international law is hardly equipped to deal with all moral quandaries that arise in connection with warfare; just witness the many recent discussions on humanitarian intervention and warfare against terror, none of which find clear-cut solutions in international law. An explicitly ethical approach to war can address questions about which international law is (and probably should be) silent, such as the intention, character, and virtue of those who fight – or of those who make the decision to do so.

Seen in this context, the contributions to this book are, excuse the expression, a God-send. The ethics of war – often simply named after its most famous constituent tradition, "just war" – has been seen as an exclusively European tradition. Hence, in confronting terrorism, or in debating civil war in non-Christian countries, the existence of a culture clash has often been taken for granted. It is a task of primary importance for philosophers, theologians, and historians of ideas and religion to show us whether, and how, such a clash can be avoided. The authors in this volume have performed a great service in that regard.

As we have made our way through this learned and informative collections, where do we stand? A multitude of challenges come to mind, and I will touch on some of them. First, should the ethics of war be *more* or *less* closely attached to ideological or religious ideas? On the one hand, it seems that the realist tradition in international politics – which dissociates politics from religion, ideology, and moral principle – constitutes the worst enemy of restraint and decency in war, since it does not let ethics play a distinct part in political and military reasoning. Realism in this sense, also known as "power politics," is certainly not the exclusive property of the Western world. Thus, we seem to have a common, worldwide enemy on our hands: the subordination of military matters to political expediency. Yet, as several chapters in this volume show us, wars undertaken on ideological or religious grounds often eclipse normal rules of military and political behavior, because the stakes are so high. Where military honor and decency would call for a certain restraint, indeed honorability, in the use of armed force, wars waged for a "higher purpose" easily let go of such restraint, as several events during the crusades of the Middle Ages and the religious wars of the early modern period remind us. It was not until the sixteenth and seventeenth centuries – the time of the religious wars – and the writings of such Spanish theologians as Francisco de Vitoria and Francisco Suarez that the moral dangers of religion as a ground for, and motivation in, war were explicitly and systematically warned against in the Christian tradition. Before that, a tradition of *jus in bello* – restraint and justice in war – applicable to all human beings, did exist, but not as an integrated part of the just-war framework presided over by church and state.[3] The latter also tried to restrain war and even to detach it from purely churchly matters, yet far too often failed to stop the most inhuman brutality in the ostensible name of religion.

This tension between an overarching theory of the justice of war and the more mundane preoccupation with the practice of war is not unique to the medieval and early modern Christian world. Another variant of it is well captured in Torkel Brekke's chapter on Hinduism and just war. He alerts us to the tension between divine kingship and contractual kingship, where the former sees war as an end, or at least as a means to the greatest and holiest ends, while the latter urges caution and restraint in the use of armed force, since war is merely a means to more realistically attainable goods in this world, such as security and prosperity. In the West, the latter view has been called "regular war," as distinguished from "just war," in the terminology of Peter Haggenmacher.[4] The difference between Christianity and Hinduism resides in the Christian "regular-war" perspective's emphasis on a chivalric or professional code of *jus in bello*, whereas the Hindu *arthashastra* tradition is more purely consequentialist rather than duty-centered. Yet, we notice a crucial distinction materializing: that between grand ideas of justice and righteousness on the one hand and political ideas of expediency on the other. It is not certain that the former can always accommodate the needs and concerns of ethics better than the latter, since the more overarching, "deep" view will be prone to incorporating ideas about the lack of worthiness of the opponent, with a focus on his moral flaws and the evil of his cause. And once the enemy has been robbed of his – or indeed her – humanity, there are few hindrances to treating him or her inhumanely.

As is so often the case in ethics, the worth and dignity of "the other" turns out to be our most crucial challenge. What does it mean to be "the other" – the enemy – in war?[5] Is "the other" devoid of rights? Are, thus, general rules against violence and killing largely set aside in war, as one confronts the totally "other"?

All the traditions surveyed in this book, along with the world's many manifestations of Christianity as well as other religious traditions, hold the taking of life to be wrong under normal circumstances. Human life is valuable, yet feeble, and hence it demands protection.[6]

If one is not a pacifist, however, one is bound to hold that there are times when another person's life may be taken with impunity. Yet, very few non-pacifists hold that this implies a total abolition of the duty not to kill. It is only *in some specific cases* that one may kill justly. The real-life tragedy of war often resides in the looseness of that "specificity." What may initially have been conceived of as a limited endeavor to punish transgressors or defend one's homeland is easily transformed into campaigns of looting, rape, revenge, and indiscriminate killing – or even if such blatant crimes are avoided, destruction becomes much more widespread than military necessity strictly speaking demands. Indeed, instances of ruthless behavior in war, even within cultures that value life highly and punish murder harshly, are so widespread historically that we cannot ignore them. What was originally an extreme exception to the most basic and widespread of rules – the duty not to kill, the duty to respect the integrity of "the other" – becomes instead a sanction for violence and brutal domination.

Why does this happen? Is "culture," widely understood, part of the explanation? Does religious or social belonging – everything from the overarching categories of being a Christian or a Muslim, to the more specific identities of being a Sinhalese Buddhist or a member of the *bushi* in medieval Japan – create the feeling of belonging to an in-group whose moral restrictions apply only to one's own kind?

In my view, this is the real moral challenge raised by this book: How can we find resources within the various traditions for recognizing human dignity beyond one's own "in-group"? How can we all come to take seriously the gravity of taking life, even in war, in a way that the various religious traditions – Christianity included – have too often failed to do in practice?

The seed to an answer, I believe, lies in the double movement of global dialog and local reflection. The quest to restrain war, protect civilians, outlaw the most indiscriminate weapons, and find peaceful solutions to entangled conflicts requires both a global, cross-cultural consensus about the nature of the problem, as well as local self-understandings equipped to finding adequate solutions.

Searching within each tradition and each faith in order to find those features that highlight restraint in armed conflict, is not the same as arbitrarily picking out threads to fit the tapestry one happens to be making. We are rather trying to cut to the center of all ethics: the protection of life. Each tradition has its narratives, its vocabulary, and its web of meaning that together comprise what we can broadly call ethics. From these there will inevitably arise reflections on the legitimacy of violence and warfare, either fully brought out as in the Western just-war or the Islamic *jihad* traditions, or more indirectly as in traditional Japanese and Chinese thought. Using these intelligently and respectfully as sources for a cross-cultural ethics of war is the grand task that this book sets before us.

In doing so, the contributions to this volume give us some reason for optimism. Parallels to such categories as "legitimate authority," "just cause," and "right intention," well known from the Western just-war tradition, are not hard to find in the various Asian reflections on justice and war. Ideas of protection, restraint, and peaceful conflict resolution are also widespread, although differently emphasized and formulated. The relativist skepticism to an effective ethics of war – i.e. the stand that our views on individual dignity and peaceful coexistence are simply so different that preaching universal standards is naive, bordering on the absurd – is effectively countered by the manifold reflections found in this book. On the other hand, the contributions promise us no quick fix. It is a truism that the further we move toward generality, the more we tend to obscure the real-life conflicts. Pious manifestations of worldwide humanity and respect for life do little in themselves to restrain the horrors of war, and are not indicative of true consensus. Yet, when we manage to locate deeply rooted concerns about the legality and legitimacy of war, and strong formulations about the inherent value of life, we have tracked down more than mere platitudes. Rather, we have come closer to finding those resources that can help us isolate and condemn indiscriminate brutality in war.

It is our common duty to contribute to that process.

Notes

1 For the most current figures on armed conflict, see the databases www.pcr.uu.se and www.prio.no/cwp/armedconflict, containing statistics and quantitative analysis, gathered and updated by Uppsala University and the International Peace Research Institute, Oslo (PRIO). See also yearly updates in the *Journal of Peace Research*.
2 See Rawls, John (1993) *Political Liberalism*, New York: Columbia University Press, ch. 4.
3 See Johnson, James Turner (1981) *The Just War Tradition and the Restraint of War: A Moral and Historical Inquiry*, Princeton, NJ: Princeton University Press, for good descriptions of this development.
4 See Haggenmacher, Peter (1992) "Just War and Regular War in Sixteenth Century Spanish Doctrine," *International Review of the Red Cross*, no. 290 (September–October): 434–45.
5 The terminology of "the other" is inspired by Emmanuel Lévinas. For an instructive collection of essays on the ethics of "the other" and on the concrete meeting and contact between human beings as a basis for morality, see Jodalen, Harald and Arne Johan Vetlesen (eds.) (1997) *Closeness – An Ethics*, Oslo: Scandinavian University Press.
6 Richard Miller, following W. D. Ross and James Childress, speaks of the duty not to kill or injure others ("the duty of nonmaleficence") as a prima facie duty – a duty that is usually binding, but which may be overridden in exceptional circumstances; see Miller, Richard (1991) *Interpretations of Conflict*, Chicago, IL: University of Chicago Press: 16. Miller connects this to a basic "presumption against war," which he claims to find in the just-war tradition. Other scholars, among them James Turner Johnson, has argued against this view, and has instead emphasized that a "presumption against injustice" is the essence of the just-war tradition (see Johnson, James Turner (1996) "The Broken Tradition," *The National Interest*: 27–36). The latter disagreement should not obscure the fact that the prima facie duty not to kill or injure other human beings is a basic constituent of most systems of ethics, and that this has obvious bearing on the ethics of war.

Bibliography

Haggenmacher, Peter (1992) "Just War and Regular War in Sixteenth Century Spanish Doctrine," *International Review of the Red Cross*, no. 290 (September–October): 434–45.
Jodalen, Harald and Arne Johan Vetlesen (eds.) (1997) *Closeness – An Ethics*, Oslo: Scandinavian University Press.
Johnson, James Turner (1981) *The Just War Tradition and the Restraint of War: A Moral and Historical Inquiry*, Princeton, NJ: Princeton University Press.
Johnson, James Turner (1996) "The Broken Tradition," *The National Interest*: 27–36.
Miller, Richard (1991) *Interpretations of Conflict*, Chicago, IL: University of Chicago Press.
Rawls, John (1993) *Political Liberalism*, New York: Columbia University Press, ch. 4.

INDEX

Abravanel, Isaac 48, 53–4
Abu Hanifa 84, 90, 96
Abu Yusuf 84, 90
ad bellum criteria 8
adat 23
adharma 133–4
Adipurana 132
Afonso V of Portugal 53
agape, centrality of 17
Ahab, king of Israel 46
Ahad Ha-am (Asher Hirsch Ginsberg)
    62, 75 n. 111
Aho, James 114
Alexander II 56, 57
Alfonso II of Naples 53
'Ali ibn Abi Talib 99–100
Almain, Jacques 11–12
Alter, Yehuda Leib 43
al-zakat 99
Ambrose 4, 45
American Civil War 56
Amiel, Moshe Avigdor 63
Amir, Yigal 44
Amoghavarsha, king 132
'Anas, Malik b. 84
Ancient Greek wars 2–3
Anscombe, Elizabeth 17
Anselm, St 5
anti-war movement (mid-1960s) 18
apostates, Islam and 99, 100, 102
Aquinas, Thomas 6–10, 11, 12, 13, 14, 17,
    18, 51, 115, 120, 136, 160
Arama, Isaac 53
Aristotle 1, 6, 7, 10, 11, 19, 81
arms trade, Judaism 47–8
artha 122, 123, 125, 128, 133, 137
arthashastra tradition 113, 114, 118, 121,
    122

Artson, Bradley 47
Asa, King of Judah 43, 51
Ascher, Saul 61
Ashi, Rav 48
atomic bomb 17
Augustine, St 4, 5, 7, 10, 45, 160, 185–6,
    189
authority of kings 115–16
Awza'i 84
al-Azhar, Shaykh 104, 105

Bahya ibn Paquda 49
Bakr, Abu 99
Balaramayana 130
Bandaranaike, S.W.R.D. 148–9,
    151
Bandaranaike, Mrs Sirimavo 149
Bar Kochba Revolt (131–135 CE) 42
Barhaspatya Sutra 114
Basham, A.L. 121
Bauddha Peramuna 148
bellum hostile 177
bellum justum 44
bellum Romanum 177
Ben-Hadad, king of Syria 46
Berlin, Naftali Zevi Yehuda 56–7
Bernard, St 5–6
Bernhardi, Friedrich von 15
Bhagavadgita 114, 132, 134
Bharadvaja 127
Bharuci 140 n. 51
Bhaskar, Bhagchandra Jain 134
bin Ladin, Usama 102
Bodin, Jean 115
Boniface (governor) 4
Boydston, Jo Ann 15
brawling (*rixa*) 120
Brockington, J.L. 119

Buddharakkhita, Venerable Mapitagama 148
Bulliett, Richard 103, 104
Bunyan, John 22
Burke, Edmund 16
bushi 159, 160, 161; courtier values and 164–7; ethics in war 167–8; honor 168–9; non-combatants and 175–7; prisoners of war 171–4; private warfare 162–4, 166; surprise attacks and 169–71

Cakkavatti Sihanada Sutta 147
Calvin, John 22
Celsus 3–4
Chandragupta Maurya 114
Chi You 189
chivalry: European 172; Hinduism and 117–19, 129, 135; Japan and 177
Christian Church: (975–1274) 4–6; pacifism 2–3
Civil Rights movement 60
Clausewitz, Carl von 54, 56, 60, 135
Clooney, Francis X. 114
compassion, Judaism on 46–7
competent authority 44, 67
Confucianism 21, 161
Confucius 21
conscientious objection 61
Constantinople, sack of (1204) 7
corporeal war 10
Crusade: First 5, 58, 97; Second 5
cultural genocide 68

Dahiya, Kahina 48
Damian, Peter 5
danda 125
Davidson, Donald 20
Dead Sea Scrolls 42
deception, Japanese and 169–71
Declaration on Jihad against Jews and Crusaders (1998) 101–2, 103, 104
defense *see* self-defense
democracy 16
Dewey, John 14–16
dharma 23; Buddhism and 145–56; Hinduism and 115, 117, 123–4, 125, 127, 128, 133, 135
dharmashastra 113, 121
divine kingship 115–16, 122
double effect, principle of 9
Douglas, Mary 22

droit de guerre 166
Dubois, Abbe 21
dueling 11
Dundas, Paul 134
Durkheim, Emile 22
Dutugemunu, King 148, 149, 150–3

economic paradigm 18, 19
Ellis, Marc 67
environment, Judaism and 40, 47, 66
Ephraim, Shutelah ben 46
ethics: definition 39; in war 167–74
Evans-Pritchard, E.E. 22

al-Farabi 50, 81
Ferdinand of Spain 48, 53
Ferrante I of Naples 53
Fingarette, Herbert 21–2, 23, 24
Finley, M.I. 1, 2
Ford, John 17
Franklin, Benjamin 15, 22
Frederick II 8
French Revolution 54

Garlan, Yvon 3
Geertz, Clifford 1, 22, 23–4
Gempei Wars (1180–85) 166, 172
Geneva Convention IV Relative to the Protection of Civilian Persons in Time of War 68
Geneva Conventions and Protocols 202
genocide: cultural 68; Judaism on 51
Gershom, Levi ben (Ralbag; Leo Hebraeus; Gersonides) 52–3
Gersonides 52–3
al-Ghazali 98
Gikeiki 167
Godaigo 160
Goldstein, Baruch 44
Gordon, Judah Leib 62
Goren, Shlomo 65
Goseibai shikimoku 162
Gratian 10, 51, 160
Greenberg, Irving 67
Gregory IX, Pope 51
Gregory X, Pope 6, 8, 10
Grotius, Hugo 13–14, 18, 19, 54
guerre mortelle 177
guile, Japanese and 169–71
Gulf War, first 18
Gunawardana, R.A.L.H. 150

Hacohen, Israel Meir (Hafetz Haim) 57, 63
Hafetz Haim 57, 63
Haganah 62
ha-Gelili, José 46
Haggenmacher, Peter 203
halakha 44, 45, 48, 55, 57, 58, 64, 67
Halevi, Chaim David 48, 66
Hall, H. Fielding 145
Hallisey, Charles 153
Han shu 195
Hananiah, Joshua ben 43
Handiqui, K.K. 133, 136
Harrington, Sir John 198
Harsah, King 129
Harshacarita 129
Hauerwas, Stanley 145, 147, 153
havlaga, policy of 63, 64
Heesterman, J.C. 121, 123
Heiji monogatari 167
Heike monogatari 167
Helbo, Rabbi 46
Helgeland, John 3
Hemcandra 132
heroism 117; Hinduism and 129–31, 137
Hertz, J.H. 59, 60
Herzl, Theodor 62
Heschel, Abraham 60
Hideyoshi, Satake 170
Hideyoshi, Yoshimasa 170
Hiroshima, atomic bomb attack on 17
Hirotsune, Taira 170
Hirsch, Samson Raphael 58
Hobbes, Thomas 18
Hocking, W.E. 15
Hogen monogatari 167
holy war 5, 53
Homer 2–3
honor, Japanese 168–9
hostage taking, Judaism and 69
Howard, Michael 1, 15
Huainanzi 194, 197
Huan Kuan 194
Humbert of Romans 6, 8
Hunter, David G. 3
Hyrcanus, Eliezer ben 41

Ibn Adiya, Samuel 48
ibn al Numan, Hasan 48
ibn Nagrela, Ismail 49
Ibn Sina (Avicenna) 81
Ibn Taymiyya 98–102
idolatry, Judaism and 52

Iehira, Kiyowara 165
Ikegami, Eiko 167
in bello criteria 9
Inden, Ronald 116
Indic law 23
infanticide 20
inferentialism 30 n. 112
Ingalls, D.H.H. 130
Isaac, Rabbi Abraham 62–3
Isabella of Spain 48, 53
Israel Defence Forces 55, 63–5, 66
Israel, modern, military defense in 65–7

Jabotinsky, Vladimir 62
Jainism 132–4
Jakobovits, Chief Rabbi Lord 66
Jannai, Alexander 42
Jansen, Johannes J.G. 104
Jewish Peace Society 60
jihad 49, 50, 97, 204
Jinasena 132
John of Legnano 10, 11
John of Salisbury 54
Joseph II of Germany 55, 58, 61
Judah bar Ilai, Rabbi 45
jus ad bellum 18, 41, 57, 159, 160, 177,
    186; Aquinas and 8, 9; in China 197;
    in Deuteronomy 40; Hindu lack of
    119–21, 137–8; Islamic tradition and
    89, 91; Judaism and 67, 69
jus in bello 18, 159, 160, 167, 177, 186,
    202, 203; Aquinas and 8, 9; in China
    197; in Deuteronomy 40; Hinduism and
    117–19, 121, 137–8; Islamic tradition
    and 89, 92; Judaism and 65, 67, 69–70
just war tradition 5; Aquinas and 6–10,
    13; Dewey on 15–17; in Early China
    185–99; Japan and 160–74; *see also*
    jus ad bellum; *jus in bello*

Kach movement 44, 72 n. 31
Kagetoki, Kajiwara 173
Kahane, Meir 44
Kahanism 44
Kalischer, Rabbi Zevi Hirsch 62
Kamandaki 113–14, 128–9; *Nitisara* 113
Kant, Immanuel 15, 16
karamyoga 138
Karelitz, Yeshayahu 63
karma 134
karmayoga 114, 115, 116, 134, 136, 137
Kathasaritsagara 124

Kautiliya Arthrashastra 113–14, 118,
    122–9, 133, 137, 203
Kautilya 114, 121, 122–9, 133, 134, 136,
    137
Kelsay, John 146
Kemmu shikimoku 162
Kemper, Steven 145
Kern, Martin 192
kibbush rabim 45
kibbush yahid 45
Kishinev pogrom (1903) 62
Kissinger, Henry 14
Kitab al-Asl (Book of the Foundation)
    86
Klimheit, H.J. 119
Köhn, Hans 60
Korean war 56
Korehira, Taira 165
Korehira, Yuri 173
Koremochi, Taira 169–70, 175–6
Kumaratunga, President Chandrika 154 n.
    13
Kunifusa, Minamoto 165
Kutayuddha 135

Lambton, Anne 81
Lamm, Maurice 61
Landes, Daniel 47
Las Casa, Bartolomé 12
Latter Three Years' War (1083–87) 165
League of Nations 16, 54
legal paradigm 18, 19, 20
legitimate authority 204
Lele of the Kasai 22
Leo Hebraeus 52–3
Levine, D. 49
lex duellorum 11
Li ji 194
Liberation Tigers of Tamil Eelam (LTTE)
    147, 148, 153
Lienhardt, Godfrey 22
Lippmann, Walter 15
Liu Bang 192
Lombard, Peter 11
Lü Buwei 189
Lü shi chun qiu 189, 192, 193, 194, 195,
    197, 198
Luther, Martin 115
Luzzatto, Samuel David 58–9, 60

Machiavelli 113, 115
Magnes, Judah 60

Mahabharata 113, 114–17, 126, 128, 129,
    135, 136
Mahavamsa 147, 148, 149–51, 152
Mahendrapala 130
Maimonides, Moses (Rambam) 50–2, 56,
    66
Maine, Henry 1
Manu 115, 116, 123, 125
Marcus Aurelius 123
martyrdom, Islam and 105–6
Masakada, Taira 164, 176
Maurya, Chandragupta 123
al-Mawardi 94–7, 101, 102
Medina, Sir Solomon 48
Megasthenes 122
Meir, R. 20
Mencius 187, 194
Mendelssohn, Moses 58
Michaelis, J.D. 58
Michitaka 163
milhemet ha-reshut 47
milhemet hova 44
milhemet reshut 44, 57
Mill, John Stuart 14
Minatogawa, Battle of 160
Miura Yasumura 163–4
Momigliano 1
Moroto, Fujiwara 169–70, 175–6
Motohira, Fujiwara 165
Mu'awiya, governor of Syria 99
Muchikane, Fujiwara 163
Muneyori, Taira 165
Muslim shields 96–7

Nagasaki, atomic bomb attack on 17
Nahmanides (Ramban) 52, 66
Naishadhiyacarita 129
Nambokucho wars 172
Napoleonic wars 54
narrative, theory of 153
natural slavery, doctrine of 12
Neglected Duty, The 102, 103, 104
Netanel ibn Fayyumi 49–50
Nicholas I, Czar 56
Niditch, Susan 60
Niebuhr, Reinhold 17
niti 133
Nitivakyamrita 133, 134, 136
non-combatants 69–70; Islam and 92–3,
    99; Japanese and 174–7; Judaism and 54
Norikage, Amano 173
nuclear war 17

Obeyesekere, Gananath 146
Okimi 176
Onia, Rabbi 46
Origen 3
outlawry of war movement 16

pacifism 3; Buddhism and 147; Judaism
    and 60–1
Pale of Settlement 62
Pancatrantra 124
Peace of God movement 4–5, 167, 74 n. 70
Peloponnesian War 3
Perera, S. 149, 150
Philo of Alexandria 46, 47, 59
pillage 27 n. 49
Pizarro brothers 12
Plato 1, 81
Prado, Abraham 48
prisoners of war, Japanese and 171–4
private warfare, *bushi* and 162–4
proportionality, principle of 45
prudence 117, 121–9, 137; of Somadeva
    132–6
punishments, Chinese 195
purity of arms 52, 64

al-Qa'ida 81, 101, 104
al-Qaradhawi, Yusuf 105

Rabbinowitz, Nahum 66
Rabin, Yitzchak 44
rajadharma 115, 121
Rajashekhara 130
Rajatarangini 130, 131
Ralbag 52–3
Ramayana 113, 118, 119, 130, 136
Rambam 50–2, 56, 66
Ramban 52, 66
Ramsey, Paul 17, 18
rape, Judaism and 39, 45
Rashtriya Svayamsevak Sangh (RSS) 119
al-Rashid, Harun 85
Rathana, Venerable Athuraliya 147
Ratwatte, General 153
Rava (Babylonian sage) 43, 51
Rawls, John 19, 201
rebels, Islam and 99–100, 102
Redemption, concept of 63
Refael, Rabbi Shilo 66
regular war 203
reputation, Japanese 168–9
right intent, doctrine of 51

Roman wars 3
Ross, W.D. 153
Rousseau, Jean-Jacques 18
Ryan, Alan 15

Sacks, Jonathan 44
sacrificial violence, Hinduism and 114
Sanehira, Kiyowara 165
Sanemasa, Usami Heiji 173
al-Sarahsi 86
Schreiber, Moses 56
Scotus, John Duns 11
Second Scholastic 12, 13, 17
sedition (*seditio*) 120
Sefer ha-Hinukh 47
self-defense; Aquinas on 9; Judaism and
    45, 56, 57, 69
Seneca 20
Seneviratne, H.L. 150
Sepúlveda, Juan Ginés 12
Sereni, Enzo 60
al-Shafi'i 82–3, 84, 97
Shang Jun shu 195–6
Shapira, Anita 61
Shari'a: reasoning 23, 82–5; war and
    85–103
shastra 122
Shaviv, Yehuda 66
al-Shaybani, Muhammad ibn al-Hasan 84,
    86–91, 93, 97, 99, 102
Sherman, Avraham 66–7
Shigemune, Minamoto 165
Shigetada, Hatakeyama 173
Shmuel (Samuel) ha-Nagid (Ismail ibn
    Nagrela) 49
Shu ji 194, 197
Silva, Nalin de 148
Sima fa 188, 189, 195
Sima Qian 192, 193
Singer, Peter 19, 20
Sinhala-Buddhist just war 149–53
siyar 86
Somadeva Suri 131, 132–6
Somarama, Venerable Talduwe 148
Song of Roland 5
Soto, Domingo de 12, 13, 14
Southern, Richard 4, 5
spiritual war 10
Stein, Burton 132
Stein, Otto 122
Suarez, Francisco 53, 202
Subandhu 129

Subhashitaratnakosha 130
Sueharu, Inunoshoji 165
suicide, Islam and 105–6
al-Sulami 97–8
Sunzi 186, 187, 188, 189
surprise, Japanese and 169–71

al-Tabari 93
Takaie, Sho Shiro 173
Takauji, Ashikaga 160
Talmud 39, 55, 57
Tantrakhyayika 124
Tattvarthasutra 134
territory of Islam 86
territory of war 86–7
terrorism 69
Thera, Venerable Sobitha 151
Thucydides 1, 3
tohar ha-nesheq, concept of (purity of arms) 52, 64
Tomomura, Yoki 163–4
Tosefta 47
Toshio, Kuroda 175
Trench, battle of (627) 98
triangulation 20, 23
Truce of God movement 4, 167
Truman, Harry 17
Tsunemasa, Taira 173

United Nations 54–5; Charter 69, 201, 202; Weapons Convention (1981) 68
universal corporeal war 10
Universal Declaration of Human Rights 201
Urban II, Pope 5, 8, 51
utilitarianism 19–20

Vajiranana, Venerable Palane Siri 145
Vasavadatta 129
Vidyakara 130
Vietnam War 17–18, 56, 60–1
virtue (character) paradigm 18
Vishalaksha 127
Vishnvardhana, king 132
Vitoria, Francisco de 12, 13, 14, 17, 53, 202
voluntarism 28 n. 60

Walzer, Michael 18, 19, 159
Wang Man 196
War Against Terrorism 60
Warrant of Pursuit and Capture (*tsuibu kanpu*) 162
Warsaw Ghetto Uprising 58
Watt, W.M. 88
Weber, Max 16, 22, 23
Wei Yang 195
Wilcock, Evelyn 60
William of Tripoli 8
Wilson, Woodrow 15
Wingate, Captain Orde 63
Wink, André 121
Wittgenstein 20
World War I 15, 56, 59, 60
World War II 56, 60, 173
Wu, Emperor 194
Wuzi 188

Xun Kuang 188
Xunzi 188, 193, 197

Yadava, B.N.S. 129, 131, 135
Yashastilaka 133, 136
Yasuhira, Fujiwara 173
Yehuda, Tzvi 63
yi bing see just war in Early China
Yogashastra 132
Yom Kippur War (1973) 48, 66
Yorichika, Minamoto 165
Yorifusa, Minamoto 165
Yorinobu, Minamoto 163, 176
Yoritomo, Minamoto 159, 160, 170, 172, 173
Yosef, Chief Rabbi Ovadya 66
Yoshiie, Minamoto 165
Yoshisada, Nitta 160
Yuddhakanda 118

Zaehner, R.C. 20, 22
Zemba, Menahem 57–8
Zionism 55, 61–3
Zoroastrianism 20
Zuo zhuan 187
Zydenbos, Robert J. 134

CPSIA information can be obtained at www.ICGtesting.com
Printed in the USA
LVOW101002140512

281632LV00002B/9/P